Man with the Killer Smile

The Life and Crimes of a Serial Mass Murderer

Mitchel P. Roth

Number 13 in the North Texas Crime and
Criminal Justice Series

University of North Texas Press
Denton, Texas

©2022 Mitchel P. Roth
All rights reserved.
Printed in the United States of America.

10 9 8 7 6 5 4 3 2 1

Permissions:
University of North Texas Press
1155 Union Circle #311336
Denton, TX 76203-5017

The paper used in this book meets the minimum requirements of the American National Standard for Permanence of Paper for Printed Library Materials, z39.48.1984. Binding materials have been chosen for durability.

Library of Congress Cataloging-in-Publication Data

Roth, Mitchel P., 1953- author.
Man with the killer smile : the life and crimes of a serial mass murderer / Mitchel P. Roth.
　pages cm
Includes bibliographical references and index.
ISBN-13 978-1-57441-883-5 (cloth)
ISBN-13 978-1-57441-889-7 (ebook)
　1. LCSH: Hassell, George Jefferson, 1988–1928. 2. Mass murderers—Texas—Biography. 3. Mass murder—Texas—Farwell. 4. Assassination—Investigation—Texas—Farwell. 5. BISAC: TRUE CRIME / Murder / Mass Murder. 6. HISTORY / United States / State & Local / Southwest (AZ, NM, OK, TX)

HV6248.H37 R68 2022
364.152/309764092 [B]–dc23
　　　　　　　2022038223

Number 13 in the North Texas Crime and Criminal Justice Series

The electronic edition of this book was made possible by the support of the Vick Family Foundation. Typeset by vPrompt eServices.

to

Teresa Ancira

Contents

	Prologue vii
Introduction	George Jefferson Hassell, the First "Texas Bluebeard" 1
Chapter 1	George J. Hassell: The Early Years 11
Chapter 2	First Love, Last Love 25
Chapter 3	Whittier 35
Chapter 4	On the Road 49
Chapter 5	Farwell, Texas: The Last Mile 59
Chapter 6	Kill Them All 77
Chapter 7	The Last Victim 87
Chapter 8	Suspicion 91
Chapter 9	The Lindops Move In 97
Chapter 10	Auction Day 101
Chapter 11	The Noose Tightens 109
	Photo Gallery
Chapter 12	Suicide 115
Chapter 13	Exhumation 121
Chapter 14	The Jig Is Up 127
Chapter 15	Picking a Jury 135

Chapter 16	Life or Death: The Trial of George J. Hassell	145
Chapter 17	Verdict	163
Chapter 18	It Was a Good Job	175
Chapter 19	Appeals and Reprieve	187
Chapter 20	Urge to Kill: Dr. Jekyll or Mr. Hyde?	209
Chapter 21	Riding the Thunderbolt	221
	Epilogue	237
	Appendix	247
	Endnotes	251
	Bibliography	299
	Index	307

Prologue

"I had started it, and I finished it." December 1926

Thanks to plenty of rain and high crop prices, 1926 had brought prosperous times to farmers in the West Texas Panhandle. The mood was festive and optimistic. No doubt, the farm and ranch families around Farwell, Texas, were counting the days until Christmas, which was less than three weeks away. Prohibition was in its sixth year, and the Great Depression and Dust Bowl were still several years distant on the horizon—nothing to worry about yet. But murder was in the air at the Hassell farm on the outskirts of Farwell, the last Texas town before the New Mexico border.

In 1926, Susan Hassell, a forty-year-old farm wife married to her late husband's brother, George, was looking forward to December, as she always did, with her birthday on Christmas Eve and Christmas to follow. But hell would be unleashed on the Hassell ranch on the cold, windy night of December 2. Prone to the bottle and fits of rage, the burly man with the smiling blue eyes was in no mood to quarrel with his third wife over his bootleg whiskey and his sexual abuse of his stepdaughter.

He had retreated out to the barn, where he knew his pint of illicit whiskey was always waiting for him. Once he sucked down enough liquid courage, he headed back into the cramped five-room house to his bedroom, where his wife and two-year-old stepson, Sammie, snuggled together in bed. When she heard him come back in, Susan continued to admonish George, who stood at the bedside as the child slept beside her. He laid down next to her, close enough for her to get a familiar whiff of his cheap whiskey. She was none too pleased. Although we only have his words for what followed, he admitted to picking up a ball peen hammer and striking his wife in the face and head at least twice. He continued to pound her with the hammer before wrapping a stocking around her neck and strangling her to make sure she was dead. When the baby boy woke up, Hassell choked little Sammie in the same fashion as he had his wife. Once he grasped what he had done, he realized that he had "best go on and kill the whole outfit," meaning the rest of his eight stepchildren.

No one knows exactly what drove him to murder the whole family, because he never provided an explanation. What is certain is that when he set his mind to do something nefarious, unlike with the more benign goals he established during his life, he usually followed through. He went from room to room in the house killing each child in very personal ways—using primitive cutting tools and his bare hands rather than firearms—ending their lives when they had barely begun. He used a straight razor to cut throats, stockings to strangle, and an axe to bludgeon skulls. There were only seven children in the house, because the older stepson was out of town. After wiping out most of the family, Hassell had only to wait a few days for the remaining stepson's return. Then he would finish him off with a shotgun blast while he slept. By the time Hassell concluded his bloody rampage, he would take the lives of nine family members ranging in age from two to forty.

Introduction

George Jefferson Hassell, the First "Texas Bluebeard"

As the year 1926 drew to a close, people no doubt pondered the many celebrities of the day who had left the earthly stage for good, such as Harry Houdini, Rudolph Valentino, Eugene Debs, Annie Oakley, Mary Cassatt, and Claude Monet. By the end of the year, they were joined by the nine members of a farming family killed in cold blood. News of George Jefferson Hassell's murder of his wife, Susan, and his eight stepchildren made bold newspaper headlines throughout the United States and beyond. The mass murder in Farwell, Texas, said one local reporter, was "the blackest crime" in the history of the West Texas Panhandle.

George Jefferson Hassell (1888–1928) was the first multiple murderer in Texas to be accorded the sobriquet, "Texas Bluebeard."[1] He might have been the first killer dubbed "Bluebeard" in Texas, but he was certainly not the first in the United States. According to one leading crime historian, the first American serial killer to be tagged with the "Bluebeard label" was San Francisco physician Dr. J. Milton Bowers, who poisoned three wives between 1873 and 1885.[2] In 1927 George J. Hassell joined the ranks of other state- and place-specific American Bluebeards, a wide-ranging cast of characters that spanned the country from West Virginia to California. Among them were Harry Powers, the "West Virginia Bluebeard"; the

"San Francisco Bluebeard," James P. Watson; and the Los Angeles "Bluebeard Barber," Robert S. James.[3] This small fraternity of mass murderers and serial killers might not be well known, yet in terms of depravity their crimes rank among the vilest in American history.

The epithet "Bluebeard" has fallen out of use in recent years, an era marked by the crimes of so many notorious mass murderers and serial killers. The term, which is shorthand for a certain type of multiple murderer, dates to the late seventeenth century. By most accounts, it is not based on specific historical events, but it can be traced back to a 1697 French folktale published by Charles Perrault, often regarded as "the father of the fairy tale." The legend revolved around a man who used his wealth to lure women into marriage. After each marriage he told his new wife that she could have egress to any room except one. However, curiosity got the better of his seven wives and each was murdered in turn. Since then, a man (or woman) who murders a series of spouses has been labeled a "bluebeard."

Although Hassell was dubbed the "Texas Bluebeard" by newspaper reporters, he did not necessarily fit the traditional profile. He had no wealth with which to lure women into his web of deceit, but he did murder at least two wives in a row, albeit nine years apart. In between, he traveled extensively and later boasted that he had "three wives during his thirty-nine years of existence, has lived with seven other women from three months to three years each and had affairs with other women in each of the thirty-seven states [or twenty-seven] in which he has been employed."[4] Whether this boast was true or not, none of these women ever came forward after George's notoriety became public knowledge. This led to speculation that some of them could have been victims as well. Others have suggested that if there were more victims, he would have shared that information before he died.

From a modern criminological vantage point, Hassell fits the criteria of both a serial killer and mass murderer.[5] What distinguishes his crimes, according to serial killer authority Eric Hickey, is that it is exceedingly rare to hear of a serial killer committing a mass murder or even having "the opportunity to enact a second mass murder or to become a serial killer."[6] In 1992 the FBI defined a serial killer as someone who kills three or more people in three or more separate events or locations, with cooling-off periods between homicides. More recently, in 2005 the FBI lowered the threshold to a minimum of two victims, again with a cooling-off period between each killing, which can last from days and weeks to years.[7] Hassell's murders fit both definitions.

Serial killers typically follow a pattern in their killings, usually exemplified by the type of victims selected or the methods and motives for killing. Some commit their homicides within the confines of their own home and have a personal relationship with their victims, as in the case of Hassell, while others kill for pleasure, profit, and other reasons.

Besides being a serial killer, Hassell also fits the description of a mass murderer, defined as one who kills four or more people in one incident and in one place.[8] Unlike the serial killer, whose goal is to elude capture and continue killing, the mass murderer usually gives little thought or concern to the possibilities of capture or death. Indeed, after both of Hassell's mass killings he not only buried the victims near or under his residences but continued to inhabit each home for a time.

Hassell's killing of his two families not only makes him a mass murderer but also a family annihilator. According to criminologists Ronald M. Holmes and Stephen T. Holmes, family annihilators are distinct from other mass killers, because of how they pick their victims: "only because they are family members and there is a perceived need to eradicate the family."[9] When it comes to comparing family annihilators like Hassell, there were only five recorded cases of "familicide" in the first twenty-five years of American history.[10] Familicide and domestic violence have been studied extensively in recent years. A familicide, according to domestic homicide researchers Marieke Liem and Frans Koenraadt, entails the killing of an intimate partner and at least one child.[11] Others describe it as the act of a "patriarchal head" murdering an entire family.[12] Some social scientists use the term to refer to the killing of four or more family members within a twenty-four-hour period by another family member, who is almost always male. In the case of Hassell, he killed his common-law wife and three stepchildren in 1917 and in 1926 murdered his wife and her eight children.

In the American colonial era, it was rare for people to kill their parents, siblings, adult children, aunts, uncles, cousins, nieces and nephews. Indeed, "relatives almost never killed one another for money or property, and they never killed one another over issues that often led to murder in many modern societies."[13] According to research published in 2010 by the sociologist Neil Websdale, there was just one recorded familicide in colonial America prior to the 1780s, a 1755 Pennsylvania case.[14] More recently, Harold Schechter, the dean of true crime nonfiction, has traced the first postcolonial case to 1782, when William Beadle crushed his sleeping wife's skull with an axe, cut her throat with a knife, and then killed his three kids.[15] The crime was eerily reminiscent of Hassell's murders. But unlike Beadle and other family annihilators, George Hassell did not kill himself in the aftermath, although he did make a half-hearted attempt at suicide three weeks after he buried his nine victims in a cellar pit, just outside the back door of his Farwell, Texas, farmhouse.

Between 1900 and 1999, familicides comprised almost half of the 909 mass murders recorded in the US.[16] Some sixty years after Hassell's last family massacre, the criminologists Jack Levin and James A. Fox asserted that "the annihilation of an entire family by one of its members is the most frequent form of mass murder." Levin and Fox explain that in most cases these massacres are the unintended consequences of mental illness, quarrels over seemingly insignificant issues, marital disputes, or some form of physical or mental abuse.[17] This certainly holds true for Hassell.

Hassell was the stepparent of eleven of his thirteen victims. Studies of child murderers, according to Dr. Michael Stone, indicate that "the risk of a child dying at the hands of a stepparent is many times higher than the risk by a biological parent."[18] Likewise, the psychiatrist Adrian Raine reports that "the less related two individuals are, the more likely it is that a homicide will take place ... Stepparents are a particularly pernicious case in hand."[19] However, we will never know whether the victims would have been killed if they had shared Hassell's DNA.

That said, at the time of Hassell's last family massacre in the late 1920s, the murder of multiple family members, was rare and unfathomable to most Americans despite that murder in general was common. Although the country was on the cusp of an era of modernization that would see the discovery of penicillin and the invention of the iron lung, the aerosol can, television, bubble gum, and Pez candy, some things were not changing.

While Americans continued to murder Americans, and the yellow press fed the stories to an increasingly receptive readership, familicide remained beyond the pale.

It is unsurprising, then, that George J. Hassell remains an outlier in the history of multiple homicides. He is unusual in that he fits the modern definitions of a serial killer, mass murderer, and family annihilator. Other multiple murderers may have had more victims, however, except for a couple of cases where husbands killed two of their wives and a small number of family members in separate incidents over time, none have surpassed the brutality of Hassell's crimes. Hassell also stands out because he killed thirteen family members in three separate incidents over a nine-year period, which means that he can also be regarded as a serial mass murderer, among the rarest forms of multiple murder.[20]

During the 1920s, crime, or perhaps the fear of it, emerged as one of the country's leading social issues, especially for urban centers, where murders were most common. Hassell's Farwell slayings stand out for being committed in the rural heartland, where multiple murder is extremely rare, both in the past and in the present. Helped along by a bevy of highly publicized murder cases, this lethal decade featured such "crimes of the century" as those committed by Nicola Sacco and Bartolomeo Vanzetti (1920), Nathan Leopold Jr. and Richard Loeb (1924), and the "dumb bell murder" by Judd Gray and Ruth Snyder (1927), who became the first woman to die in the electric chair. Newspapers, true detective magazines, and radio stations figured out that crime news sold, and they ran with it, sticking to the time-honored journalistic adage "if it bleeds it leads."

Reporters relished recounting the life and crimes of George Jefferson Hassell for a readership eager for increasingly lurid stories. It was common to see his crimes touted under such headlines as "THIS TEXAN WAS BUSY FOR ONE 20-YEAR PERIOD," which accompanied a scorecard tallying his "thirteen murders, six marriages, enlistment in the army and navy and a prison term for desertion ... crowded into a twenty-year period." The media circus ended only with his execution on February 10, 1928.[21]

What should we make of this double mass murderer, the killer of two of his own families and, most probably, of his brother, Thomas? During his brief time in the spotlight, between his arrest around Christmas 1926 and his execution less than two years later, he was observed and studied by sociologists, criminologists, penologists, reporters, and "alienists" (the psychiatrists of that era). The story of Hassell's life and crimes is not a classic whodunit. Like the vast majority of mass murderers who are killed or are captured after the crime, Hassell was caught not long after his bloodiest familicide; however, he had been able to elude capture for a previous mass murder for almost a decade. This book is not even a *why*dunit, since the perpetrator was never able to provide a rational explanation for why he committed his crimes in the first place. Hassell's crimes should fall instead into a different category, a *he*dunit (to propose a new category). From the first, he never denied committing his last mass murder in Farwell, Texas, and was even eager before his execution to admit to additional murders committed in 1917.

If there was one quality that linked George Jefferson Hassell to his life and crimes it was his unmistakable affinity for women. He loved women, and apparently, they loved him back. One reporter with a talent for understatement was impressed by the womanizer, writing, "Women apparently played an important part of his life. Hassell recalled his first 'trouble' as connected with a fifteen-year-old girl" when he was just eight years old. Of course, behind Hassell's winning smile and charming extroversion lurked the mind of a predator, one that contemporary social scientists have a better understanding of today. Perhaps people trusted each other more in the early twentieth century or were just more naïve. But the sciences of criminology, psychiatry, and psychology were still in their infancy in the late 1920s, and researchers had only a slight grasp of the evil that people are capable of. Moreover, the average citizen, in the words of Eric Hickey, would find it "disconcerting to learn some of the nicest people you meet lead Jekyll and Hyde lives."[22]

The clinical psychiatrist Michael Stone has studied hundreds of killers, past and present, over the past forty years, including serial killers and mass murderers. Hassell possessed several of the traits exhibited by psychopaths and sociopaths, especially what Stone refers to as "superficial charm" and "glibness." Like many other serial murderers, he had a talent for saying the right thing at the right time if it suited his purpose. In his relationship to his known victims, he was more than capable of telling the women and children that he loved them if it suited his ultimate objectives. According to Dr. Stone, "Even under the best of circumstances, the psychopath is incapable of meaningful or enduring relationships with others—especially love relationships," and conversely, he can walk away from them "in a heartbeat if something better" comes along.[23] Likewise, the criminologist Kim Davies has noted that psychopaths can be "quite charming." Some are very intelligent, but "don't appear to have capability to be remorseful." These descriptions of psychopathic behavior certainly ring true in any consideration of the life of George Hassell.[24]

Over the years, it has become de rigueur to turn to psychologists and psychiatrists for the best insights into the mind of a killer. Yet, the terms *sociopath* and *psychopath* have often been used interchangeably to describe someone who murders without conscience, as in the case of Hassell. However, these terms have distinct meanings. Psychopaths are classified as individuals with "little or no conscience," while sociopaths have a "limited" ability to feel remorse and empathy. In recent years these terms have been replaced by the category "antisocial personality disorder," which is characterized by narcissism, pathological lying, lack of empathy or remorse, early onset of behavioral problems, impulsive behavior, and no guilt in harming others.[25] Moreover, these individuals tend to place their needs above those of others and do not fear the judicial consequences of their actions. George Hassell's traits and life story are replete with all of these characteristics and more.

It is easy to play "Monday morning quarterback" when reexamining a killer who committed a series of crimes almost a century ago. However, modern psychiatrists and criminologists have tools that at least can give us a peek inside the mind of George Hassell. According to criminologist and psychologist Adrian Raine, "the best assessment tool for [measuring] psychopathy" is Hervey Cleckley's psychopathy checklist, introducd in his 1941 book, *The Mask of Sanity*.[26] In the book he describes "the psychopathic person as outwardly a perfect mimic of a normally functioning person, able to disguise the fundamental purposeful destructive behavior ... Despite the seemingly sincere, intelligent, even charming external presentation, internally ... does not have the ability to experience genuine emotions." It should be noted that Cleckley's adoption of the label "psychopath" in the *Mask of Sanity* brought the term into popular usage.[27] Unfortunately, the term *psychopath* has become a "catchall slang term for pure evil."[28]

Cleckley's checklist of behavioral characteristics suit Hassell well—superficial charm and noticeable intelligence; absence of delusions; absence of nervousness, unreliability, untruthfulness, and insincerity; lack of remorse and shame; suicide threats rarely carried out; failure to follow a life plan; poor judgment; and failure to learn from experience.[29]

This is the first comprehensive published account of the life and crimes of George Jefferson Hassell. My research stands as a corrective to previous accounts of his life, beginning with the place of his birth, which was in Smithfield, not Smithville, Texas. Between 1917 and 1926 he murdered at least thirteen people, including a common-law wife and her three kids and his brother's wife, whom he married, thus becoming stepfather to her eight children. He was a man of contradictions. Someone who could profess his love for children one minute and the next, strangle his own stepchildren as they slept or attempted to fight back. Most people who came into contact with George during his adult years described him as "a huge brute of a man." In fact, he seemed to grow in size with each telling. However, his prison records indicate that he was under five foot eight. Photographs of him indicate a powerful-looking man with large hands and long arms.

George J. Hassell did not leave much of a paper trail. Most what is known about him comes from his myriad interviews with reporters, his confessions, the trial transcripts, and reminiscences of those who crossed paths with him in Texas, Oklahoma, and California. Hassell controlled his life narrative until the day he died. Indeed, much of what was written about him, from the peak of his notoriety to the present, is based on his confessions. As this book will reveal, some of these tales do not hold up to the scrutiny of the *actual* historical record of George J. Hassell's life.

I have taught college courses on serial homicide and mass murder for more than twenty-five years and never in that time came across the subject of this book—that is, until one of my students alerted me to the fact that he was related to George Jefferson Hassell, whom he proudly informed me was "the fifth white person electrocuted" in the Texas state penitentiary in Huntsville. I then asked him if he had any family information or historical documents (a habit I developed early on, whenever someone alerted me that they might be privy to little-known historical information). He told me that he had a short unpublished manuscript written and researched by family members in the late 1980s.[30] He was kind enough to make a copy of it for me. I held onto it for a number of years with the intention of eventually writing a book on George J. Hassell and his murderous life. Finally, I found myself between book projects and decided to begin researching this book.

At the time I received the document, which the family titled "George Hassell Murder Story," I was unaware of both the exceptional nature of George Hassell's crimes and the research conducted by his relatives. What I have learned is that the family had been researching the Hassell story for more than thirty-five years. Members managed to travel to the Farwell, Texas, locations twice in the 1980s, the last time in 1988. Their timing was impeccable, since they were able to interview several people who had taken part in the trial, including the last living grand and petit jury members. They were also able to obtain interviews with surviving members of the Lindop family, who George lived with briefly after the murders. What's more, they interviewed the last surviving member of the exhumation party that dug up the bodies of his nine Texas victims.

Following in their footsteps, in 2020 I visited the family mass grave at Mount Olivet Cemetery; the former Clovis Baptist Sanitarium, where George was treated after his unsuccessful suicide attempt; the courthouse; the county jail; local history museums; and other sites. However, as luck would have it, the actual murder house, which the Hassell descendants were among the few modern researchers to visit, was long gone by the time I reached Farwell in 2020.

When I decided to devote myself to this project, I figured that someone else would have probably beat me to the story. However, as of 2022 the only published works on George J. Hassell's life and crimes are a modest number of articles in various newspapers, a thirty-eight-page book chapter, and a roman à clef about George Jefferson Hassell. They all offer interesting insights into the case, but for the most part what has been written about Hassell has been a retread of what prior authors and chroniclers had published, errors and all. Much of their evidence was based on George's numerous interviews with reporters as he was transferred between a handful of jails and prisons in Texas between 1926 and 1928. Other information for this book was gleaned from newspaper interviews with individuals who had known him in his twenties and thirties, as well as documents held in the Texas State Library and Archive (TSLA) and the Texas Department of Criminal Justice Archives. My research on this case over several years has found and corrected a number of historical errors in his storytelling and the accepted accounts of his life.

Man with the Killer Smile resurrects the life and crimes of an unforgettable villain previously lost to history. He joins a stable of Texas killers, such as John Wesley Hardin and William Longley in the nineteenth century, as well as the twentieth century's Dean "Candyman" Corll, Joe "Bluebeard of South Texas" Ball, Kenneth "the Broomstick Killer" McDuff, and "Railroad Killer" Angel Maturino Resendiz, on the roster of the Lone Star State's most despicable murderers.

Curiously, Hassell is not mentioned in any of the published compendiums of America's worst serial killers and mass murderers. Even the king of narrative true crime, Harold Schechter, leaves him out of his comprehensive 2012 tome, *Psycho USA: Famous American Killers You Never Heard Of*. Hassell's saga and crimes intersect with the growth of cities such as Whittier in California and Abilene, Fort Worth, and Farwell in Texas. *Man with the Killer Smile* chronicles the continuing evolution of the Texas criminal justice system in the 1920s, including its prisons, judiciary, and the death penalty. Hassell cast a long dark shadow over the roads he trod during this era, introducing another major crime figure to the rich history of Texas crime and punishment.

Chapter 1

George J. Hassell: The Early Years

> *"Hassell as a boy ... turned out to be thoroughly shiftless and unworthy."*
> —Sid Ross, 1906

Husband, father, uncle, embezzler, mass murderer, serial killer, family annihilator, philanderer, child molester, and military deserter, George Jefferson Hassell was many things to many people, most of them bad. Much of what is known about his early years comes from the copious newspaper interviews he gave in the heyday of his infamy, between 1926 and 1928. Other information can be gleaned from interviews with those who knew him in his teens and twenties. Like any autobiographical information, much of Hassell's own chronicle of those years should be taken with a healthy dose of skepticism.

He is among the least-known multiple murderers in Texas, let alone American history. Consider the fact that in August 1888, the first of Jack the Ripper's five murders took place in the East End of London. Dozens if not hundreds of books have been written about this crime spree, which was considered among the most notorious of all time. The first Ripper murder took place just one month after the July 25, 1888, birth of George Jefferson Hassell in Smithfield, Texas, a short distance from Fort Worth in Tarrant County.[1] He would go on to eclipse the murder spree of the British Ripper, in number of victims if not fame, during the years 1917–1926. Yet, George remains among the least-known mass murderers and serial killers in history. This is his story.

George J. Hassell was the youngest of seven children. Most in his paternal lineage had been farmers. He would follow in their stead, with sporadic jobs in various other low-paying and labor-intensive positions, such as tenant farmer, oil field roustabout, thresher operator, railroad worker, and merchant marine chef. If George took after anyone in the family, it was probably his paternal grandfather, Spencer Tomlin Hassell (1825–1916). Born in Hickman County, Tennessee, he moved to Anderson County, Texas, in early 1845 and lived in Palestine, Texas, for the rest of his life. Like his future grandson, Spencer was brought before the Texas justice system on more than one occasion, appearing in front of a court twice in 1887 alone. On May 7 of that year, he appeared in the local district court in Palestine, after a plaintiff, W. L. Warrington, sued him for slander and defamation of character. The jury agreed with the plaintiff and rendered a verdict against him to the tune of $750.

Spencer was back before the district court on December 5, 1887. The case achieved some local notoriety, due no doubt to his prominence in the community and of the crime itself. He had separated from his wife earlier in 1887, and they had reportedly "amicably" split up the property between them. However, shortly afterwards, their former homestead burned to the ground in a suspicious fire. Spencer was arrested on suspicion of setting it but was not held in custody as the investigation proceeded, and he was subsequently acquitted.

Hassell's grandfather had a colorful backstory. He enlisted in the Confederate Army on July 11, 1863. During the Civil War he rose to the rank of sergeant in the Confederate cavalry, as a member of Company E, 37th Regiment, Terrell's Texas Cavalry. He was honorably discharged on the banks of the Trinity River following the Confederate surrender.[2]

While his grandfather's life is well documented, except for what Hassell revealed in newspaper interviews little is known about his parents. George's father, James William Hassell (1850–1910), was born and died in Anderson County, Texas. His mother, Martha Jane Stovall, was born in St. Augustine, Texas, in 1851 and would outlive her husband by four years (1851–1914). Hassell would sometimes use his mother's maiden name while on the lam. Martha died in Bexar, Texas, on April 21, 1914.[3] His parents had tied the knot in 1872. By 1900, the family was living in Cloud Chief, Oklahoma, once the county seat of Washita County but by the twenty-first century little more than a ghost town.

Hassell's first years were spent on family farms, where he, the youngest child, was known as "Jeffie," probably short for Jefferson. He always claimed that much of his early life was "a faint memory of especially striking experiences."[4] He boasted that he began chewing tobacco before he was six and that by the time he was on trial for his life in 1927 he could expectorate tobacco with a marksman's skill. Reared in the Methodist faith, by the time he was convicted of the mass murder of his family in Farwell, Texas, in 1926 he professed no attachment to any particular church. His mother, he claimed, was a Bible student who was regarded as an "expert reader and a good church worker in the community in which she lived."[5]

During his sojourns in various small county jails on his way to the electric chair in the late 1920s, Hassell enjoyed regaling reporters with his exploits, holding forth on his purported youthful religiosity as well as his murders as an adult. Only in conjunction with his courtroom confession in 1927 and the reminiscences of who crossed paths with him when he was young, can his interviews with journalists be said to offer the best information on his early years.

Hassell recounted that the first punishment he ever received was from his mother, for chewing tobacco as a wee lad. In his words, his mother "took him to the barn, kneeled and prayed for him and then forced him to repeat every prayer after her." He was fond of boasting that he had also been a student of the Bible when he lived in Oklahoma, bragging he "was regarded as one of the best men at public prayer in the country in which he lived" and could outpray any man in his county. He explained how he had begun to reveal his dual nature early on, telling a reporter that had "he prayed at church in daytime and chased about with girls at night."[6]

His troubles with—maybe a better phrase would be "his weakness for"—the opposite sex appeared to have begun quite early. He seemed proud that he had had his first affair at the age of eight, if he was to be believed, with a fifteen-year-old girl. One reporter wrote, "From that time on the story of his relations with women is as unbelievable as the fact that he murdered as many people as he claimed."[7] However, George took solace in his claim that despite having had affairs in more than thirty states, he "never so far as I know wrecked a home."[8]

He was fairly consistent in his numerous confessions and interviews with journalists. But this did not mean there weren't holes in many of his stories. Perhaps, having crammed so much living and killing into a twenty-year period, he was confused about past events, but it is more likely he was trying to inflate his reputation in any way possible. While the main events rarely varied in retelling, the years and order of his travels between 1900, when he was twelve, and 1920 often differed by a year or more.

Accounts of his life, most of which are journalistic, have erroneously noted that Hassell had just "entered his teens" when his mother died. Government records indicate otherwise. Since she actually died in 1914, that would have put him at twenty-six years of age. Likewise, his father was supposedly poisoned by his second wife in 1904 or 1905. Again, records put that death in 1910, when Hassell was actually twenty-two. These dates punch holes in the credibility of much of Hassell's accounting for his early years and make one wonder what else he lied about.

His oft-told version of his life has him leaving home in 1901 after his mother Martha died, which would have put him at around thirteen. But as noted above, she wouldn't actually die for another thirteen years. He perhaps used these dates to suggest that he was out on his own and more independent at a much earlier age than he actually was. Indeed, there is a stark difference between leaving home as a young teenager and in one's mid-twenties. Meanwhile, his father, James, remarried after his wife supposedly died in 1901. The variation in timeframe is important here. Hassell claimed his father was fatally poisoned by his new wife in 1904 or 1905, which would have made him sixteen or seventeen. He liked to tell reporters that when he got wind of this malfeasance, he was intent on exacting revenge and that this was probably the first time he considered the mass murder of family members. It sounds good on the face of it, but it was likely just more of his bluster.

The recorded events in his early life suggest that the story about Hassell's father being poisoned by his stepmother and his revenge plot was fabricated, a figment of his imagination. However, in light of the carnage that accompanied his later years, it is worth recounting here. In his telling, he had been in Fort Worth the night before the purported poisoning, spending money he had embezzled from his employer, when he heard of his father's death. Shortly after, he returned to his hometown of Smithfield, intent on shooting every member of his stepmother's extended family, which included three children as well as a niece and her husband, when they jumped out of their beds after he created some ruckus to wake them up. He claimed he laid down, waiting for the family to fall asleep. But by the time he woke up, the sun was shining in his face. He said that he had drunk too much whiskey and passed out before he could carry out his first mass killing—alas, if he had not consumed so much whiskey and had stayed awake, he would have added a stepmother and five step-relations to his ultimate list of victims. This tale of thwarted revenge is a great story. The only problem with it is that both of his parents were still alive at this point in time, and in fact his mother would outlive his father by four years. Moreover, there is no evidence that there was ever a stepmother in the picture. Perhaps, the only morsel of reality in this telling was that he had demonstrated a weakness for alcohol earlier in his life and used it justify his misbehavior during his violent episodes.

Hassell often mentioned that his dad was quick to punish him, noting that one particularly savage beating "caused him to leave home and become a wanderer." He usually claimed it was in 1899, when he was only eleven, but he probably conflated several examples of his father's brutality. If his father was as brutal as Hassell claimed, his early life would fall in step with those of the many other psychopaths who have endured poor parenting and childhood trauma on their way to adulthood. In this version of his saga, when he left home, he ended up in "Cardill [sic]," Oklahoma.[9] This story sounds implausible, but it is representative of the penchant for prevarication and running away that would characterize him for the rest of his life, whether avoiding confrontations, evading the consequences of his murderous deeds, or deserting from the Navy and Army under different names. Moreover, it is possible that he became inured to domestic violence on the home front of his youth, further contributing to his increasingly brutal domestic crimes.

In Hassell's telling, his father sent him a letter that convinced him to move back home after the aforementioned beating. Instead, in 1906 he pulled up stakes once again, this time lighting out for the small towns of Tuscola and Ovalo, Texas, in southern Taylor County. Both towns were separated by less than three miles. There he found work driving a freight wagon for Sidney Peters (S. P.) "Sid" Ross (1871–1945). The son of a Baptist preacher, Ross had settled in the Abilene area in 1898 and, by 1906, was in the ginning business in Tuscola and then in Ovalo. Ross and R. C. "Bob" Malone ran a cotton gin together in Tuscola. Although cotton gins and mills dotted the southern plains until the mid-1900s, few survive today. But in the 1920s cotton farmers were dependent on local gins for removing seeds from the lint and cleaning it in order to prepare it for milling. Hassell arrived in southern Taylor County before trucks were used to carry the cotton to the gins. Freighters were needed to haul it in wagons, which were usually pulled by teams of horses or, in some cases, oxen.[10]

Cotton farming dominated much of the regional economy between the Civil War and World War Two. Indeed, while much Texas mythology hinges on oil and cowboys, "it was agriculture that supplied most Texans with their living before World War Two."[11] Twenty years after Hassell worked for him, Ross was interviewed by a reporter after the 1926 murders in Farwell. He remembered the boy well. He told a reporter that he and his partner "liked the boy" as well as the sister he had, who was living near Fort Worth, "a splendid woman who wrote him letters filled with sisterly advice, and he used to read them to me."[12]

It wasn't long before Ross and Malone came to trust Hassell enough to send him to Abilene "with cotton seed for the oil mill, money for the bank, and money to buy supplies"—a decision they would soon regret. Due to the lack of a railroad connection at Tuscola, everything had to be freighted.

Thus, Hassell's job entailed driving a wagon the twenty miles between Tuscola and Abilene and back. On one journey in late fall of 1906, he drove a "cotton caravan" to Abilene. Upon arriving in Abilene, as Hassell related in 1927 from a Texas jail cell, he committed his "first crime." In his telling, "Ross gave me $100 to put in a bank and I had $40 which had been paid for chickens. I met a companion and bad company. We had some drinks and they proposed to me to go to Fort Worth and we took the money and we left." Crime and drink were steadfast companions to Hassell until his death. And so was his predilection for lying. Once arrived in Abilene, he "left the teams in the wagon yard here, threw off the cotton in a yard, and with the money he stole at the gin, disappeared."[13]

Hassell was the only one who claimed that he had accomplices in this incident, probably due to unwillingness to take all the blame for his criminal actions and untrustworthiness. His early tendencies toward fabrication and lack of self-control and his predilection for liquor fit the characteristics of many psychopaths. The researcher Hervey Cleckley would have instantly recognized early signs of developing psychopathy in Hassell at this age. His stealing, deceit, and selfish nature, combined with a "poor work history," were all predictive of a future life of crime and duplicity.[14]

When Hassell did not return to Tuscola on time, Ross went to Abilene to investigate. Once he learned of the theft, he brought it to the attention of the authorities. He would later recount that "Hassell as a boy, was unworthy of the confidence I placed in him, and turned out to be thoroughly shiftless and unworthy."[15]

Police tracked him down to his sister's home in Fort Worth. On March 11, 1907, he was indicted for embezzling fifty dollars from his employers, as well as for forgery and passing a forged instrument. Two days later he plead guilty and was sentenced by Judge J. H. Calhoun to a term of not less than two and not more than ten years imprisonment. Besides the embezzlement, he had fraudulently endorsed a check made by Chandler-Hall Grocery Company to W. R. King. The $3.40 check was signed by P. T. Hurt to "Malone & Ross," on the Citizen's National Bank. Once Hassell accepted the embezzlement charges, the others were dismissed.[16]

Hassell would later claim that his employer tried to convince authorities to allow him to work off his debt instead of going to prison. There is little evidence to support this, but even if the effort had been made, it obviously failed, for he began a two-year sentence, beginning on what was probably the Burleson and Johns Share Farm in the vicinity of Hillsboro, Texas.[17] He would often bring this up when coming up with excuses for why he turned to homicide. In January 1928 he even told reporter John L. McCarthy, "I firmly believe if they had allowed me to work out the money, I took from Sid Ross that I would never have committed any other crime."[18]

With respect to this episode, Hassell can be observed refusing to take responsibility for his actions. In his copious interviews he claimed to have been seventeen at the time, which would have put him in jail around 1905. In fact, George was already eighteen (pushing nineteen) when he entered the Texas state prison system on March 13, 1907. His earliest prison records described George as being just over five foot seven and 180 pounds, wearing size nine shoes. This runs counter to subsequent descriptions that portrayed him as a large bear of a man. But it might have been more attributable to his considerable girth or sheer body mass. In any case, it is clear from his state prison records he was no taller than five foot seven. His complexion was described as fair, his eyes grey (or in some cases blue), his hair light or chestnut. Several scars marked his body, including one on the bottom of his left foot and another inside the joint of his right elbow. As to his other traits and status, prison records indicate he was unmarried, had a tobacco habit, and while poorly educated, could read and write.[19]

Hassell's stint in confinement would confirm the worst of the Texas prison system's reputation. In an interview shortly before he was executed in 1928, he told *Amarillo News* reporter John L. McCarthy that he had "suffered every abuse and privation in the pen or work farms" but worked hard and was awarded a trusty position.[20] His later screeds against the incarceration of teenagers alongside adults in leasing and farm camps were no doubt based on the brutal and unrestrained treatment of inmates there. No facility in Texas was more violent than the prison farms. Prisoners were routinely whipped until they lost consciousness, and in other cases they were raped and physically abused. In November 1901, for example, an assistant sergeant at the

Clemens State Farm discovered two prisoners engaged in sodomy. Both were disciplined in the most humiliating fashion. First, they were subjected to a brutal whipping, and then they were forced to perform the sexual act in front of other inmates in the camp.[21] If Hassell never witnessed any of these episodes in person, he certainly would have been privy to such stories from other prisoners.

Prisoners were often shifted from one camp to another. According to one investigation from this period, an inmate was transferred fifty-four times in seven years. This inmate also reported being whipped at the Hill County Farm, which is where George entered the convict leasing system.[22] The inquiry into prison conditions further revealed that mattresses were only changed once a year, at least at the Burleson-Johns Camp where George began his sentence, which lasted from May 12 to June 6, 1907.[23] The food was reported as being "tolerable," and farm work usually involved harvesting cotton, corn, and alfalfa.[24]

Since the 1890s, Albert Sidney Burleson (1863–1937) and his brother-in-law, C. D. Johns, had operated the three-thousand-acre share farm in Bosque County, using a force of about 150 state prisoners. Shares were divided so that the state received 60 percent of the crop, but the farm earned substantial income for its owners.[25] Texas inmates "have always been expected to pay their own way ... to defray the costs of incarceration through inmate labor." In 1866 the Texas Legislature established the Board of Public Labor and directed its members to secure contracts with private interests for the use of inmate labor. The prison superintendent was then requested to organize prisoners to work on farms, railroads, public utilities, river channels, iron mines, and so forth.[26]

Hassell's first experience with the prison system began under the administration of Governor Thomas M. Campbell (1907–1911). During his term in office Campbell enlarged the prison farm system. In 1908 the Penitentiary Board paid $160,000 to the Imperial Sugar Company for 5,235 acres along with stock and equipment. Hassell would soon be laboring in the sugarcane fields, which gained their own notoriety for brutal conditions. According to an article appearing in the *San Antonio Press* just months after Hassell was released, "if a guard approached a man, knee deep in cane field mud and slush, he must snap to attention with head bared to the blazing sun." Confronted by an array of reports about the punitive regime, Campbell responded that "everyone had to realize that some criminals must undergo the pain of the lash lest they become incorrigible."[27]

In 1909, the same year Hassell was released, an investigating committee report contained the following comments, as if verifying his worst accounts of inmate treatment. One committee member reported that "after witnessing with my own eyes accounts of brutality and hearing with my own ears talks of atrocious and brutal treatment at the hands of certain sergeants within the penitentiary system ... I cannot find it in my heart to endorse the use of an instrument by which death has been inflicted upon human beings; neither can I endorse a modification of the punishment by the strap or a bat," which was a twenty-four-inch leather strap, four inches wide, with a wooden handle.

The Texas Legislature was forced to act in response to the newspaper accounts portraying inhumane conditions throughout the prison system, but by the time it did, Hassell had already been released and would not enjoy the fruits of the subsequent investigation. It is unknown whether Hassell was ever lashed or otherwise physically mistreated while working on prison farms. However, it is clear that when the committee investigating the penitentiary system made its findings known in November 1909, those hoping for less physical punishment were disappointed, particularly by the recommendation that convicts "must be whipped in the presence of disinterested citizens and of a prison physician" who was tasked with making a detailed report of the punishment as well as the physical condition of the man before and after the ordeal.[28] But although there was a preexisting rule that the skin should not be broken by the lash, the committee identified many men bearing permanent scars on their backs and bodies.

Hassell was next shifted over to the construction of the Trinity and Brazos Railroad and probably confined at Camp Wright, which was located near present-day Maydelle, Texas. Camp Wright was created in 1906 to house convict workers and chain gangs that built the Mewshaw State Sawmill in 1908. The prisoners were tasked with hauling wood that would be turned into charcoal for the Rusk Prison iron foundry.[29] While we do not know the specifics of his railroad camp experience, according to the investigative committee a similar labor camp "[showed] that the brutality of the guards and sergeants in this camp exceeded that of any other camp visited by this committee; that the convicts were poorly fed, half clothed, and they were driven to their work with the lash, like galley slaves, from early dawn until the somber shadows of evening put an end to their sufferings and gave them relief from the bullwhip."[30] After his stint at Camp Wright, he was transferred between September 5 and October 23, 1907, to the Texas Turpentine Company, where he worked from October 23, 1907, to November 1908.[31]

According to the investigation, the railroad company "failed to make the necessary sleeping quarters [for the convict workers] after repeated demands had been made [to rectify conditions]." Investigators "considered [these conditions] detrimental to the health of the men."[32] As a result, the Texas Prison Board ordered the superintendent to take charge of the men and declare the lease contract with the Trinity & Brazos Railroad "null and void on account of failure" to provide adequate sleeping quarters. The lease was canceled on September 1, 1907.[33]

Based on this information, Hassell would have labored beside legions of other inmates building the state's fledgling roads. He did not speak fondly of any of his work assignments, reserving his greatest enmity for his time on turpentine and cane farms, a part of his incarceration he described as a "hell on earth." He would later describe the Texas prison system as an "awful place for anyone to be, especially a youth or young man."[34] During this era, East Texas still boasted "vast virgin stands of longleaf pines." Resin was harvested from these trees for the distillation of turpentine. Turpentine camps were located in the forests, isolated from the prying eyes of town or city folks.

Hassell was leased out to the Texas Turpentine Company, which was located in Jasper, Texas. In 1908, which corresponded to Hassell's prison stint, the Turpentine company employed over eight hundred prisoners. According to Texas Prison Board minutes, when it came to leasing convicts for mining or turpentine work, the minimum prices were set at $40 per month. Ordinarily, the minimum for leasing prisoners began at $28 per month for white convicts and $30 for Black convicts.[35] Turpentine work, like mining, was abolished in 1910. The state had never been a big supporter of loaning prisoners out to turpentine companies, due to the "unusually hazardous" nature of the work."[36]

The writer and folklorist Zora Neale Hurston (1891–1960), best known for her association with the Harlem Renaissance, was sent by the Works Progress Administration (WPA) to visit the turpentine camps thirty years after leasing ended. Although the work was no longer performed by prison labor, Hassell probably would have recognized the miserable process. Hurston observed that the process required chippers, pullers, dippers, and wood choppers. The chipper "is the man who makes those little slanting cuts on pine trees so that the gum exudes and drains down into the box." A puller was "a specialized chipper, [who] chips the trees when they have been worked too high for the chipper." Dippers are responsible for "[scraping] out the gum with the dipping iron and [putting] it back in place and [passing] on to the next face." Hassell never mentioned which task he performed. Between the smell of hot resin and the tropical humidity of East Texas, unpaid convicts no doubt dreaded the turpentine assignment.

Hassell's prison experience did not get any easier when he was assigned to harvest sugar cane in Brazoria County beginning on November 1, 1908, probably for the House family. By the end of the nineteenth century, the Edward M. House (1858–1938) clan was wealthy and influential in Texas society. His father, Thomas W. House, who died in 1880, had come from England and opened a mercantile business in Houston. Having invested his lucre in agricultural lands and grown cotton and sugarcane, by the time he died he owned more than 250,000 acres touching parts of 63 counties.[37] According to Texas prison historian Robert Perkinson, "Harvesting sugar cane is one of the most grueling tasks in agriculture, as the stalks have to be cut, stripped, crushed, boiled, and processed in a blistering race against spoilage."[38] Trading the East Texas turpentine camps for the Brazoria sugarcane fields did little to ease the rigor of Hassell's daily life, and before he knew it, he had joined hundreds of convicts "swinging machetes and rolling the cane."[39]

In 1899, Texas purchased more than five thousand acres of "exceptionally fertile" soil perfectly suited for this crop. This region had long been described as the "Sugar Bowl District of Brazoria County."[40] The state invested in a large-capacity sugar mill that could grind nine hundred tons of sugarcane every twenty-four hours. Prison officials were confident there would be work for as many as four hundred prisoners. The Brazoria prison farm, later named the William Clemens farm in honor of the chairman of the prison board, proved so successful that in 1908, it established three more agricultural units, just in time for Hassell, who was only halfway through his prison stint.

Between 1906 and 1908, the number of prisoners working on state farms rose from 338 to 1,065.[41] Like other leasing initiatives, the idea was to extract as much labor as possible from inmates on state farms, often almost killing them in the process. Profitability was foremost on the minds of all farm managers. To that end, meager resources were devoted toward providing prisoners with adequate food, medical care, and living quarters. Indeed, conditions did not improve until sugarcane leasing was abolished.

The Texas Penitentiary Investigating Committee report found that the "excessive work from first light to last, seven days a week," was "devilish and corrupt." In 1910, the contract lease system was abolished and "the state reestablished its total responsibility for running prison operations." But not before Hassell was seemingly marked for life by what he witnessed and experienced in the convict leasing camps. Prior to 1909, he had no record of violent behavior, but before the end of the next decade he was well on his way to becoming a serial mass murderer.

After being released from prison two months early on March 13, 1909, Hassell was given five dollars, which he spent most of on a pair of shoes, saving his last dollar for a meal and a bed for the night, leaving him flat broke. He would always claim that after he was released, he was walking down a street in Galveston when he saw a military recruitment sign that said: "Men Wanted." He decided to use his mother's maiden name, telling one reporter that "it wouldn't do to go in the army under the name I had in the pen,"[42] and enlisted under the name "George J. Stovall." If this was true, then like most of his actions throughout his life, he behaved on impulse, not putting much thought into what he was getting into. Resorting to an alias, however, was a strategy he would use often in the coming years to operate just beneath the radar of the authorities.

His Army career, if he had one, was short-lived. According to Hassell, he was first posted at Fort Sam Houston in San Antonio. He would later allege that in 1909 he was in Dallas, either with his unit or to visit some type of exposition, where he managed to find trouble once more by getting into a dust-up with a cook. He told a reporter years later that he "punched out one of his eyes."[43] He was arrested for the fracas and decided to desert a week later, heading back home "to my people near Fort Worth." It is possible that he made a cameo appearance in the Army and then returned to his sister's house. Alternatively, perhaps it was after this that he went back to ask Sid Ross for his old job back.

Indeed, his ex-employer remembered Hassell returning to Taylor County when he got out of prison in 1909. He went back to Ross and Malone and said that he was reformed and asked for a job. It is very possible that his short stint in the Army had actually taken place and that he neglected to inform the ginners that he had actually deserted. Anyway, succumbing to his superficial charm and sociopathic persuasiveness, they rehired him. Ross remembered him as "a great workman, and Malone [his partner] and I had hoped he had learned his lesson."[44] The ginners would rue the day they fell for Hassell's promise to turn over a new leaf.

Chapter 2

First Love, Last Love

"The only woman I ever loved."

Only a few months out of prison and having possibly deserted from the Army, Hassell was back on familiar turf in Taylor County. His former employer, Malone and Ross, had given him another chance. Initially, they put him to work at their Ovalo gin. It must have been around this time that he met and married a local woman, Minnie L. Laughlin, "daughter of a fine old Ovalo pioneer," Joel G. Laughlin, who was born in 1849. Ross described Minnie as "a splendid little woman" and "hoped she could make a man of him."[1] It would seem by his description that Ross was familiar with her family.

Of his three known wives [one was common-law], Minnie was the only one to escape his clutches alive—barely. She has presented a tantalizing mystery for researchers attempting to chronicle her life or death. She left even fewer traces than her notorious husband. The common conceit was that she disappeared intentionally, going to great lengths to shield her son and herself from his infamous father.

What records that are available indicate that she was either born in 1889 or 1890, in the area of Ovalo and Buffalo Gap, Texas.[2] Except for her age and the 1910 US Census, records of her family and early life are hard to come by.[3] The last time she appears in any public records [as Minnie L. Laughlin] is in the 1920 US Census, which lists her, at twenty-six, living with her father, seventy-one, mother, sixty-one, and her son by George, Delbert Laughlin, who was nine. Most of what is known about her short family life with Hassell was revealed in his confessions and interviews in the late 1920s. A rare documentation of their marriage, also in the 1910 US Census, dates from just five months after they married. The couple appears in its pages as man and wife for the first and only time.

It is easy to envision the magnetic young man with the disarming smile, grey-blue eyes, and well-practiced charm sweeping Minnie off her feet. Although only separated by a year in age, Hassell must have seemed worldly to the country girl as they set off on what would become a rocky two-year marriage, with most of that time spent apart. However, from the very start, at least according to Hassell, Minnie's parents tried to convince her to get out of the relationship. Most likely they knew her suitor was an ex-convict, out of prison just nine months when they tied the knot. Despite her parents' misgivings, they were married in Buffalo Gap on either December 9 or 15, 1909. Minnie's parents' machinations must have become more difficult in the fall of 1910, when Minnie gave birth to a son, who they named James Delbert. Little could she predict that the interference of her parents would probably save her and the baby, given that Hassell would go on to murder at least eleven stepchildren and two domestic partners over the next sixteen years.

Like with every other aspect of the story, we have only George's later versions of events and scanty genealogical records to go on. However, a letter in his Texas Penitentiary Execution file offers a more credible explanation for why his first wife and son took off. In the early fall of 1964, George's son wrote to the assistant director of the Texas Department of Corrections (TDC) seeking information on his late father. According to James Delbert Laughlin, he explained, "In my later years I have found out that I was born to George Hassell. They [the three of them] only lived together a short time and upon their separation, my mother returned to her maiden name which I also use. I understand he was the murderer of a woman and her three children in California and also the murderer of a wife of his deceased brother, which he had later married himself, and her eight children [also his nephews and nieces] ... *I can remember that he made attempts on the lives of my mother and myself in which he failed* and for which I am thankful for my life today" (italics in original). James Delbert went on in his letter to beseech the Huntsville warden, W. E. Moors, and then Assistant Director of TDC, Richard C. Jones [not Johnson] to fill him in on the rest of the Hassell saga. He was grasping for the truth and said, "I have heard his story in so many different ways, I would like his own story firsthand, of how, where and why he could have done such things." He ended by asking whether he could obtain a copy of Hassell's confession if he came Huntsville. Whether this ever came to pass or not is unknown.[4]

Now that Hassell was married, with a young son in tow, his former employer Sid Ross gave him another chance to make good. According to what Ross later told a reporter, he not only hired Hassell back but let him [and probably his family] live on a farm he owned in neighboring Nolan County. In fact, it appears that Ross built a house for Hassell on spec and furnished it as well. All his tenant had to do was farm the land "on halves," and Ross would purchase all supplies. This arrangement didn't last long. Several months later Hassell was again back to check-forging. Years later, Ross recalled how Hassell got ahold of one of his checks, "which had already been cashed in the bank at Trent. It was yellow with age, and he must have found it on the prairie. He took it to the bank and cashed it again." The check was for twenty dollars, and Ross was reimbursed by the bank. However, Hassell, according to Ross, had already "left his crop, deserted his wife and baby and disappeared." Meanwhile, his benevolent employer still had to pay for the furniture and supplies he had provided to George. In the end he decided not to prosecute his wayward employee and hoped he had seen the last of him.

Hassell might have come from a farming family, but as time would tell, he still had a lot to learn about agriculture. Perhaps that is why he never mentioned in any of his interviews that Ross had helped get him started on his own farm. Depending on whose account you believe, either Ross got him started on his Nolan County spread before the family split up or Hassell rented a slice of land on his own and tried his hand at farming and settling down. Regardless, there is much more to the story in Hassell's account than Ross mentioned in his 1926 interview.

Hassell recounted that after he married, the family moved to Ovalo, in an unincorporated part of Abilene, where he found employment with one "Ace Edwards."[5] Named for its location within an oval-shaped valley in southeastern Taylor County, Ovalo was an early camping place for buffalo hunters and a stop for trail drivers going through Buffalo Gap. Perhaps Ovalo offered better prospects to the young Hassell family, especially after the Abilene and Southern Railway Company laid tracks near it in May 1909. The 1910 Texas Almanac described Ovalo, which was established in 1908, as "a new town on the Abilene and Southern Railroad, twenty miles south of Abilene, TX." In less than twelve months, Ovalo boasted forty-six businesses, "two good church buildings," a two-story brick schoolhouse, "distinct industries," and "several houses of brick and cement structure."[6]

Maybe looking to be closer to the "big city," Hassell moved the family twenty miles away, to Abilene. George liked boasting that he found work laying the city's first pavement. Once this job was over, he allegedly worked as a night watchman some 180 miles away in Fort Worth and was even given a police commission, although this, like so much else, cannot be substantiated. He said he continued in this work "until he grew tired of it" and moved on to a farm in Hobart, Oklahoma.[7] It seemed no matter how hard he tried, he was unable to put down family roots anywhere, and moving once more, they were back in the Fort Worth vicinity, some 224 miles from Hobart. Hassell never explained how the family traveled from place to place. He never mentioned having an automobile, so we can only assume he and the family moved around by train, especially as more lines moved into the region, connecting to more and more small towns. His transient nature falls in line nicely with Cleckley's psychopathy checklist, particularly "his inability to follow any life plan, aimlessly drifting from person to person, job to job, and town to town."[8]

Hassell would usually stick to his story, which was that he and Minnie had agreed that she would go back home with the baby to be near her family,[9] while he would go north to Kansas to earn some money working in the wheat fields.[10] He also insisted in later interviews that they promised to write letters to each other every day, and he never wavered from his contention that he wrote her every day. However, he claimed that he did not receive any letters back from her for the first week or more—that is, until he received a letter by registered mail in which she told him "she was through with him." He angrily tore it up. He would later recount that this "ruined my life." He was quick to blame their separation on interference by his in-laws, especially once he found out that his letters to his wife were being intercepted by her parents, as were her letters to him. Hassell would always explain, "they didn't like me. I had been a convict and they thought I was bad."[11]

Every journalistic account of this interlude in the Hassell saga likewise has Minnie's parents interfering in their marriage, though some accounts have Hassell leaving Minnie, while other suggest she left him. A better explanation for the estrangement lay hidden for decades in a letter in the Texas State Library Archives, James Delbert Laughlin's 1964 correspondence seeking more information on his infamous father. Rather than a love story gone awry, as Minnie and George's son explained, he and his mother left Hassell for their own protection because Hassell had been trying to kill them. In any case, Minnie's parents could not have realized how prescient they were in distancing the former lovebirds from each other.

Shortly after receiving the registered rejection letter from Minnie, Hassell later claimed, he enlisted in the Navy in San Francisco under his real name. However, he feared that his earlier desertion from the army at Fort Sam Houston under the name "George Stovall" could be revealed through a fingerprint record. Hoping to avoid arrest, he deserted the Navy soon after joining.

Sources vary as to the next sequence of events in Hassell's life. By some accounts, after he deserted the navy, he joined the Army again under his real name, hoping the Navy would never find him. Like many of his plans, this proved to be a poor move on his part. Just days after his last desertion, the authorities tracked him down in Oklahoma and he was arrested.

Convicted of fraud and desertion from both branches of the armed services, Hassell later recounted that he did a total of three years' time, at the Fort Leavenworth Penitentiary in Kansas and in two naval prisons: Mare Island Naval Prison, California, and the Marine Disciplinary Barracks in Norfolk, Virginia.[12] If he served time in military prisons for his desertions, it was probably sometime between 1911 and 1914, but the sequence of confinement is confusing according to his various confessions and the lack of any prison records indicating his penal life. However, it is probable that he served this time and in three different military prisons. It appears he most likely did his first stint at Mare Island on the West Coast. He has said that he was then sent to Fort Leavenworth in Kansas for his army desertion and then to Norfolk, Virginia, for fraud and desertion.

No matter the order of his incarceration, Hassell had already been toughened up during his two-year stint as a teenager in the infamous Texas penal system and was probably better equipped than most to handle time behind bars. Whether it prepared him for the military prisons is unknown, because he never goes into any detail about his prison stints. Undoubtedly, he became even more inured to violence during his terms inside what some have described as America's toughest prisons. Again, we only have his later interviews to account for his experiences at any of these prisons.

Mare Island was the Navy's first land-based prison. Opened in 1868, it was better known to servicemen as "Old 84" (after Building 84). Moreover, it had a reputation as "one of the toughest federal prisons."[13] Sailors and Marines who served time there included convicted deserters, mutineers, men who conspired to rob and kill superior officers, and the like. Most likely, Hassell did his time at Mare Island rather than Norfolk during this time period. because Mare Island had a much larger disciplinary barracks. In 1912, Norfolk held just twelve miscreants, while Mare Island had close to two hundred prisoners.

Hassell's probable years of confinement, between 1911 and 1915, coincided with a time period when more than half of the prisoners in naval disciplinary institutions were convicted of desertion. The naval prisons were overcrowded but were no longer the brutal regimes of the late-nineteenth century, when floggings and double irons were common. Hassell was fortunate that his sentences corresponded with a growing prison reform movement and a move towards less draconian conditions. By 1914, military offenses such as desertion were being treated less seriously, as attempts were made to reduce the number of inmates and military costs. The implementation in 1915 of General Order 110 "targeted offenders with little or no potential for immediate discharge from the service." Likewise, it was intended to "rid the Navy of large numbers of chronic liberty offenders."[14] If anyone fit this criterion, it was the deserter of multiple services George Hassell.

Once freed from naval prison confinement, Hassell, by his account, tried to "affect a reconciliation" with his wife, Minnie, who was still residing with her family, back in Texas. Apparently, this did not go well, and he would use this sequence of events to explain his murderous familial behavior in the years to come. He was always adamant that she was the only woman he ever loved (and the only one of his three wives and live-in partners he did not kill). Hassell would always claim that his turn to evil began after his wife rebuffed his attempts to reunite. Until his dying day, according to one Texas reporter, he would persist in claiming that his first failed marriage "was responsible for the queer quirk to his makeup which led him to deeds of violence."[15]

Hassell would use his recollections of unrequited love as part of a narrative to explain how he ended up on death row. Whether he ever loved his wife or anyone else is unknowable, but Hervey Cleckley's research on psychopaths found other examples in the Hassell mold, "profoundly disturbed individuals" who were not just "incapable of love" but cared only for themselves.[16] Likewise, according to the criminologist-psychiatrist Adrian Raine, a psychopath is so egocentric that he might be able to offer verbal signs of affection but not emotional love.[17]

Hassell was not one to give up easily, and during his numerous interviews he usually mentioned how much he wanted to meet his son again.[18] He went shopping in Fort Worth for some "little suits" he could take up to James Delbert in Winters, Texas, where the family had put down roots. He claimed he was allowed to see the boy, but only briefly. According to this claim, he gave the young child the clothes and then was off again.[19]

The next time Hassell allegedly saw Minnie and James Delbert, they were living in Abilene. He later told a reporter, "I went there to see my boy," who by then had "been taught his papa was dead and they agreed to let me see him if I wouldn't reveal my identity. I agreed to this so I could see him." The last time Hassell saw the boy, who was then about fourteen and whose mother had remarried, was in 1924, when James Delbert was reportedly living in Jarrell in Bell County. This time, when he went up to the house, or so he claimed, "they threw rocks at me. My boy said, 'you are not my papa, you are just pretending you are my papa, and he threw stones at me. I had a kodak [camera]. I wanted a picture of him. I asked a doctor in the little town to get me a picture of him," but there is no evidence he ever received a picture of his son, let alone asked for one. In any case, Hassell next went to Waco, Texas, and worked for a relative named Sam Hassell for a short time, another example of his peripatetic work history and inability to settle anywhere for any length of time.[20]

By the time Hassell was twenty-five years old, if he was to be believed, he had served five years in four of the nation's toughest prisons. At each of these facilities, corporal punishment was common and guards could dole it out on their own authority. Hassell must have considered himself a hard guy at this point, someone who could "take a trimming" from brutal guards. It is very possible that his future lack of compassion and empathy for others was linked to the cruel treatment he received in various penal institutions. Whether this is true or not, few killers were ever more brutal than George J. Hassell. As his trial for his last murders would demonstrate, he developed a demeanor in which he never expected compassion from others, and he never showed it toward someone else. But according to Hassell family lore, "he was never to become a mean person, always well-liked by everyone, he simply didn't care about the suffering of any other human being."[21] And as for his ex-wife and son, there is no evidence they ever tried to contact him again while he was alive, and they vanished into the mists of history.

It should be noted here that the ginner Ross would see Hassell one last time. George apparently returned to Ovalo around 1916 or 1917 "and asked ... for work." Ross said, "He told me he had joined the Navy and deserted."[22] His employer had learned a thing or two since the first time he hired the ne'er-do-well and "refused to give him work but did give him a stiff talk." Ross remembers Hassell listening attentively and thanking him for his advice, telling him "he was going to turn over a new leaf and when he left, he promised to keep in touch with me." Ross never heard from Hassell again.

Chapter 3

Whittier

> *"Mrs. Vogel and the children had disappeared simultaneously a number of years before."*
> —January 21, 1927

It is unclear exactly which military prison Hassell last paroled out of once he had served his sentences for fraud and desertion. Military prison records offer information on neither George Hassell nor his alias, George Stovall. Leavenworth Penitentiary, in fact, has no record of him ever being incarcerated there. Most evidence suggests he was out of prison by 1914 or 1915. We only have his often-picaresque accounts to go by. Like so many facets of George J. Hassell's saga, his time in California leaves more questions than answers. In one of his last interviews, Hassell told the assistant Huntsville penitentiary physician, Dr. E. L. Angier, that after he was released from the Norfolk naval station brig in 1914, he headed back to Texas to attempt a rapprochement with his first wife, Minnie, and his son, James Delbert.[1] So, this is probably the closest we will get to settling the question of which prison he was paroled from. He claimed that he worked his way back to the Fort Worth area from Virginia, where he had purchased some clothing for his estranged son before delivering them to the child's residence in Winters, Texas. He was allowed to see the boy, albeit briefly. Once more rebuffed by Minnie, he was encouraged to hit the road.

Hassell liked to brag that after he left Winters, "I started trotting the globe again. I can't name the different states I have seen but I have been in 37 different states of the union."[2] How long he was on the road and where he went are matters of conjecture, since it is highly unlikely that he traveled so widely in the 1910s and in such a short time period.

In most of his accounts, he made it only forty-five miles after leaving Winters, ending up in San Angelo, Texas. As with many of his unverifiable tales and anecdotes, there are several versions of how Hassell met his next female companion and first-known adult victim. The least likely scenario but most widely repeated account has him hooking up with a woman in San Angelo. With a knack for attracting women, in San Angelo he met a Mrs. Marie Vogel, who reportedly owned a boarding house. If this was true, it is possible that Marie fell for him after he rented a room from her.

Born Marie Sirlin in Pennsylvania in 1885, Marie Vogel would have been three years older than Hassell. Information later provided by her sister, Mrs. Gertrude Hoffman of Pittsburgh, identified her parents as Mr. and Mrs. A. L. Sirlin. Marie had three brothers and, besides Gertrude, another sister. Records show that she was married in 1910 to John J. Vogel and living in San Diego with their only child, Gerald, who had been born in California. The husband worked as a "washer," whatever that entailed.[3] It most probably was an unskilled job such as laundry worker attendant or dishwasher.

Hassell claimed he was drawn to Marie by the fact that "she had a boy about the size of my boy." Despite his subsequent inclination to manually strangle children, he told a Huntsville prison physician that "we both loved children and soon became great friends."[4] By Hassell's account, she had left her husband before they met and they would go on to live relatively happy lives together in Whittier, California. Sometime between 1915 and 1917, Marie adopted two more children. Some accounts suggest that all three of her kids were adopted. Hassell declared he was "crazy about those three kids." Whenever he lamented his subsequent murders of Marie and the children, he would add that "nobody ever lived who loved children more than I did."[5] However, on one tragic night in June 1917, his actions contradicted his professed paternal love for the kids.

George and Marie, soon after meeting in San Angelo, Texas, were out on the road, possibly with little Gerald along. This brings up several questions. If they did meet in 1914 or 1915, it would have been less than five years after Marie had been living in San Diego with her husband and son. It begs the question: what would have made Marie relocate 1,100 miles away from San Diego to San Angelo, Texas, in the first place? There is no evidence that she had any friends or relatives in the area. It is possible that Marie separated from her husband in San Diego and ended up in San Angelo, where she might have opened her own boarding house. It is also conceivable that they decided to leave San Angelo together for California, since her husband was living there and perhaps she wanted to formally arrange for custody of young Gerald—that is, if he was actually with George and Marie to begin with. Another question comes up: by what means of transportation did George, Marie, and the seven-year-old travel from San Angelo to California? It's difficult to reconcile this arrangement with the events to come.

Hassell loved regaling anyone who would listen with his tales of past escapades, especially the story of how their money ran out in Deming, New Mexico, about halfway to California. He told a reporter that he found temporary work on a hay ranch, one of the more strenuous farming duties, but he said he wasn't making money "fast enough." As usual, he looked for an easy score, an easy way out, and he convinced Marie to partner up with him in the con known as the "badger game."[6] There is no record indicating whether she was familiar with this scheme previously. This confidence game is a clever extortion ruse with a long history, in which a male victim is tricked into a compromising position with a woman, making him vulnerable to blackmail. Once they are in the room together, suddenly an indignant "husband" appears, in this purported case it was George, gun in hand. In his words, "we pulled a stunt on a guy there in order to get—we were supposed to get $2,500 out of it, but instead of that we got $100. I was supposed to go away and be gone that night and he was to slip in the room ... I was planted outside and after he had gone in there, she gave me the signal and I went in, but our scheme did not work [as planned]."[7] This story makes one wonder where little Gerald was while this con game was playing out.

To be successful, the ruse had to be believable to some degree. If it goes as planned, the man will buy his way out of his predicament by paying the culprits. In some cases, he might be threatened with being accused of rape if he doesn't pay up. Hassell suggested they might have done this more than once. But apparently, the $100 [$2,500 in 2020 dollars] score was not insignificant and was enough to get them to the West Coast.

After considering numerous versions of the San Angelo, Texas, and Deming, New Mexico, interludes, there is a good likelihood that these incidents never took place and were merely more of the fanciful accounts Hassell recounted to reporters while he was behind bars, probably to bolster his reputation. Marie's mother, who had no reason to lie, visited her daughter in California in 1916 and has suggested that Marie and George probably met each other there when her daughter was working as a housekeeper at a doctor's ranch in East Whittier.[8] Years later, her mother identified George as a ranch hand employee named "Baker," and clearly recalled how "Hassell acted 'queerly' at times and was always sullen."[9]

Mrs. Sirlin was always convinced that Marie had actually moved to California around 1906,[10] and had already been there for ten years when she and Hassell probably got together. She never mentions that Marie lived in San Angelo, Texas. How and where George and Marie met up varies in specifics and, unsurprisingly, Hassell's memories often conflict with Mrs. Sirlin's. In the end, we have only their stories to go by since Marie was dead and buried in 1917. George and Marie probably lived on the ranch either as a couple or independently of each other for at least a year between 1915 and 1917.

Most striking in her mother's account was that she remembered Hassell, Marie, and the three kids being the only occupants of the ranch at the time.[11] Gerald has been identified, more or less, but it has never been satisfactorily explained where exactly the other two children came from, especially since they were both under three years of age. Unsurprisingly, the available explanations differ. "We both wanted children," according to Hassell.

In his telling, Marie's sister ran an orphan asylum in Colorado. Hassell later claimed he wrote to the sister from California and, using his typical subterfuge told the sister that Marie knew a rich family that wanted to adopt two babies in the two-year-old range. In this version, Marie's mother was planning a trip to California from Pennsylvania and transported the two kids out to the ranch on the way out.

When the mother arrived with the two children, Hassell told reporters, he continued to pretend that the children were "for a rich couple" and told Marie's mother the couple had gone out of town.[12] However, this story contradicts the mother's later claim that the kids were already in California when she arrived. Marie had confided to her mother that she and Hassell were posing as man and wife in order to keep their jobs on the ranch. By then, they were living under the aliases Mr. and Mrs. George G. Baker.[13]

Mrs. Sirlin left the ranch and returned to Pittsburgh and never saw her daughter and three grandchildren again. It wasn't long after she returned to Pittsburgh that Sirlin received a troubling letter from Hassell stating that Marie and the kids decided to move to Australia. Ten years later, Mrs. Sirlin told reporters that it "was the last time she heard of her."[14]

In 1917, the couple now known as the Bakers and their three children, all under the age of eight, were living in Whittier. They figured that the only way they would be able to keep the kids was to leave their pasts behind and continue posing as a married couple, but in a new town. Hassell found work in the local oil fields, and they were able to save enough to make rental payments on a small cottage at 263 Whittier Avenue (now a four-unit apartment building at 7242 Whittier Avenue). They moved in sometime in March 1917, and there, Hassell remembered, they "spent many happy hours planning on the future."[15] Nonetheless, it is hard to imagine, considering his poor work history and rather nomadic existence, that any long-range plans were considered by the couple, or at least by Hassell, who by most accounts was incapable of such deliberation.

Ten years later, as he sat in a Texas prison cell, investigators focused on connecting him to his Whittier years. The first record of him in the vicinity came from the personnel files of the Southern Counties Gas Company and his employer, the Standard Oil Company. Although earlier dates in March have been mentioned in other articles, his verifiable official dates of residence at the South Whittier Avenue home lasted from March 26 to August 30, 1917.[16]

Their arrival in Whittier was propitious, as the city was well on its way to making the transition from a sleepy Southern California town with "rural Quaker roots,"[17] into a bustling city on the rise. Settled by Quakers around 1887, by the beginning of the twentieth century agriculture was central to its economy, with thousands of carloads of lemons and oranges shipped by rail from there each year. Once oil was discovered in the area towards the end of the nineteenth century, Whittier was truly on the ascent. But despite the construction of concrete sidewalks, power lines, and water mains, in the early 1900s much of Whittier still had a "Wild West" frontier flavor "with unpaved streets and roughhewn structures." Indeed, much of Whittier's streets, which were graded and oiled in the 1910s, remained unpaved well into the 1920s.[18]

Between 1900 and 1912, a great deal of activity took place in the Whittier-Olinda oil fields east of town, which is where Hassell probably toiled. The landscape around the town was dominated by wooden oil derricks. As oil production in June 1917 reached 96,000 barrels a month, according to Whittier historians, some "sections of the Whittier Hills were a veritable forest of derricks."[19] George was among the hundreds of oil field workers drawn to the area for jobs as America entered the First World War. The influx of new families and workers paralleled the construction of new homes, larger schools and churches, and "the beginnings of metropolitan atmosphere indicating the 'city was passing through the period of adolescence usual to the big-town–small city jump."[20] Photographs from the period show a proliferation of automobiles as horse-drawn vehicles still plied the roads, and as early as 1915, there were several soda fountains in business as more and more merchants catered to the "leisure and amusement" needs of the community.[21]

Hassell had only been in the Whittier neighborhood for several months when his common-law wife and her three kids disappeared. Their next-door neighbors knew he was an oil field worker, but little else about him. Mrs. S. C. Shanker and her daughter, Mrs. Myrtle Larkin, would regularly stop by when he was at work and pass time at the Baker house with Marie, who they described as a "quiet, unassuming sort of woman."[22]

Ten years later, George confessed to what was still an unreported Whittier mass murder. He told reporters from behind bars, "I got off work at midnight one night" and "my wife was in bed but not asleep when I got home." He would always stick to his story, which was that at around 2:00 a.m. "we were home, absolutely the two most satisfied persons in the world, laughing, talking and kidding, when the first thing I knew I had her by the throat and had choked her and the babies to death." He finished the deed by tying "a stocking around her throat."[23] Although she presumably struggled, Hassell likely made short work of Marie and then the kids.

In another version, Hassell stated that late on a June evening in 1917, he argued with Marie over whether or not he should register for the draft. This seems rather farfetched considering his three previous desertions from the armed forces. There are other accounts as well, in which he asked Marie whether it might be a good idea to add several years to his age so he would be above draft age.[24] We only have his words to go by to try to understand what set him off. He did admit that after drinking some whiskey he accused Marie of stealing some money: "I lost my temper and choked the woman to death." Since this fits the pattern of other murders he would commit in the following decade, it might indeed have been his drinking compounded with his psychopathy that led to the deaths. The psychiatrist Michael Stone noted that when a psychopath is involved in a marital dispute, an "argument goes from words to lightning fast action that is unplanned and unforeseen at the beginning, whether married or not."[25] Likewise, in his study of serial killers, criminologist Eric Hickey observed that domestic murders can be triggered by what most people would view as a "trivial remark, simply a minor insult or provocation."[26]

The most likely scenario in this sequence of events was revealed in a 1935 interview with Parmer County Attorney J. D. Thomas, who was involved in the trial and investigation of Hassell's Farwell, Texas, murders of 1927. He remembered Hassell telling him that "everything seemed all right" between him and Marie until she "began to get on my nerves and the house was always cluttered up by the kids. One night when I came home, she began to argue because I wasn't giving her enough money. We had a hot time of it for a while and then I got mad. I went over to her and grabbed her by the neck. She went purple and started to struggle. Before I knew it, I had choked her."[27]

However, Hassell mentioned a different trigger for his rage, telling Parmer County Attorney Thomas, who probably knew George as well as anyone ever would, that "the kids were running around screaming and crying. I grabbed them off one at a time and choked them too. Then I went down into the cellar and started to dig. When I got through, I had dug out a good-sized hole. I threw the woman in there and the kids after her and covered up the place."[28]

Hassell's account of killing the three children varies. He told one reporter that "he was pleased to find out he could do that task in such a quiet manner that it did not awaken the ones still sleeping." One Hassell family member in the 1980s attributed his strength to a lifetime of manual labor, noting he "worked at many jobs with his hands and they were very strong."[29] After killing Marie, he probably sat on the edge of the bed figuring out his next move. It didn't take him long to decide to go into the next room where the kids were sleeping and manually strangle the life out of each one. George first choked the eight-year-old that reminded him so much of his son, before throttling the two younger children. The best explanation for the deed he would ever come up with was: "something came over me and I did it."[30]

Hassell's method of killing his young charges would not have surprised researchers who study domestic homicide. The Canadian evolutionary psychologists Martin Daly and Margo Wilson, among others, have noticed that homicides committed by stepfathers "differ from those by biological fathers not only quantitatively, but qualitatively."[31] Hassell might have established a superficial kinship with the kids, but unlike a biological parent, who is less likely to use "brute force" to kill his "genetic offspring,"[32] Hassell, sharing no DNA with his victims, killed them up close and personal, brutally, with his hands, ligatures, and bludgeons.[33] The psychiatrist Adrian Raine also noted this discrepancy between methods of killing utilized by biological parents and stepparents. He found that the likelihood of being killed by an unrelated person is ten times greater than by a genetic relative.[34] In both of Hassell's family annihilations, the same pattern of physical brutality was repeated. In both cases, he attacked and killed the adult women without warning and then methodically killing the rest of the family.

Although Hassell seemed incapable of strategizing in his professional life, he demonstrated a frightening capacity to plan ahead when it came to covering his tracks after his murders. Most accounts of his Whittier murders suggest he had probably set his plan in motion two weeks earlier, when he dug a small tunnel five feet under the back of the house. He always denied that digging the tunnel was premeditated, but it is hard to believe that he did not dig it ahead of time with the intention of turning it into the family crypt when the time came to eliminate his family.

The way George liked to tell it as he sat on the Texas death row in 1927, was that his wife was a spiritualist and "at night said she could hear voices. She went as far as to make a trumpet for them to talk through." George recounted that one night "she had a vision that a light came from the sky and struck the floor of the home. She said the light pointed to buried money." So, he dug a hole under the house in compliance with his wife's wishes, but the "money must have been buried deeper, for I didn't find it." Two weeks later he killed his family and buried them in the excavation.[35] If any of this is true, she might well have had some type of premonition that some kind of treasure was buried there, but as one reporter put it, "she little dreamed her own body would constitute the only treasure."[36]

In order to dig the space, Hassell would have had to squeeze through a trapdoor on the rear porch and tunnel his way under the house over the course of three days and nights. The houses in the neighborhood stood close enough together that one did not necessarily have to eavesdrop to detect strange happenings next door. Mrs. Clara Shanker, the closest neighbor, would later remember seeing Hassell carrying out a heavy trunk and "other small bundles into the garage." She watched him closely enough to see him crawling out from under the north side of the house on several occasions by way of a ventilator. His actions really began to attract her attention when she noticed that every day he was under the house throwing out dirt and rubbish. Once he noticed he was being watched, he remarked to Shanker's daughter, Myrtle Lark, that he was "just cleaning out the basement." She would always remember how he acted in "a very peculiar manner."[37]

A few days later, he "dug a large hole in the garage floor, telling anyone who asked that he wanted to be able to get under his car to work on it."[38] He then hauled his truck into the garage. Myrtle Lark clearly remembered strange odors emanating from the house around this time. "Later," she said, "I noticed him burning rags in the kitchen stove. I smelled the rags burning for many nights."[39]

By the time the pit was completed, it was long and deep enough so that Marie's body could be laid flat on her back. Once her body was positioned, he stacked the children on top of her, in order from the largest to the smallest with their heads facing south and then packed the dirt in tightly around them. Hassell's account, however, does not jibe with the actual positions of the bodies when they were excavated ten years later. Newspaper accounts and eyewitnesses from 1927 claimed that each of the victims had actually been placed in the grave face down, with stockings and rope tied in in square knots still intact and wrapped around their necks and heads.[40] Hassell would later, in 1935, add some minor details that checked out, including burying a set of false teeth with "the woman."[41] Since the neighbors would later recount George carrying dirt out from under the house after the murders, it is likely that the 1935 version was closer to the truth. Perhaps he started digging the pit several weeks earlier, only realizing when it came time to bury the bodies that more digging was required to entomb all four victims for posterity.

Having dealt with the bodies, George concocted a story to explain their absence as he continued living in the house, a ritual he would follow after another familicide almost ten years later. Once George was confident that no odors of decomposing bodies were in the air, he felt more and more comfortable. After several months of living in what would later become known locally as the "death house," he was confident enough to tell his neighbors that Marie and the kids had moved back east and he was going to join them. This probably made sense since Marie's people were in Pittsburgh. Other sources have him telling neighbors that they had gone up to San

Francisco at the request of her sister. He even told a neighbor (Shanker) one morning that Marie had eloped with another man.[42]

After killing and burying Marie and the kids, he later recounted, "I didn't leave as one would have expected anyone to do, but in fact, it hardly broke my daily routine of living." As stated previously, he was clearly capable of meticulous planning when his life and freedom depended on it. The clinical psychiatrist Michael H. Stone has studied psychopaths and other killers extensively. His findings suggest that the actions of killers similar to Hassell would have coincided with those of other modern killers he has studied, who were likely "to stretch out their actions to include some planning after the fact, often to hide evidence of what they have done."[43] Hassell might have acted on an "ungovernable impulse," but his subsequent actions reveal "malice aforethought."[44] Stone never studies Hassell, but he explains scenarios similar to the ones Hassell found himself in, where the killer might be caught off guard by his crime, "surprised and alarmed" at what he had done, and do his best to cover it up and elude justice.[45]

Hassell had to first get rid of all of Marie's clothing and possessions. He packed them in trunks and later admitted that he "stored them in Los Angeles and came back to Whittier" with another woman in tow. He then said, "I made her leave, and I went to Los Angeles and got another woman—she was married but separated from her husband. I would tell her name, but she may be living with her husband now."[46] It is unclear which of the women he was referring to when he commented that several months later he "brought a woman he introduced as his housekeeper and child to live with him."[47] They had been together for a few months when one night Hassell decided to flee. He sent the housekeeper and her child to the motion picture theater one evening, and by the time they returned home, he had vanished. But evidently the woman stayed long enough to close up the house for him. Curiously, he returned three months later to retrieve a "bundle" left by the previously mentioned woman at a neighbor's house.[48]

Since George continued to live in the house after his family's disappearance, it appears that although the neighbors might have been suspicious, they were not alarmed enough to contact local law enforcement. Once he too disappeared, neighbors contacted the police. A local constable, Bob (R. B.) Way, was the first officer to respond to the neighbors' suspicions. Ten years later the constable would weather a storm of criticism led by Los Angeles newspapers claiming that he failed to make a diligent investigation at the time of the murders. Way responded to the critiques by sending a report to the sheriff's office, in which he presented the facts of the case based on his records of the events of 1917. He explained that

> after the Fall rains had commenced, I was called by occupants of the Shanker home at 230 Whittier Avenue and was shown a depression in the ground on the rear of the lot ... and informed there had been an excavation inside of the garage. [The garage had since been moved to a new location immediately adjacent to the spot.] This left the former excavation exposed and recent rains had settled the earth in a manner that made the prior excavation clearly defined and visible by lines of demarcation which separated the firm structure of earth from the spongy. Mrs. Shanker then informed me that a former occupant of these premises had dug the hole and she had suspicions that it had been used for some unlawful purpose. I do not recall any suspicions on the part of Mrs. Shanker, only that the party had been seen taking a trunk in the direction of the garage. I do not recall any conversation regarding the basement of the house for I am sure if there had been, I would've made a thorough search at this time. Consequently, with help of other parties (whose names I do not remember) we removed the dirt from the place mentioned above without results.[49]

Way also reemphasized why he never searched under the house, which was because "nothing was ever said to him at the time about Baker being under the house."

Of all the actors in this strange saga, it seems that Marie's sister, Mrs. Gertrude Hoffman, was the driving force of the search for the mother and children. She reportedly wrote to authorities in Whittier on more than one occasion over the next decade seeking information, but the only thing they could tell her "was that Hassell, Mrs. Vogel and the children had disappeared simultaneously a number of years before."[50] Several years after their disappearance, Constable Way of Whittier received communication from relatives in Pittsburgh asking him to look into the case of the missing

"Baker" family. However, by his account, the information he was given was "so meager no trace could be found" of the family.[51]

Hassell left town, disappearing for good, at least in the guise of Mr. George G. Baker. He reassumed his real name and moved on to the next peripatetic chapters of his life. It didn't take long for his neighbors and the community to forget that he and his family ever existed. But the murders would come back to haunt Whittier in the years to come.

Chapter 4

On the Road

"He was a good workman, but as to his human side nothing is known."

Hassell buried Marie Vogel and the three children deep in the clay soil beneath their Whittier love nest sometime in the early summer of 1917, probably in June. Barely had the family been "gone" when neighbors remembered him "keeping house with [a] woman over the secret grave of his murdered victims" for several months before vacating the cottage for good.[1] He must have felt relieved to be out on the road again, most importantly all by himself. Now he could relax more under the comfort of his real name, George Jefferson Hassell, leaving his "George Stovall" and "George G. Baker" avatars behind. One less thing to worry about or hide from authorities.

He apparently traveled around the western states, joining the Merchant Marine for a time and working a variety of unskilled jobs ranging from threshing crewman to oil field roustabout. He claimed that his travels took him to a range of cities including Los Angeles, San Francisco, and Salt Lake City. Employment records introduced during his 1927 trial confirmed that he worked in oil fields in California between 1922 and 1923. His final employment in California was in the San Joaquin Valley, where he worked for the Associated Pipe Company of Fresno (though he never worked in Fresno itself). Although he worked on the pipeline for more than a year, his fellow workers had nothing to share with authorities, remarking that he never volunteered anything about his personal relations and family.[2] Nor did police find any indications that he committed a criminal offense in Fresno County. Company records indicated that "he was a good workman, but as to his human side nothing is known."[3]

After working for the pipe company, Hassell claimed to have married another woman for three months. But there is no record to substantiate this, and no woman ever came forth to acknowledge the relationship. Hassell purportedly left this "wife" and joined the Merchant Marine corps, probably in San Francisco, on July 15, 1923, as a cook on ships plying the Pacific Coast. But the only evidence of his merchant marine days are aging newspaper photographs of him cloaked in a cook's uniform. He later mentioned in his confession that for the most part he "was following the sea in the Merchant Marine." He claimed to have served as a water tender on the *Admiral Farragut*, in San Francisco, before moving on to Galveston, Texas, in the summer of 1924, where he found work on a tanker traveling back and forth to Tampico, Mexico.[4]

One of Hassell's more curious claims was that after wandering through parts of the West he returned to Whittier for a short spell, where he said, "without emotion, [he] often passed the house where the woman and children were buried."[5] Hassell seemed to enjoy entertaining investigators and journalists during jailhouse interviews with stories about his drive-bys of the old cottage on South Whittier Avenue, knowing full well the bodies were still buried undetected under the house. In placing him in the context of other multiple killers and their predilections, his inclination to return to the scene of the crime is significant, particularly because it aligns some of Hassell's behaviors with what is now known about serial killers. Killers in the category of "organized serial killers," for example, have been known to revisit the locations of previous crimes, "especially before they think it has been discovered," perhaps to relive the event or revel in their murders and the fact that the victims were still undiscovered.[6]

And of course, if Hassell had his way, Marie and the children would never be found until he wanted them to be.

Hassell often recounted that "there was a period in my life that I never wrote to any of my folks at all, something like five years." It is unclear which years he is referring to, but it must have been sometime between 1917, the year of his Whittier murders, and 1924. Since his parents were already dead, his reference to his "folks" must refer to his older brother, Thomas Virgil Hassell, or perhaps other siblings. On several occasions George Hassell traveled to visit his brother and his large family on their Blair, Oklahoma, ranch. These visits took place between 1920 and 1924, which is when he finally put down roots in Texas that would hold him there until the end of his life. Except for these visits and his oil field employment, there is little in the way of a paper trail to track his wanderings in these crucial years.

Tom and his wife, Susan Ferguson, were both nineteen years of age when they applied for their marriage license on September 3, 1902, in Kiowa County, Oklahoma Territory. According to the application, both parties offered consent letters written by their parents. The marriage took place the following day at Cordell in Washita County, Territory of Oklahoma. Of George Hassell's six brothers and sisters, it appears he had the closest relationship with Thomas, who was his older brother by five years, born on June 23, 1883.

Like his father and family members before him, Tom Hassell worked as a farmer for most of his adult life, settling with his family on a farm near Blair in southwestern Oklahoma in 1921. His brother-in-law, J. V. Ferguson, knew Tom relatively well and remembered him starting a crop of mostly cotton in 1924 but dying in July before the crop could be harvested. Nonetheless, the cotton went for a pretty good price that fall, falling just short of fifty bales. Susan's brother later testified at George Hassell's trial that Tom "tried to specialize in raising good stuff in the way of good turkeys, hogs, and so forth; I understand they took some prizes for their cotton. It was a variety of half and half cotton."[7]

Tom was well-known locally. After he died in a mysterious ranching accident in 1924, the local newspaper made note of it, reminding the community that he had worked in the Hobart, Oklahoma, area for the "old Ash-Harris lumber company." Tom was remembered fondly as having "moved here with his family in the early days." He also "drove delivery wagons for other business concerns here prior to that time." After Ash-Harris quit business in Hobart, Tom went to work for Hobart Ice & Bottling Company, where he was employed until failing health made a change of occupation necessary.[8]

As noted previously, Hassell made a point of visiting Tom's Oklahoma farm on several occasions as he gallivanted across the West. According to Hassell family lore, "it was always a treat for the family to see 'Uncle George' as he would have money for ice cream and candy. Best of all, he had stories to tell about what he had seen and done so he was popular with all, but especially the females." On one of his visits, George Hassell no doubt was impressed with how much more mature his eighteen-year-old niece, Nora, looked since the last time he saw her.

Nora Lorraine (1903–1973) was Tom's brother's oldest child. By the time 1926 was over, she would be the only living child from that union. She would go on to marry six times. According to ancestry and family records she married her first husband, Irby Truman McGee, on April 1, 1921, in Cordell, Washita County, Oklahoma. The following year they had a daughter, Georgia, in Kiowa County, Oklahoma. If family records are correct, they moved to California with Irby's parents and siblings. This account conflicts with Hassell's claims that Nora, who subsequently gave birth to his illegitimate child, had traveled to California with him in 1922.[9]

In his telling, Nora was still living at home in 1921, unmarried and without a child. He claimed that she was keen to visit her uncle's old stomping grounds in California. He had probably filled her head with visions of the Golden State. In 1922, supposedly, Nora convinced her mother to let her uncle take her on a road trip to California. Hassell later recalled that "it was a pleasant trip," and he later admitted that he "didn't get in a big hurry as they were sleeping together every night." By the end of the year, she had given birth to her uncle's child, who she named Georgia, after the baby's father.[10] Since Nora could not have had the same child with both her first husband, McGee, and her uncle, it raises the question of which story is more likely to be factual.

By the time Hassell arrived on the scene, Susan and Tom had been married twenty-two years and had eight kids, with another on the way. It was common for young farm wives to have their first child shortly after marriage. Farm families remained consistently larger than other families in Texas. One description of a farm wife fit Susan well: "She represented millions of Texas women at the turn of the century who led lives in relationship to their families and rarely had an existence away from the farm."[11]

In one of his last interviews, Hassell recounted that his brother "had a pretty good crop started—I had been to his place before he started the crop and he told me that he was going to work a pretty good sized crop and if the oldest boy stayed at home [Alton] he would get through alright." Although George Hassell had visited Blair, Oklahoma, over the years, according to his brother's neighbors "he was not well known here."[12] But few if any people could ever say they really knew Hassell.

Tom's mysterious death on July 1, 1924, would set into motion a series of tragic events. There are several mysteries connected to this sequence of events that deserve examination. The main question is whether Hassell was present when his brother was killed in a bizarre ranching accident. The second is what actually caused Tom's demise. As to the first, Hassell always claimed he was not present when his brother was mortally injured by a mule kick. He usually insisted he was notified of his brother's death by letter from his brother's widow in Oklahoma. However, this seems too convenient. Since the ever-itinerant roustabout was never in one place for long, it is unlikely that Susan would have known where to send the letter to notify him that Tom was dead and that she needed help caring for their farm. Hassell claimed that once he was notified of his brother's death, he "begged automobile rides back to Oklahoma" and finally joined the widow and her brood of kids.[13]

Hassell clung to his well-worn story that he was in New Orleans in July 1924 waiting for a ship when he got word that his brother Tom had died in a ranching accident at home in Blair, Oklahoma. He might very well have been in New Orleans waiting for a berth when he heard of his brother's death and had nothing to do with his demise. However, the historical research conducted by members of the Hassell family argues otherwise, noting that he had lost his seaman's rating in February, five months earlier, so it was "hard to believe he would sit in New Orleans waiting for a ship when he was no longer a sailor."[14]

Most accounts suggest that Tom died from being kicked by a mule. Since his younger brother was the only witness, no one challenged this story at the time. However, his death certificate noted he died of a "strangulated hernia" (also known as an inguinal hernia).[15] It is not uncommon for this condition to be fatal if not treated promptly, however it is difficult to reconcile the mule kick with the official cause of death, since strangulated hernias originate internally. Some hernias lack any identifiable cause, but typical sources include chronic coughing, strenuous activities, straining during bowel movements, a preexisting weak spot in the abdominal wall, heavy lifting, or increased pressure within the abdomen.[16] In any case, Susie collected on a $1,100 insurance policy, which would amount to a little more than $16,000 in 2020.

From the get-go, residents of the rural community were mystified by the longtime farmer's tragic death on July 3, 1924. The death of the family patriarch, with a widow and eight children left behind and Susan marrying Hassell shortly after, might have left neighbors with questions related to Tom's untimely demise. On the other hand, there were probably others in the community that accepted the death as accidental and refused to make assumptions. It was not until his brother's bloody family annihilation in 1926, along with the revelation that he killed another four people in 1917, that observers began wondering how many others he might have killed, including his brother.

During an interview with the *Clovis News*, Hassell may have implicated himself in his brother's death when he shared a story about a vision he had: "I don't believe in visions but one night I saw a vision about the first night I was out with the thresher. This old Hoopie was cut down and I had a bed in it [and] I was laying there—I don't remember my brother kissing me but once in my life before and that the last time I visited him. When we parted, he kissed me, we kissed one another, and this was the only time. That was the vision I had."[17]

Newspapers wasted little time digging into the mass murderer's background, beginning with the mysterious death of his brother and his marriage to the widow just a few months later. On December 26, 1926, a Montana newspaper featured the headline, "Slays Brother to Get Widow, then Kills Her and Her Eight Kids." The story indicated that Farwell authorities were interested in the death of his brother in Blair, Oklahoma, in 1924. But Tom's death was accepted as an accident by family members—that is, until the Hassell familicide was revealed.[18]

Hassell always stuck with the story that he was the only person that Susan could turn to for help. He added that since he was "footloose to go and help her I felt my duty," meaning that it was his responsibility to help her with the farm. He slipped in a caveat that seems designed to alleviate suspicions as to his intentions. He told the reporter, "I had no intention and thoughts of marrying her at the time." Susan, he said "was very ignorant of the ways of the world. You understand what I mean, an awful good woman, and of course I got there about July 10, after he had been buried." Moreover, he insisted, "I don't see how anybody can link me with having anything to do with his death with me in New Orleans and he in Blair."[19] Perhaps Hassell, like Ophelia in the Shakespeare play *Hamlet*, "doth protest too much," or at least is attempting to convince himself that he was neither present nor responsible.

Shortly after Hassell's arrest, he went further in explaining his sudden marriage to Susie, telling the reporter that they had thought the children would be better off if they married four months after Tom's death. Hassell recounted, "I told her maybe the people thought she was not showing respect enough but the way we looked at it we were keeping the children together and were under control and we got married."[20] According to a relative on the Ferguson side of the family, the marriage of Susie and George "was one of convenience. Susan had eight kids and was pregnant and George Hassell was there to provide the muscle to keep the family intact and help prevent the loss of the farm" that her late husband "had worked hard to keep afloat."[21]

Hassell asserted that after his brother died, he and his nephews "laid the crop" and he bought an "old Hoopie" so that he could drive to work the harvest up in Kansas. He said he was "fixing to go on when I got a letter from her stating she would be glad if I would come back and help her pick cotton. So that night on my way back I stayed all night with one of her brothers, J. W. Ferguson, at Bray, Oklahoma. He was having his [farm] sale the next day and he tried to get me to stay over, but I went on down with the folks."[22]

As soon as he returned to the Blair farm, he began assisting with the farm work and discussing marriage with his widowed sister-in-law. Susan was a Russellite and a student of the Bible and supposedly consulted it often for advice. Hassell said they consulted the Bible together and arrived at the conclusion "that they might be married without disrespect to the husband and brother," who was dead and buried only a few months.[23]

George Hassell and Susan may have wasted little time getting married, but it was not unprecedented for a brother-in-law to help out a widow of a large family in a rural setting. He married Susan Ferguson on October 7, 1924, at Lawton, Oklahoma. Three non-related witnesses signed the marriage document, but it is unclear whether any family members attended or even how they might have felt about the union.

Susan, who preferred the less formal "Susie," was two years older than Hassell. According to their wedding license, they continued to reside on his late brother's farm in Blair.[24] One of Susan's Ferguson descendants more recently suggested, "My best guess is that the marriage was one of convenience. Susan desperately needed help, and George was there to provide the muscle to keep family intact" and help prevent the loss of the farm that her husband "worked so hard to keep afloat."[25]

Once he married Susie, he became responsible not just for her but for eight stepchildren, his nieces and nephews. One might well wonder, what was he to gain by killing his brother, marrying his widow, and taking in her eight kids? Hassell had few prospects for the future. His oft-mentioned weakness for women might have attracted him to Susan, especially with her having a healthy insurance settlement. Others have speculated that he and Susie might have had a relationship prior to his brother's death. It certainly would not have been beneath Hassell's questionable ethical standards to have had an affair with Susan while Tom was still alive.

Susie's extended family, the Fergusons, had met Hassell previously, but like almost everyone else who crossed his path, they admitted they really didn't know him. On one occasion, however, the Fergusons were afforded an excellent insight into his simmering temper. During 1926, they visited her family several times, and the last visit was to a family reunion. Most of the large Ferguson clan was there, as were all of Susie's kids. One of her brothers, J. V. Ferguson, later remembered that something came up that night that Mr. Hassell took exception to, and "he seemed to talk a great deal and kind of got mad, and some of them tried to pacify him and so forth, and he really got pretty sore." In other words, "he didn't let his family sleep in the house, and he taken them all outside. I didn't go outside, and don't know what he said out there. No sir, he didn't abuse the Ferguson family. But the next morning he got up raving some more, and I finally got all of it I could stand, so I just says to him, 'Mr. Hassell, you have said enough now, and I don't want another word out of you,' and he never returned another word to me."[26]

***

George J. Hassell, his new wife Susan, and the eight children left their Blair, Oklahoma ranch for Parmer County, Texas, in December 1925. It is undetermined what brought the Hassell clan to Farwell. Perhaps the idea was to give the children some new scenery and a chance to start over, away from the ranch where their father tragically lost his life. In any case, when the family headed down to the Texas Panhandle, none of them had an inkling that in little more than a year they would all be dead and buried, victims of the worst family annihilation in Texas history.

Chapter 5

Farwell, Texas: The Last Mile

" ... didn't use enough judgment to leave ... ought have walked out."

There is no record of how the Hassell family, now numbering ten hardy souls, made it down to Farwell. With Susie's recent insurance settlement and the sale of their farm goods and crops, there is reason to believe that they traveled by train or at least partway by automobile, since Hassell owned a vehicle, though it is doubtful that the ten of them could fit into it. The Hassells would have traveled about 240 miles due west to reach Farwell on the "western side of the Texas Panhandle," where they settled down as tenant farmers on the outskirts of town. This living arrangement was common at a time when, according to Texas historian Stephen Harrigan, "almost half of all farmers didn't own land they worked." The population of Texas had increased from eight hundred thousand in 1870 to over three million by the beginning of the twentieth century. Although much of the expansion took place in urban areas during this time period, almost 80 percent, according to Harrigan, "still lived rural lives."[1]

During the administration of Miriam "Ma" Ferguson (1924–1926), the first female governor of Texas, there were more than sixteen thousand miles of state highways and almost one million cars on the road.² As the Hassells made their way down to the Texas Panhandle from Oklahoma in December 1925, they no doubt saw a mixture of traffic, both horse-drawn and gas-driven. It is unknown whether any of the family members kept a journal describing the sights and sounds on their trip, but if someone did, they would have recognized some of those recorded by the Bam White family as it traveled from Colorado to Amarillo and the Texas Panhandle by horse and wagon in the winter of the following year. The writer Timothy Egan recounted how the Whites drove "past fields that had just been turned, the grass upside down. People in sputtering cars roared by, honking, hooting at [his] cowboy family in the horse drawn wagon, churning up dust in their face."³ As the rig bounced along the uneven road there was always fear, especially in winter, that a horse might drop dead," what Egan described as the "nineteenth century equivalent of a flat tire."⁴

Dozens of new towns sprang up in the Texas Panhandle between 1900 and 1930, including the community of Farwell. Compared to their former domicile in Blair, Oklahoma, the town of Farwell must have seemed a welcome change of scenery to the provincial members of the Hassell household, who were probably familiar with little besides their small farming community in Oklahoma.⁵ In these new surroundings, the newly married Hassells, Susie and George, and their pack of eight children no doubt hoped for better years to come.

When the iconic artist Georgia O'Keefe spent time in the south Panhandle town of Canyon, Texas, in 1916 and 1917, she described it as having a "quiet and untouched" feel where she could "work as she pleased." But by the mid-1920s, more and more farmers and other settlers were moving in. Nellie M. Perry (1864–1953) visited her brother on the Texas High Plains often between 1888 and 1925, a span of years that coincided with the birth of George Hassell through his family's arrival in Farwell, Texas. During these years she saw the lonesome plains of West Texas become increasingly populated, to the point that by 1925, so many settlers had moved in that neighbors, at least what were considered neighbors by Panhandle standards, had become "commonplace."⁶

Before the 1920s most Americans grew up and remained on farms and in small villages where culture revolved around rural neighborhoods and their local schools, churches, and stores, while "the economy centered on crops and weather."[7] The Hassells settled quietly into their far from commodious abode outside the town of Farwell, Texas, just spitting distance from the Texas-New Mexico border. In December 1925, they rented a farm from Judge James D. Hamlin, a local landowner and businessman. During the winter months the Hassell farm was "a bleak looking place." If one looked from the house in any direction to the countryside beyond, there was no other home in sight. Except for a "few stunted trees about the place," the flat landscape seemed to go on to infinity.[8] From another perspective, it might have looked like an isolated farmstead on the southern plains, but in reality, rural life relied on services from small towns like nearby Farwell, which was about three miles to the east. Newcomers might find social interaction lacking out on the prairie, but in town they could shop and mingle with locals.

It has since been demolished, but to find the Hassell home in 1925, one would drive "about four miles east and a little north" of town, "where the westbound Santa Fe trains say goodbye to Texas and hello to New Mexico." Locals knew that the only way to get there by automobile was to "take the Amarillo highway which angles north out of Farwell, and drive until you see a road cutting off from the highway and pointing directly east. Turn on the road and drive about two miles to where the road winds around a sink hole in a sort of hair pin curve. To the left, right off the point of this turn" stands "a small frame and stucco house, with a small lean-to addition clinging to the rear, set perhaps 75 feet back from the gate." In a little more than a year, everyone in Parmer County would know by heart how to find the Hassell home, "the scene of the most revolting and gruesome crime in the annals of the Southwest—perhaps in the country."[9]

***

Llano, the Spanish word for plains, conjures up the character of the region where Hassell and Susie would make their last home. Many travelers over the next centuries would remember a featureless landscape that "seems to go on forever."[10] Perhaps one Parmer County, Texas, farmer put it best, commenting that "this land looks like it was fit for nothing but to hold the world together and was about to fail in that."[11]

When Zebulon Pike scouted the region in 1806, he compared it to Africa's Sahara Desert in his report to President Thomas Jefferson, informing him that it "would take a hundred generations to settle the blank space on a map." Shortly after, Stephen Long dubbed the region the "Great American Desert" in 1820, and this name soon found its way onto American maps and was accepted as a fact of life by any settler considering moving there. Long wrote, "I do not hesitate in giving the opinion that it is almost uninhabitable by a people depending upon agriculture for subsistence." Indeed, its reputation proved a barrier to agricultural settlement for decades to come, and its reputation remained a "cartographic fact until after the Civil War, when it became the Great Plains."[12]

But one should never judge the land by first impressions nor always accept the word of an explorer. Those hardy enough to toil the fields and innovative enough to bring crops to fruition would find that despite its aridity,[13] the soil was excellent for cultivation, and since the 1920s, the Llano had become "one of the leading wheat, cotton and sorghum producing areas" in the United States.[14] But, as the historian J. Evetts Haley noted, it took time for the first farmers in the Texas Panhandle to master dry-land farming, commenting that they "often moved into new agricultural areas before they had mastered the most efficient way to use the land."[15]

The great experiment went into effect July 16, 1920, ushering in Prohibition and the so-called Roaring Twenties for many city dwellers. The flappers, hip flasks, speakeasies, and bootleggers were the iconic images coming out of Chicago and New York City, not so much in the rural Panhandle, where the Roaring Twenties was more a whisper than a roar and where farmers and merchants were much more clandestine in their use of intoxicating beverages. As the Dust Bowl historian Timothy Egan put it, while alcohol prohibition was taken seriously in much of Texas, not everyone was a teetotaler.[16]

Panhandle inhabitants from all walks of life were known to imbibe spirits from time to time, even during Prohibition. John Darlington Hamlin, a lawyer and businessman and Hassell's landlord, had struggled with the bottle off and on for years. He had been in the Farwell area since its inception and was considered among the town's elite. As early as 1909 he noticed "a goodly population of church people who were violently opposed to liquor in all its forms." By the time of the passage of Prohibition, he claimed in his autobiography that he "was one of the few men in public life living in the Panhandle who took the stump in favor of its repeal." He would later take a "second whiskey cure" in a Sanitarium in Denver in 1936, but it didn't last, and he continued to drink well into his sixties.[17] While Hamlin and other upstanding citizens might drink in private, others, in many cases younger and inexperienced drinkers, sometimes demonstrated in public the darker side of drinking. In 1925, the same year Hassell reached Farwell, the essayist Nellie M. Perry witnessed a very public display of drunkenness at a local football game. The crowd seemed more interested in watching a local deacon trying to help a young "drunken fellow" get away from the crowd before he was "run in by the local marshal."[18]

***

The agricultural development of the Texas Panhandle was made possible thanks to the unintended consequences of one of the largest business deals in Texas history. In 1879, the State voted to allot three million acres of land in the Panhandle that could be used to fund the building of a new capitol building in Austin. Texans didn't have to wait too long. When the building burned down in 1881, the Texas State Legislature moved quickly with a scheme to rebuild it. The project was taken on by Taylor, Babcock and Company of Chicago, of which the Farwell brothers were principals.[19] Charles B. and John V. Farwell, at the time, were Chicago's "largest suppliers of wholesale dry goods." The younger brother, John, had been drawn to Texas history and lore since his youth on the family farmstead in New York state. Their vision spurred the transition of what was cattle country into a region of small farms in the years to come, and their names would live on, with the town named in their honor.

In 1882, a deal was struck with what became known as the Capitol Freehold Land and Investment Company of Chicago, or "Capitol Syndicate." In return for funding the capitol building project, Texans agreed to hand over three million acres of land in West Texas, land that would become the fabled XIT Ranch.[20] At its zenith the XIT was the largest ranch in the world, or what cowboys reportedly described as "the damnest ranch in the world."[21] None of the Syndicate's principals had ever been on a cattle ranch prior to the project. Although they were in their sixties at the time, the Farwell brothers poured their energies into the project, even directing the survey of the Farwell townsite after selecting the location as a central point from which the company could later administer the sales of converted XIT ranchland to farmers. One local historian suggested that the "XIT was established as a temporary institution to secure the use of land until the time of the farmer came."[22] But until the turn of the century, Parmer County "remained unorganized," and except for XIT cowboys and a smattering of settlers, it remained mostly unpopulated.

Ranching still dominated the region at the turn of the century, according to the 1900 Census. However, the following year the Syndicate began putting up XIT lands for sale "in order to meet its obligations." Pioneers began arriving from more developed areas to the east around 1905, from East Texas and other points east of Texas, with little understanding about what it took to farm semiarid country. As they came and settled their plots of land, cattlemen and cowboys no doubt watched curiously as they brought in their farm horses and tools. One Parmer County historian noted that until the coming of the first farmers into the region, "no plow had broken the soil and to the ranch owner and cowboy, [it was] sacrilege to take native grass from cattle."[23]

It wasn't long before the former cattle country was divided into ninety-four pastures and surrounded by almost fifteen hundred miles of fencing. Most of the land was sold in small tracts to farmers, and by 1912, the last of the XIT cattle had been sold.[24] The liquidation of XIT holdings in the early 1900s led to one of the region's greatest periods of immigration and "turned the Syndicate into a genuine colonizer of the grasslands of Texas."[25]

Land speculators and entrepreneurial boosters had no trouble enticing new residents to West Texas, promising a land that was "so healthy that if a man wants to die, he will have to go somewhere else to do it."[26] Concomitant with the campaign to subdivide and sell off XIT lands to farmers, small ranchers, and land speculators, the town of Farwell was established in 1904 and incorporated as a city three years later. After some debate between surrounding towns, Farwell was named the county seat.

The land grants that would become Farwell consisted of almost 586 acres, further subdivided into blocks, streets, and alleys.[27] Before the town could be platted out and surveyed, workers had to burn off grass that stood almost four feet high over the entire area. Settlers mused about the abundance of blue quail and antelope living in the grasslands.

Farwell expanded in the first decades of the twentieth century as real estate developers continued to parcel off XIT lands to attract more settlers. The town was considered "booming" in 1910, boasting a population of eight hundred, and it even had its own newspaper, the *State Line Tribune*. In its early days, many locals felt its future seemed limitless. But any future progress was predicated on sustainable rainfall. During a three-year span prior to 1910, the area experienced little rain, and no crops meant no money. Droughts and crop failures were never far from the minds of the local farmers, but as long as it rained, the area "blossomed like a flower garden."[28] Since few farmers had the resources to drill their own wells, families continued to rely on cisterns or haul water from neighboring farms until 1910, when a public water tank was approved.

Kitchens, for the most part, still utilized coal stoves in the early years, since there was no reliable electrical system at the time outside city limits. Meanwhile, automobiles entered the fray in 1912, competing with horse-drawn carriages and other vehicles on local roads. Over the next seventeen years, "favorable rains" meant "fairly good crops."[29] The tight-knit but homogeneous community of Farwell was developing all the trappings of a growing town-consciousness, as neighbors helped neighbors in the direst of times. Picnics, holiday celebrations, and other social occasions were often marked by public gatherings at country schools.

Bill Mersfelder was one of Parmer County's earliest residents and in his role as part-time peace officer was familiar with George J. Hassell, having guarded him at the county courthouse and the local jails following his arrest in 1926. He had moved to Farwell's neighboring town of Bovina around 1900, hoping to open a general store and restaurant. The Farwell brothers had not started selling land yet, so there was nowhere for him to start his business. He improvised, locating his business "in a large dug out on railroad land southeast from where the depot at Bovina now stands. This was the first private business established in Parmer County limits." Bovina's restaurant took off as the hard-riding cowboys from the XIT, who had worked the range for months, needed somewhere to spend money and decompress after long hours in the saddle. At the turn of the century, Bovina was described as "the largest live cattle shipping point in the world."[30]

One former Parmer County sheriff said that county residents "were as much or more law abiding than they are now."[31] The county, at least according to a 1974 history of it, was "tame by most frontier standards" and there had never been a saloon in the county to speak of. While there was some rustling, there was a law against wearing pistols in the towns and it "was enforced too."[32] There was little crime, aside from vagrants breaking into businesses on their way through town. Nonetheless, there was plenty of demand in the first decade of the twentieth century for some type of formal law-enforcement apparatus, with residents expressing displeasure that there were no local law officers in the county.

Parmer County sheriffs were always elected, not appointed.[33] Statewide, Texas sheriffs often established good working relationships with the sheriffs of neighboring counties. They might cement the relationships by either meeting with each other in person or speaking on the phone. According to Texas historian Thad Sitton, there were several reasons for this from a criminal justice and jurisdictional point of view. It was common for bandits and other groups of malefactors "to cluster along county lines" and move back and forth across multiple jurisdictions. Ultimately, informal cooperation between neighboring sheriffs was essential for fighting any organized outlaw activity. This held true "even if they personally disliked each other."[34] But the sheriffs' "most fateful and intimate relationship was with his county judge," since "sheriffs brought most of their criminal cases in county court."[35]

By 1908, Parmer County had its first jail, and two years later Farwell maintained a city constable (the unfortunately named W. M. Shitley), who held the job for a decade. Nothing symbolizes a town's stability like a newspaper, and in 1910 Farwell introduced the *State Line Tribune*. That same year, Richard Coke Hopping (1875–1954) was voted Parmer County sheriff (1910–1918). He penned his autobiography in the early 1950s and recounted that in the earlier days, "Texico, Bovina and Farwell were wicked, wild and gory, and enticed rowdies, murderers and gamblers. The rustlers were still mavericking the calves and yearlings."[36]

In order to tame the Llano Estacado, the sheriff's office would need a rugged man full of courage, and by most accounts Hopping fit the bill.[37] Born in Hood County, Texas, Hopping was raised on a ranch. Married at seventeen, he was managing a ranch by the age of twenty. He trailed a herd from East Texas to New Mexico, before settling near Portales, New Mexico, where he mixed ranch work with being county sheriff. Hopping's stint as sheriff coincided with the exodus of many of the troublemakers and riff raff that seemed common in the county prior to his taking office. Hopping later suggested that they more likely moved on because the entire county was becoming increasingly well organized. In any case, he moved to Lubbock in 1926, the same year Hassell committed his last murders.

George Hassell would have noticed the variation in headwear in the Panhandle, especially as he moved from place to place throughout the West. According to one county history, "Our Western men preferred the smaller brimmed hat because of wind." By comparison, the chronicler noted that Stetson hats which were often given as gifts to Texas Rangers and celebrities, were especially handy for protecting one's face from sun and dust, or to blindfold a steer or smother a grass fire."[38]

By the time the Hassells arrived, Farwell was enjoying heady growth. The 1920s saw the population double in size. Indeed, by then a crudely graded road connected Farwell with Amarillo, passing through the Parmer County towns of Bovina, Hereford, and Canyon. A similar road linked the town to Lubbock via Muleshoe and Littlefield.[39] Most of the towns in the vicinity of Farwell began as cow-camps for the XIT in the 1880s and would experience divergent growth patterns and varying levels of success attracting settlers.

The Hassells would have found Farwell to be on the ascendant, boasting a new bank, hardware store, grocery, and butcher shop. Just three years earlier, W. W. Hall had opened his Texas Grocery as well as "the first tourist cabins in this section of the country," according to a history of

Parmer County.⁴⁰ Hall was evidently ahead of his time or overly optimistic, building tourist accommodations in Farwell at a time when this type of convenience was rare. Promotional materials described six cabins "made out of cotton sack ducking." Hall explained that they were actually closer to tents than cabins, since "the sides could be rolled up and there was a kerosene drop light in each cabin ... One dollar per night."⁴¹ Hall supplied the kerosene, located in a barrel in the middle of the lot. At the time, the only modern provision was a water hydrant, also located in the middle of the lot, to be shared by all six cabins. His optimism might have paid off for a while, with customers reporting "that these were the best accommodations to be found between St. Louis and the West Coast."⁴² In any case, Hall quit operating the cabins and the grocery store in 1928.

Although built some twenty-seven miles northeast of Farwell, newcomers and locals alike couldn't possibly miss the Syndicate Hotel built by the XIT Land Company in 1925 to accommodate land buyers brought to the area when ranchland was being marketed to farmers. When it opened in 1926, one local historian suggests that it "looked out of place in the midst of flat farmland, miles away from anything else."⁴³ The Hassells would have been impressed "by the nine room two story stucco structure."⁴⁴ The first floor offered a lobby, dining room, office, bath, kitchen, and living quarters for those who ran the hotel. Upstairs were two large bedrooms capable of accommodating a dozen beds each, two smaller bedrooms, a hall, and a bath. A windmill pumped water, which was piped throughout the building. Large coal stoves supplied heating and cooking. Guests and prospective buyers typically spent two nights there and received five meals.⁴⁵

The year before the Hassells moved in, a Ford Agency was already operating in Farwell, and in 1925 two partners opened the Fox Drug Store (after the town had done without one for twelve years). Other businesses they would have been familiar with included the Farmers Grain Company, which advertised lump and nut coal for sale, and the OK Wagon Yard featuring "Chick Chow" to make chickens grow.

By the mid-1920s, Farwell had some "modern utilities" with further infrastructure improvements such as streetlights already in the works.⁴⁶

In 1916, ten years before Hassell was arrested for murder, work had begun on the courthouse where his trial would later take place.[47] In addition, a new county jail, which Hassell would become familiar with in due time, was built behind the courthouse, on 3rd Street. When Parmer County officials moved into the court building the following year, they found the edifice "modern in every respect," indeed, many regarded it as "the pride and joy of the entire community."

Perhaps a harbinger of the sinister forces on the horizon, Farwell was hit with a series of fires beginning in 1913 when an entire block of the business section was burned to the ground, a suspected arson. And in 1920, the popular Farwell Inn became another fire victim. One local historian noted that "fire was basically a determining factor in the moving of most of the business section to the new Main Street in 1921." Nevertheless, residents and newcomers had visions of a growing urban entrepot, and prospective home builders bought up lots to house an expected crush of new residents.

The Hassells arrived in town at an auspicious moment. While it is unclear exactly what brought the family to Farwell from Oklahoma, surely the clever advertisements of land boosters must have played some role or at least caught the Hassells' attention. Perhaps one of them, before they left Oklahoma, came across the 1924 pamphlet titled "Capitol Reservation Lands," that extolled the region's virtues and was intended to "spur land sales in Parmer County, advertising a half million acres for sale as farm homes."[48] The booster literature described 160-acre tracts of land selling for affordable prices with reasonable terms of payment. It also made note of Farwell's proximity to larger cities such as Lubbock and Amarillo.

Land speculators and prospective farmers were drawn by the area's reputed rich soil and lands, which were at an altitude of three thousand to four thousand feet, "offering invigorating atmosphere conducive to health and energy." Moreover, if promotional materials were to be believed, the soil was "underlaid with an inexhaustible sheet of soft water from 50 to 225 feet" deep." Promoters claimed that "the efficient farmer had never had a complete crop failure." Among the staple crops were wheat, broom corn, oats, millet, sorghum Kaffir corn, and "almost every variety of vegetable," all "yielding abundantly." Indeed, "Kaffir corn and milo maize were considered the pioneer [most significant] grain crops" of this region.[49] During the fall, no business was busier in the town than the elevators, "when threshing of hand cut maize, went on for weeks at a time." The maize was cut in the fields and farmers hauled it into town by the wagonload.

Parmer County was notable for "the number and quality of Hereford Durham and Angus Cattle that thrive on native grasses here." What's more, the availability of "pure water and abundance of grain" made the region ideal for raising hogs." One local farmer referred to hogs as a "mortgage lifter."[50]

***

No one could ever deny that George Hassell was an industrious worker. Neighboring farmers remarked on how Hassell made improvements to his landlord's property, something seldom required from tenant farmers. One neighbor, J. O. Ford, a farmer for thirty-four years, would later testify at Hassell's trial in 1927 that he had taken notice, commenting, "I thought he was about the best renter to fix up a place that I ever saw." When Hassell took over the place, the property was pretty run-down, and he built fences and "leveled the ground around the house and garden." What most piqued Ford's interest was his use of a machine commonly called a "fresno" (Fresno scraper) to level holes on the place, something he thought "was out of the ordinary." Indeed, Ford added, very few landowners, let alone their tenants, did that.

In contrast, Ford was not as generous in his appraisal of his neighbor's farming methods. As a fellow farmer, he paid close attention to the methods others used to raise crops and livestock. Driving past the Hassell spread almost every day, Ford likely paid more attention to it than others. He described Hassell's farming methods as "out of the ordinary, or abnormal." Moreover, he "did not admire his farming, that is, his method ... his method of cultivating his crop, I didn't like that. I didn't think he did that part right." On one occasion, Ford noticed Hassell filling up holes in the fields with his fresno. He went over and asked him if he could borrow it, but Hassell responded somewhat cryptically that he needed it for something.

Former Parmer County Attorney J. D. Thomas in 1935 remembered Hassell "as a burly man ... possessed of a remarkable physique—a giant of a man—and was very industrious ... Indeed, the entire family was industrious." This description, as noted earlier, runs counter to his penitentiary records, which place him at average height and perhaps 180 pounds. A "neighboring woman" remembered the family keeping to themselves, and "little was known about them" except they had "moved to Farwell from Oklahoma about a year before and had rented a farm belonging to Judge J. D. Hamlin."[51] According to a 2011 interview with the son of a Farwell bank president, a friend of one of the Hassell boys, when Hassell wasn't working on his land he could be seen driving "a maintainer to grade the roads for Parmer Co." Occasionally he would let "area children ride on the road grader."[52]

The lives of dozens of families would intersect in Farwell, but none could have been more dissimilar from each other than the Hassells and Hamlins. The Hassells were the salt of the earth, unlettered and unsophisticated, while the James D. Hamlins were cultured, educated, and part of the region's elite. The Hamlins had been in the Farwell area for about twenty years before the Hassells became part of the community. Judge James Darlington Hamlin (1871–1950), better known as J. D., had married Kate Nichols in 1906 before putting down roots in the area. Born in Kentucky, he attended the University of Kentucky and in 1897 left home in search of his fortune during the Alaskan Gold Rush. He didn't get very far, ending his adventure in Amarillo, Texas, where "he found relief from his chronic asthma."[53] In 1898, he was admitted to the Texas Bar and practiced law until 1902, when he was elected county attorney for Potter County. In 1905, he became an agent for the Capitol Syndicate, opening XIT lands to colonization and helping found the city of Farwell.

When the Hamlins moved into town, J. D. was actively campaigning to sell XIT lands to the influx of settlers moving into the Texas Panhandle and eastern New Mexico. Especially attractive to his business instincts were the railroad lines being constructed in close proximity to Farwell and Texico, on the Texas–New Mexico border. Farwell was located at the junction of two branches of the Santa Fe railroad, one branch connecting northeast to Amarillo and the other southeast to Lubbock. Hamlin had probably watched families disembarking from trains in Farwell, with the more prosperous staying at the four-story Farwell Hotel as they toured available homestead sites in touring cars. At the time, others were still arriving by covered wagons. With a virtual absence of stone and indigenous trees, many were forced to improvise, carving out sod homes and dugout structures from the prairie soil.

Great Plains historian Walter Prescott Webb described the region as one that challenged new inhabitants on every level.[54] Settlers were tested daily by the risky businesses of dry-land farming and herding. Periodic droughts and windstorms withered cattle and crops, sporadically forcing the typical family to rely on small windmills to pump enough water for the home as they tended a milk cow, some chickens, a handful of fruit trees, and vegetable gardens for sustenance.

Texas historian Ty Cashion suggested that farmers who, like the Hassells, arrived in the early years of the twentieth century were "beneficiaries of rapid and accessible transportation and the attendant flurry of town building" made possible by the expansion of railroads in the region.[55] Likewise, Great Plains sociologist Carl Frederic Kraenzel asserted that railroads proved to be "the great booster of settlement."[56]

Success and wish fulfillment are often predicated on luck and the unforeseen whims of others. Such was the case for J. D. Hamlin, who saw an opportunity to reap a large profit by joining an enterprise seeking to build a railroad cutoff from a sidetrack on the state line at what became known as Texico. Farwell and Texico, on either side of the New Mexico–Texas border, are considered twin cities, due to both their relative proximity to each other and the machinations involved in their founding. The hope was that if the Texico project saw the light of day, it would allow trains running from Chicago and Kansas City towards the Pacific Coast to circumvent the treacherous Raton and Glorieta Passes. Hamlin and a partner, John Huston, purchased land on the New Mexico side of the border and laid out the townsite of Texico. The town boomed, and a great future was forecast for the town once the Pecos Valley and Northeastern Railroad was purchased by the Santa Fe. Hamlin was confident enough that the new line would start at Texico, ninety-five miles southwest of Amarillo, that he purchased an eighty-acre townsite there.

Its location was strategic for the growth of the area. Hamlin and other investors counted on a new railroad depot to bring in settlers if the Capitol Land Company could influence the Santa Fe Railroad to locate its shops there. Hamlin and his partners offered the railroad a half-section of land to locate its shops at Texico-Farwell. But the Santa Fe held out for more land. Catching almost everyone by surprise, the railroad made a quick determination to locate its roundhouse ten miles west of Texico at what had formerly been called Riley's Switch. The railroad secretly purchased land and laid out its own townsite of Clovis, New Mexico, in 1907. With this turn of events, any hope of Farwell or Texico becoming sizable towns was terminated.

***

Farwell residents surely could not have recalled anyone making such a huge impact on their lives and town in such a short time as did George Jefferson Hassell. While locals would see Hassell doing business in Farwell and nearby Clovis, New Mexico, from time to time, like everyone else that had crossed paths with him during his lifetime, few could really say they knew him, let alone his family. While he could often be charming, even disarmingly so, some neighbors described him as "always irritable and impatient" and "often quarrelsome with his family." Those familiar with his proclivities might have associated his behavior with his occasional whiskey drinking, which he would relate, on more than one occasion to others, that his wife did not approve of.[57] One Hassell chronicler wrote that "although Hassell was very friendly and outgoing, with an awkward kind of charm, some of the men in town thought of him as a 'hick' with a sharp eye for women, a fondness for bawdy jokes and a liking for bootleg whiskey."[58]

Four of Hassell's younger stepchildren went to school when they weren't needed on the farm. They were considered "exceptionally bright." After school they typically returned home to help their brothers and sisters on the farm. A former neighbor, Mrs. N. A. Lindop, commented on how the students "made excellent grades in school—when work on the farm permitted their going to school." During Hassell's 1926 murder trial, the Lindops were living in the Hassell house, by then known as the "murder house," where Mrs. Lindop found a "faded honors slip with the name of one of the children on it." It had been issued at a previous school in Oklahoma.[59] Some might have had reservations about their quirky neighbor, but according to the Lindops, none could question his work ethic. Indeed, she noticed that he "worked all the time, it seemed, and the children did too." Moreover, "they seldom had a holiday. They worked every Sunday as far as we know."[60]

By the fall of 1926, Susie and Hassell were at loggerheads once again. Their quarreling became more frequent, and Hassell became increasingly riled by the fact that she always took the side of her children. Few, if any, community members knew that his kids were actually his stepchildren, let alone his nephews and nieces. But this was about to change. He would later state that at one point he started to pack up and leave the family, following a pattern he set earlier in life when he deserted his first wife, the Army, and the Navy. He would later admit that he "didn't use judgment enough to leave but that is the thing I ought to have done, ought have walked out."[61]

In December 1926, Farwell was in the grip of a typical High Plains winter. Hassell, his wife, and his eight stepchildren had by all appearances fallen into the rhythms of country life. Living in their cramped five-room stucco house, the family seemed to be coping with the travails of farm life. Susan's day-to-day life would be familiar to Texas farm wives elsewhere, "overburdened and undereducated" as they "toiled at many tasks." In their cramped farmhouse that she shared with her husband and eight children, she "was wife, mother, cook, seamstress, laborer, doctor, treasurer, and spiritual provider." As one historian put it, "In the story of Texas, the farm woman is an unsung hero."[62] Farm women were tasked with a seemingly endless list of chores and responsibilities. They not only contributed to subsistence activities such as feeding, clothing, and raising children but took care of family gardens, chickens and eggs, and maybe the milking of cows. Family work was usually divided by gender, with men expected to raise feed crops and cotton as well as tend to cattle and workhorses.

By the time Hassell sold his farm possessions at auction on December 22, 1926, he had amassed a respectable amount of property, including thirteen head of cattle, ten horses and mules, chickens, rabbits, and three hogs, as well as plenty of feed and farming equipment. Susie probably appreciated the gasoline iron, the wash pot with furnace, the ice cream freezer, the cooking stove, the sewing machine, and the phonograph and records that Hassell sold at auction shortly before leaving the homestead to the Lindops. But she would not have much say in what property was being sold.[63]

***

Sometime in late fall, Mrs. Hamlin noticed a pit being dug in the Hassell yard. She later estimated it was at least ten by fifteen square feet, or possibly larger, "just a square, a square hole in the ground about four or five feet deep."[64] She thought it odd that it was being dug close to the back door, only six to ten feet from the east side of the house. It was quite a project, taking place over several weeks. Hamlin later testified, "I never knew or understood what it was being dug for." She added that there was already a dugout, where Susie stored canned fruits and preserves. Several neighbors remembered seeing two of the older boys, Russell and Virgil, digging the pit, but she did not remember seeing the oldest boy, Alton, or Hassell working on the pit.[65]

The neighboring Lindop's sixteen-year-old son, Lester, remembered that the pit had been dug around the time of the Dallas Fair, which would have put it in October. At that time, "the pit looked to be three feet deep with the dirt piles around it." While being interrogated by the county attorney soon before his crimes were discovered, Hassell said that he had "dug the cellar because he thought he needed it and later found he didn't need it, and that he wanted to leave the premises in as good condition as possible and filled it in." He told others that it was meant to be a storm shelter. Neither story passed the sniff test.

A hush would fall over the Parmer County courtroom in January 1927 when Mrs. Hamlin testified that in the months preceding the Hassell family massacre she had seen the Hassell boys digging what would become the death pit. Both boys "toiled with spade and shovel for days digging the hole where they were buried." Little did they realize that "the pit would soon wrap its silent folds about them and seven others, and again unfold to yield to the nation the greatest crime of the decade."[66]

Like most people who knew Hassell, Mrs. Hamlin described him as "a pretty good worker around the place." He would sometimes stop by the Hamlin house and ask for assorted materials, such as posts, wire, gates, chicken coops, and hinges to fix doors. This went on throughout the year. Contrary to the claim in the Hassell family chronicle that Hassell asked Mrs. Hamlin for permission to create a dugout,[67] in Hamlin's trial testimony she said he never mentioned the dugout to her, nor did he ever give a convincing explanation for why it was necessary given that there was already a dugout on the property.[68] When Hamlin became aware of the pit construction, she was perplexed as to why Hassell never asked for any materials for building it. Kate Hamlin asked Susie Hassell about the pit the Friday or Saturday night before the family disappeared. The last time she saw Susie alive, Hamlin had been driving past the Hassell property and saw her standing at the edge of the dugout, so she stopped the car close to the chicken house and waited for Hassell to come out, but she never did. She then called out to Susie and "asked her how she got that splendid work done, and I commented on it." However, Hamlin never heard or understood her response: "she answered me some way—chatting—I don't know or really remember what she said."[69]

The year 1926 "happened to be a bumper year" for the Hassell farm, with Hassell raising and harvesting "an especially bountiful crop. However, few knew that his relationship with Judge Hamlin was deteriorating. Fortunately for Hamlin, Hassell mostly dealt with his wife. According to an interview with the Parmer County attorney in 1935, it was said that Hassell was surprisingly avaricious. When it came time to divide the halves of the crops with his landlord in 1926, "Hassell gave evidence of a grasping nature. He tried to take more than was coming to him, and his business relations with his landlord were anything but pleasant."[70] When Judge Hamlin heard in December 1926 of Hassell's plan to move away after the crop had been disposed of, it was probably a relief for the respected landowner. But tragedy would soon be on his doorstep.

Chapter 6

Kill Them All

"I had started it, and I finished it."

According to Hassell, when he married Susan in 1924 she was aware he had impregnated Nora, his niece and her daughter, two years earlier. If this were true, one of the most perplexing questions is why Susan, if she knew of this abuse of her daughter, would marry her brother-in-law after such a transgression. Nora had told her Uncle George several years earlier that she would stay in California and look for a husband after he went back to Oklahoma. She stayed in California after giving birth to Georgia and got married. That marriage did not last, and then she married Luke Breaux Guidrey, known as "Frenchie," who raised Georgia as his own. In the summer of 1926, Nora and Frenchie left young Georgia at home and traveled from California to visit the rest of the family in Farwell.

Hassell would never mention any of his victims, past or present, by name. Even when he spoke of his murder of Marie Vogel in 1917, he depersonalized her, insisting on referring to her as "that woman." In his later confessions and statements, he always referred to his last wife, Susie, as "the woman" and his niece Maudie as "the girl." The oldest of Susie's girls still at home, thirteen-year old Maudie was described as "a big girl" by the landlord and neighbor, Mrs. Hamlin, who was under the impression she was at least fifteen or sixteen years old," which in 1926 was below the age of consent, as it is today.[1]

It was another hot Panhandle afternoon when Frenchie and Nora arrived from California. Maudie borrowed Nora's swimsuit. Or, in Hassell's vernacular, "they put it on this other girl [Maudie], the one that was at home, put this bathing suit on and she got in a wooden tank out there at my place bathing." By all accounts, she couldn't swim, which was not uncommon in regions where there was little opportunity or reason to learn. Nora had gone back into the house, but when she came out a few minutes later she saw that her husband had not just been teaching Maudie to swim but also placing his hand on "a suspicious place" on her body. Nora went into a rage and threatened to sue him for a divorce (which she apparently did when they returned to California).

Nora and Frenchie returned home to California a couple of days later. Hassell later claimed that Nora told "the girl's mother," Susan, about it. Once Susan found out about Frenchie and Maudie, she suspected that Hassell might have sexually abused Maudie as well. Based on her experience with pregnancy, Susan sensed that, as Hassell put it, "the girl was in a family way." Susan voiced her displeasure to both her daughter and Hassell and began accusing him of having had relations with the girl.[2]

Shortly after this interlude, Susan took Maudie to an osteopath in Clovis to confirm her suspicions. She brought along one of her sons but did not reveal why they were at the doctor's office with Maudie.[3] Hassell described how their troubled relationship was getting worse, saying that his "wife talked to me all the time about the girl being in a family way and I tried to reason with her and tried to tell her things like that had happened and if it had we would have to take care of her. Three times, I think, she went to doctor around time [her] period [was] supposed to be … It was plain enough to see she was in a family way all right."[4]

It was difficult helping to raise eight stepchildren and, as Hassell would later explain, "spats began to come in frequent." Moreover, Susan "would always uphold her children, of course, and I was just kind of a lost card.

She would take the side of the children on any correction I would make, and fusses come more frequent and more plentiful." The swimming incident only heightened the tensions between Susan and her husband.

What started out as a couple of trusted, grown men teaching a young girl to swim in a wooden water tank on a hot Texas Panhandle summer day would have tragic consequences for most of those involved. At Hassell's 1927 trial, the jury and grand jury were allowed to read his full confession, but when the salacious confession was widely published in the newspapers, the lurid aspects of the Maudie incident were edited out. However, the original trial transcript lays out the sordid sequence of events.

During Hassell's 1927 trial he was asked whether he had had sex with Maudie, and he said, "Yes, I had intercourse with the girl." When queried as to what he had planned to do, he said that he told his wife only after Maudie was found to be pregnant. Ever the calculated predator, once he found out that she was pregnant, Hassell even tried to persuade "the girl, Maudie," to blame it on a cousin that she had visited with earlier in the summer. He convinced Maudie that it was in her best interest to say that the father was her cousin. Indeed, "she said her cousin had sexual intercourse with her all right but that he didn't—he said he just barely did get it in. Kinda tussle match, you know."[5] Hassell was anxious to keep Susan in the dark about his sexual predilections. He told her that Maudie had agreed to support the accusation against her cousin, that it was he who had "got her that way, and it was just about her time. I was going to help her through, and I told her she could go ahead and lay it to this boy and marry this boy and if she didn't get along, she could come back home, but her mother was awfully quiet about it and didn't say nothing to me." Hassell said that Susan "said nothing to me ... kinda indifferent," and he suspected that the girl had told her mother already.

***

The marriage between Hassell and Susan took a turn for the worse. Hassell later recounted that the arguing over his abuse of his stepdaughter went into full throttle when they were together picking cotton. It became so heated, he said, that "I started to pack up and leave and did pack up to leave but didn't use judgment enough to leave but that is what I ought to have done, ought to have walked out."[6]

Susan was looking forward to December, as she always had, with her birthday Christmas Eve and Christmas on back to back days. No doubt, the farm and ranch families of Farwell, Texas, were also counting the days until Christmas. But on the frigid, windy night of December 2, George J. Hassell launched a family killing spree in their small abode outside Farwell.

Predisposed to the bottle and fits of anger, the brawny man with the smiling blue eyes was in no mood to quarrel with his wife or listen to her seemingly endless complaints, especially after it was firmly established by a local doctor that he had left another one of his nieces (now his stepdaughter) pregnant. He had killed before and knew what he had to do, although he would never be able to explain why. In fact, nine years later the bodies still had not been discovered under the house in Whittier, California. It is likely Hassell felt that if he could get away with it once, why not again?

On the frigid evening of December 2, 1926, Hassell was lying in bed with Susie and two-year-old Sammie. His wife was once again criticizing him for his rapacious ways, no doubt bringing up his sexual violence against two of his nieces over the past four years. He got out of bed, put on some clothes, and went out to the barn to his pint of whiskey. His wife, Susie, was a Russellite, which meant keeping alcohol and tobacco out of the house. The sect was founded by Charles Taze Russell (1852–1916), who traveled widely throughout Texas in his last years.[7] Russellites did not believe in the existence of hell, nor in the doctrine of the Trinity. What is more, they did not own their own worship buildings, instead meeting in each other's homes, which functioned as de facto churches. (The Jehovah Witnesses Sect was founded in 1931, with Russellites providing the nucleus of the new sect.)

When Hassell went out to the barn, he may have intended to take a few sips, just cool off, and wait for Susie to fall asleep. But when he went back into the cramped five-room house, his wife continued to reproach him. He laid back down beside her, close enough for her to smell the whiskey on his breath, exacerbating the argument that now included his drinking.[8] On more than one occasion, he had promised Susie he would turn over a new leaf and leave the whiskey alone, a common refrain among alcoholics trying to make peace with family members. At this point, Susie was probably convinced that he was incapable of mending his ways.

In another interview from the week before he was executed, Hassell gave an alternate version of what pushed him over the edge. According to this scenario, "our first differences were about reprimanding her son. She was a wonderful mother and housewife, but green about the ways of the world, therefore she didn't understand when I refused to let her son run around with a girl who was trying to stick some man."[9] Having lived forty years, married at nineteen, and given birth to nine children, it is unlikely that Susie was naïve when it came to relations between boys and girls. Moreover, it seems that Hassell was borrowing a page from his own past: if understood correctly, he was implying that the girl might be trying either to get pregnant or was already pregnant and looking for someone she could blame for it. It sounds much like his conversation with Maudie when he tried to convince her to blame her pregnancy on her cousin, rather than on Hassell or "Frenchie."

Hassell said that once they began arguing, he got out of the bed and went and sat at the dining room table for about forty-five minutes, "with my face resting on my hands, when she came over and put her arms around me and begged me to come back to bed, and I told her I would." But first, he said, "I went out to the barn and took a pull on a pint of whiskey. When I went back into the house, she kissed me and smelled that bootleg on my breath. Something was said and I saw a hammer on the floor."[10]

The only commonality of these two versions of his last interaction with Susan was that the murder was preceded by her scolding him about his drinking. In both cases he claimed to find himself suddenly holding a ball peen hammer "weighing about a pound and a half." He hit Susie twice in the face with it. He told a jury that he did it "before I could stop myself and then I shut her wind off with my hand to keep the sound in, and all the blood commenced running everywhere and I thought I had her passed [sic] any noise and I taken a stocking and tied it around her throat to stop the noise, and about the time I had that done the little fellow [Sammie] was laying there and he commenced hollering and putting up a noise, and I just reached over and choked him. I choked him with my hand and then tied the stocking on after—he wasn't hit at all." He would later clarify his rampage, as if it would improve his image, by noting that "none of the three little ones were hit."[11]

We will never know exactly what Hassell was thinking when he commenced killing. This was not his first family mass murder, and he may have thought back to his murder of Marie Vogel and her three kids nine years earlier, when he had argued with Marie late one evening in Whittier and ended the argument by strangling her and then tying a sock around her neck and sitting on the edge of bed wondering what to do with the three sleeping children in the next room. In 1926, as he had in 1917, he decided to go in the room and manually strangle the children. In his trial testimony, he seemed quite proud of himself for being able to commit those grisly crimes in such a quiet manner and not awaken the little ones still sleeping.

Hassell had plenty of time to escape after killing Susie and Sammie, his first two victims. However, he lingered to kill the rest of the family, or as he later admitted, "So I had started, and Lord-God I would have given anything in the world if I had not made the first lick but I had started it and I finished it."[12]

He then left the front bedroom that he shared with his wife and Sammie and moved into the middle bedroom, where the youngest children slept. He made quick work of Nannie (age four), who shared one bed with Maudie, and David (age seven) and Johnnie (age six), who shared the other. Somehow, he was able to choke the three youngest ones without waking the others up, and then he "turned his attention to the still sleeping Maudie. Wanting to be sure she would not cry out to alert the older boys, he struck his pregnant stepdaughter two severe blows to the head using the same hammer that he used to kill Susan. He finished her off by choking what life remained in her."[13]

It is hard to believe that he had not planned this ahead of time. According to the Hassell family manuscript, as he committed the murders there was "no emotion, no pity, no compassion, no anger, he was just doing a job that needed to be done much like butchering the hog and beef had needed to be done, not because he was mad at them. His only concern at this point was the amount of blood splattered at this point around two rooms." However, compared to the "neat aftermath of his California murders," Hassell "could worry about cleaning up the mess later."[14]

With these six out of the way, he had only to deal with Virgil (age fifteen) and Russell (age eleven). Twenty-one-year-old Alton was still away working on a threshing crew, but Hassell must have realized that the two boys remaining at home would be no pushovers. There would be no strangling them in their sleep. They were both hardy young country boys, used to toiling on the farm, possessing the strength of most adult men. Hassell headed to the rear bedroom where Russell and Virgil were sleeping, still undisturbed by the rampage in the other bedrooms.

On his way to the boys' room, he spotted the family shotgun, which was stored in the kitchen, and took the precaution of hiding it in the dining room. He saw that Russell was not in his bedroom but instead asleep in the front room. He woke him up and told him to get in his bed. This was his first mistake, as he would later admit, noting that he should have dealt with Virgil in the bedroom first while he was still asleep and then come back and finished Russell off in the front room. When Russell returned to the bedroom, it roused his brother. Virgil woke up, groggily asking if Alton had come home yet. Hassell overheard him and told him no. Russell grabbed his clothes in the front room and went back and got in his bed. Meanwhile, Hassell built a fire in the heat stove. The boys still had no clue about the carnage in the other rooms. Virgil, according to Hassell, couldn't get back to sleep and joined his uncle in the dining room by the fire. At this point, Hassell feared that he was going to be facing two young but formidable adversaries, possibly more than he could handle. Moreover, with both boys now awake, they might discover his handiwork in the other two bedrooms. Afraid he could not handle both at once, he had to act quickly and decisively before he lost control of what was up to that point a perfectly executed mass murder.[15]

Hassell felt he could not get to the hidden shotgun with Virgil now sitting in the dining room, so he decided to deal with Russell first in his bedroom. With Virgil sitting by the stove in the dining room, he figured his course of action was to go into the bedroom and first strangle the preteen Russell, hoping his time-tested technique of manual strangulation would allow him to dispatch Russell quietly. Hassell remembered, "I just goes in there and starts choking Russell ... He was the only one I hit with an axe and he began to make a noise; I couldn't handle him in the way I had the rest of them." Russell fought back, rousing Virgil's attention in the other room. As Virgil went to see what the uproar was about in his bedroom, he saw his stepfather manhandling his younger brother and said, "Daddy, what in the world are you doing, trying to kill somebody?" Hassell yelled at him to "get out of here and attend to your business."[16]

As fifteen-year-old Virgil grabbed for him, Hassell turned his attention from Russell to the older boy. Hassell would later recount that "of course, I had to let this other fellow go and in the meantime though I was afraid so I taken the shotgun from where it was and put it in another place, and at least one of the boys said, 'Get the shotgun,' and called 'MAMA' for a little while then or called Maudie; that was the girl, and while this other boy and myself was on the floor fighting—he was kind of a chunk of a boy—Virgil hollered for Russell to come and help him, that he would get the sonofabitch ... Russell picked up a brick and hit me 2 or 3 times ... so after I seen I was going to have a pretty tussle with both of them and after they had scratched me up here and bungled me up I just swung loose from them and jumped up and run into the room and grabbed the shotgun and when Virgil walked into the room the other way I shot him right through the heart, I guess, about through the heart" after which Virgil fell in the dining room near the stove.[17]

After dispatching Virgil, Hassell went looking for eleven-year-old Russell. He had lost track of him in the struggle. At first, he thought he might have run outside. He went out the back door but couldn't spot him. Hassell rushed back into the house; time was of the essence at this point. Continuing to search for Russell, Hassell found him cowering in the corner of the closet of the boys' room and "got him down on the floor and choked him with his bare hands." To keep him from making noise, Hassell tied a ligature tight around his neck to stop his death spasms.

By the time he concluded that day's bloody work, he had taken the lives of eight family members ranging in age from two to almost forty-one. The bodies were probably still warm when Hassell decided to bury Virgil first. No doubt rushing to be done by sunrise, he went into the dining room to retrieve the body. As Hassell later described, "I think I rolled him over on a quilt and dragged him out to the cellar and I believe he was laying next to the wall on the west side."[18] Russell would be a different story. When he reached down to move him, according to Hassell, "he kept wheezing ... and I was afraid it sounded awful loud ... and I was afraid somebody might be passing and would hear it to the road, and so I gets this axe and hits him and that was the only one I hit with an axe. After I choked him and he wouldn't stop wheezing I hit him."[19] In later interviews Hassell would go to great lengths to clear the record, especially when it was rumored that he killed all with an axe, by asserting he only killed one with an axe. In any case Russell was placed against the wall on the north end of the cellar.

Hassell buried the rest of the bodies face down in the pit, "in pretty much the way he had planned but by the time he had covered them, so much area was filled in, the spot for Alton was small enough that he would have to be buried sitting up."[20] Dawn was just breaking when he went back inside to start cleaning up the mess, and what a mess it was. The walls were "splattered" with blood, and there was a lot of it "pooled on the floors of three rooms." Family chroniclers claimed that "there was blood on two mattresses, but the bedclothes had soaked up most of it."[21] Once Hassell finished his cleaning, he could relax for a short time and wait for Alton, the older boy, to return home.

In one of his last interviews Hassell said that "the impulse to kill was not satisfied until he had slain every member of his families (11 stepchildren and two wives)."[22] Moreover, he seemed proud, according to the *Abilene Morning News* on February 1, 1928: Hassell declared he "clubbed his two wives to death a few minutes after he had petted and kissed them," and that "a moment later the impulse to kill came and I committed murder."[23]

Chapter 7

The Last Victim

"He died easier than any of them."

Alton finally returned to the Hassell farm on the night of December 5, 1926. Hassell had to wait three days for his oldest nephew and stepson to get back. At twenty-one, Alton was an experienced farmhand and strong to boot. Hassell knew that the boy would present the most challenging obstacle to completing his plan of wiping out the entire family. In his confession, he explained that he had expected Alton home on Saturday evening, December 4, when he was supposed to finish his threshing job. He had waited up until midnight, but Alton didn't return.

At the time of the murders, Alton was working for G. W. Crawford, who ran a threshing machine several miles south of Bovina. Alton oiled the separator on the contraption, earning three dollars per day (equivalent to $43 in 2020). He had been working almost two and a half weeks. On the night of December 4, instead of returning to the farm as expected, Alton went home to Clovis with his boss, who had two sons of his own working with him as well, and prepared to stay the night. Crawford happened to overhear the boys talking about planning to go to a "picture show."

So, he told Alton he could go home with them and spend the night after the movie.

For farm boys, they got up kind of late on Sunday morning, December 5. It was raining and snowing a little. They hung around the house and read, followed by a late breakfast.[1] Alton stayed until two or three in the afternoon. One of Crawford's sons and a friend dropped him off at home close to sunset. This was the last time the Crawfords saw Alton alive.

***

By Sunday Hassell had only filled two thirds of the cellar pit, leaving room for his biggest and last victim. The evening was cold and windy with sleet and rain. He must have welcomed the boy warmly into the house, trying to deflect his attention from the fact that the house was silent and that there was no sign of the rest of the family. Hassell tried out his cover story as they sat down to dinner, telling Alton that the family had gone "to see Aunt Liddy down at Shallowater." Before they settled in for the evening, Hassell remembered that "we killed a chicken and went and drove the chickens up and got the ducks off the pond and sat around and played cards until after midnight."[2]

After eating dinner and cleaning up, Hassell and his oldest stepson played cards, though Hassell was probably more focused on how he would eliminate Alton. By some accounts, Alton might have been "drinking from the same jug from which Hassell said he had drawn courage to put to death the mother and small children."[3] It was getting late and Alton was likely tired, if not from imbibing with his stepfather then from his hard work on the threshing crew and what had probably been a late night at the sleepover the previous evening. Hassell and Alton had probably played cards at the table many times before. Alton trusted his uncle and apparently accepted the story about the family being in Oklahoma. Finally, the young man was ready for the embrace of Morpheus and went to the rear bedroom and quickly fell asleep.

At around 4:00 a.m. on Monday morning, Hassell realized it was now or never and that he "had to do something." So, he got up for some more liquid courage, "took me a drink of whiskey to help my nerve," and went to the side of Alton's bed as he slept and shot him in the head with the shotgun.

Hassell pulled the trigger and later told reporters he had been surprised at the noise of the shotgun. He stopped for a moment and quietly waited to see if anyone else had heard it. As if to make it sound less heinous, Hassell later qualified his confession, commenting that Alton "never knew anything about it and died easier than any of them, and I put him on the other side of the dugout and began covering the dirt in from the other side." He buried the young man with his bloody bedding. This was a different method from his treatment of his other victims. He had kept all of their bedding until he had time to burn it up.[4]

***

Hassell never knew how lucky he had been the night he killed Alton. It turned out that just before midnight, the Smith family had arrived in Farwell by train with all their belongings. They were met at the train stop by relatives, the Lindop family. The night was dark and chilly, with a steady light rain falling to add to the general discomfort, but there was nothing else to do but unload the flatcar of the two autos, put the household goods in N. A. Lindop's freight wagon, and head down the road to home. The rest of the Smith family belongings, including the livestock, were due in tomorrow and they would need to be back to pick them up, so this run had to be taken care of tonight, rain or no rain. Everything was going as planned on the old rain-slicked mud road till the Dodge slid into a ditch as it came around a curve in the road around the pond by George Hassell's gate. Trying to rock it back and forth to get it back on the road only made it worse, so N. A. decided to unhitch his mules from the freight wagon and hook them onto the Dodge. In the meantime, his son Lester went up the lane to Hassell's barn to get a shovel. Lester saw no need to go up to the house in the middle of the night to ask permission, because he and his brother, Mervin, had just recently worked for Mr. Hassell and "he went to school with the Hassell kids so he knew it would be alright. He did notice, however, that there was still a light in the dining room. At last the Dodge was free, the mules were hooked back to the wagon, Lester returned the shovel to the barn, and they were on their way. No one in this group heard the sound of the shotgun blast that came after they were some distance away."[5] And Hassell was none the wiser.

On Monday, December 6, Hassell bumped into Crawford, Alton's boss, in Farwell and they spoke briefly. Later, Crawford distinctly remembered Hassell telling him that Alton, not yet dead a day, had joined his family in Oklahoma. He was half right; he had joined his family, but in the cellar pit. Coincidentally, when Crawford went home to Clovis, his wife told him he had missed a visit from Hassell. Hassell had stopped by to notify Alton's boss that his boy "wouldn't be with me anymore and for me to look out for some other hand." The next time he ran into Hassell, he told him that he still owed Alton for his work earlier in the week and asked him if he could pay him to pass it on to his son. He wrote Alton a check for eighteen dollars ($262 in 2020 dollars), which was a week's pay, and handed it to Hassell. During his subsequent trial in January, the check with his signed endorsement was presented as exhibit 5.

Ultimately, the murder of Alton would prove to be Hassell's undoing. His trial would hinge on this murder alone, because waiting for Alton to get home so he could kill him had "made it easy to show the killing was premeditated which made it murder in the first degree."[6] Moreover, killing Alton while asleep had erased any potential for a claim of self-defense. Likewise, there were no potential defense arguments to be made about acting in the heat of passion or an argument. As a postscript: when Hassell went on trial the next month, he made sure everyone knew that while the suit he was wearing was his, everything else, including the ring on his finger, had belonged to Alton, his last victim.

Chapter 8

Suspicion

"I looked at him sharply and asked him if he had been having trouble with his family, and it seemed to startle him."

In the days following the murders, "neighbors took notice of Hassell living alone on the farm."[1] Prior to December 1926, no one who passed the Hassell spread several miles east of Farwell would have given a second thought to the goings on around the five-room farmhouse. However, several women from neighboring farms, filled with what one reporter described as "feminine curiosity," cast suspicion on their neighbor after they noticed his wife and eight kids had vanished. Their first suspicions were directed at the dugout being covered up by Hassell, leading one to question, "why should a fellow, when he is planning on abandoning a place, take the pains to cover up a dugout?"[2] One farmer persisted in asking this question for several days. Indeed, it went against traditional practices. Typically, if a tenant was abandoning his property, he would not usually take the time and effort to perform such a laborious task as filling up a dugout, especially one of such recent vintage.

His landlord, Mrs. Hamlin, was among the first to notice that the Hassell family was missing, about a week after Thanksgiving, sometime in early December. She didn't waste much time asking Hassell where the family was, and he told her they went to Shallowater, Texas. A few days later he changed the destination to Oklahoma. Still another time he explained that his wife took her household effects and rented a house in Oklahoma and signed the children up for school, adding, "That is all we can give our children, Mrs. Hamlin, is an education." Hassell explained that his wife wanted to get the children started in school at the beginning of the year, and that he would join them as soon as he sold his farm machinery, livestock, and other effects.[3]

J. O. Ford, another local farmer, had only known Hassell and some of his older stepkids for about six months. Although he admitted he had never visited the family nor entered the house, he was under the impression that the family members "seemed to get along pleasantly." Living about mile east of the family, he frequently drove by the property on his way to Farwell. Sometimes he would stop and talk to the burly farmer. Ford happened to be driving by the farm on December 14, when smoke billowing above the Hassell homestead caught his attention. It was a wet, drizzly morning, mixed with snow flurries (in other words, a typical Panhandle winter day). He decided to pull over and check up on Hassell and the fire he was tending, using the excuse that Hassell had promised to do some work for him and he wanted to discuss when it would be done. Like many neighboring farmers, they often bartered services with each other, so it wouldn't have been out of the ordinary for him to stop by. The Hassell boys were supposed to help Ford out as soon as Hassell had caught up with his own work, but it was the fire that caught Ford's attention.

Ford parked his car in front of the lane gate that leads up to the house, "right in the opening of the lane where it leads away from the highway." He got out of his car to talk to Hassell, who was tending the fire "to the north and east of the house." He "left the fire and came down and met me down about the barn before I got up to where he was." From where Ford was standing, he would later tell the court he could not make out what was burning, "but it was a big fire, about a six foot blaze." He remembered that Hassell approached him at "a pretty good gait—not in a run, but a pretty good walk." As he advanced, Ford saw he was carrying some type of stick or piece of iron that he had been using to control the fire. Ford only got to about thirty yards from the road when Hassell met him and they began talking. They walked together back down to the gate to finish their conversation. As Ford went to leave, Hassell told him about his forthcoming farm auction and hoped he would come.

Ford would later testify that it seemed like Hassell might have met him down the lane in order to keep him from getting too close to the house, but at the time it did not raise any "serious suspicion." He couldn't resist asking Hassell why he had such a large fire going on and asked him "if he was killing a hog," to which Hassell defensively responded, "just burning trash." He could be touchy, despite his usual jocular mien. Ford later testified that "he seemed bothered by something; didn't appear quite as jovial as ordinarily." Ford, smiling, had to get one more dig in at his neighbor: "Your wife run you out of the house and you are building a fire to keep warm." Hassell stoically replied, "No, they are in Oklahoma." He also casually added that since the boys were gone to Oklahoma, he would probably not be able to help him with his work as promised.

During the subsequent January 1927 trial, Ford was asked on cross-examination by Hassell's attorney, W. H. Russell, whether he had seen anything that he thought "looked funny" before having heard about the alleged murders." He reiterated that something "didn't look quite right," but explained that they had only been neighbors for six months and that they weren't one another's closest neighbors (two homesteads were closer).

Later that day Ford ran into Hassell in Farwell, and they talked about the impending auction he was having, including the sale of his livestock. Despite living relatively close to each other by farming standards, this was the first time that Ford heard that the family had gone to Oklahoma. He chalked up Hassell's less than jovial mood to the fact that "he was bothered about his folks being gone." Hassell and Ford wouldn't meet up again until the auction on December 22.

***

Mrs. Hamlin had already spoken to Hassell at the beginning of December about possibly continuing to farm on the property, and he gave her every impression he planned to do so. After being recalled to the stand during Hassell's trial the following month, she said, "Anyway, I looked at him sharply and asked him if he had been having trouble with his family, and it seemed to startle him. He hesitated before he answered me, and he didn't look me in the face for a little bit." But then, she said, he looked back at her again and rather gave the impression that there were indeed problems on the home front. Hamlin said, "I won't say that he quite said 'yes', but he gave me the impression that he had. He was nervous at the time."[4]

Over the first few weeks of December, some local residents became even more suspicious about Hassell and his missing family after noticing what looked like scratch marks on his face and arms. One day he visited Parmer County Constable R.V. Hawkins, who also acted as deputy sheriff, at his grain business office. When Hassell went in, Hawkins remarked, referring to his scratches, "How did the other fellow look?" Never one to have his manhood challenged, Hassell responded almost indignantly, "Why do you want to know?" Before he left, he made sure to clear up any suspicions Hawkins might have about where the scratches came from, telling him that his horse fell "in the stubble field."[5]

One day around this time, while he was busy hauling loads of corn, Mrs. Hamlin approached him in the barn. He told her he "was batching," which she was well aware of. Nonetheless, although the Hamlins had already eaten, she asked him to "come into the house to eat your dinner." As he consumed his meal, she noticed that his "face and hands were badly scratched up; his face and the backs of his hands. You could plainly see that they were finger-nail scratches." She asked him, "What in the world happened to your face and hands." He told her he "fell off his pony in the stubble field, and I never asked him anymore about it."[6]

Shortly before the December 22 auction, Mrs. Hamlin asked him again about his scrapes and cuts and noticed "his eyes filled with tears, and that was the only sign of nervousness ... I think Mr. Hassell showed nervousness the day I asked him about the time of the sale ... I was looking at one of the handbills, and I looked at him and I says, 'Mr. Hassell, what is

Mrs. Hassell going to say to you about selling all of that stuff.' And I think he was pretty nervous over that, he did quite a bit of fidgeting, although he answered me rather promptly. At the same time, I saw that disturbed him." In reply to all that he said, "Oh nothing; she told me to."[7] This "might have occurred the day before the sale. I was looking at one of the lists of stuff he had to sell. It was either the morning of the sale, or the day before." Hamlin continued, "There was no other times seen him in nervous condition."

Chapter 9

The Lindops Move In

"Did not see any signs of blood stains on the floor; not a bit."

A week had passed since Alton joined his family in the cellar pit. About this time Hassell contacted a neighbor, Nicholas Albert "N. A." Lindop, to see if he wanted to buy some cows, telling him he would like "to sell out" to him. The Lindops were somewhat familiar with the Hassell family, living less than two miles east of the Hassell home on what was known locally as the "White farm."[1] Hassell also asked Lindop if he wanted to take over his remaining lease and buy his unharvested crops. Over the past year, Lindop had become familiar with Hassell "and made a crop there by him, farming the land about a mile and a half from him."[2]

Initially, Lindop didn't "pay much mind" to Hassell's December 11 proposition. But the next morning, he and his wife discussed the offer and decided to go talk to Hassell about his proposal: "So, we talked with him, and he priced his stuff to me, his wheat and farming tools, and so I told him I would let him know later on."[3]

Hassell told Lindop he would sell him his wheat crop for $600. Lindop was happy to take him up on the offer, since he was going to have to move out of his brother-in-law's place in any case now that the Smith family had returned home (on the night Hassell killed Alton). What's more, Hassell offered him a price he couldn't turn down. Once Lindop got permission from Hassell's landlord, Mrs. Hamlin, to move onto the property, he went back to see him to complete the transaction for the wheat, but offered only $500, which was one hundred dollars less than Hassell's original asking price. He had meant to get to the Hassells' by 9:00 a.m., but it was so cold that he couldn't get his Ford automobile started and didn't arrive at the place until 11:00 a.m.[4] By that time, Hassell had gone into Farwell. Lindop followed him into town to finish their transaction, but Hassell backed out of their deal, not content with the counteroffer of $500. Lindop gave in and agreed to give him $600 and to "take up a note of $600 against the implements, and he [Hassell] backed out on me and I went home." The following day (Tuesday), Lindop was back in town at "Parker's store," where he caught up with Hassell again and they agreed on the previous day's offer and closed the deal the next day.

The Lindops later testified that they "did not see his family around" for some days and were not sure when they had last seen them. On December 12, the Lindops did a walk-through of the house as Hassell busied himself scrubbing and mopping the floors. He told Lindop he had already scrubbed three rooms, but Lindop said he "never paid any particular attention to that myself. I noticed some of the floors were wet." Hassell wouldn't allow the Lindops to see all of the rooms at that time, and Lindop clearly remembered seeing that one room, the middle one on the back side, had all kinds of boxes and suitcases piled up and hadn't been cleaned up yet. He would later say that "there was nothing to prevent me from going in that room, except that he stood in the door." As Lindop later recounted, "We never did get to see that room."[5]

***

Hassell stopped by the Hamlin residence to make sure it was alright to allow Lindop to take over his lease, knowing that she liked and respected the Lindops. She had no problem with the arrangement. She reportedly told others that Hassell "was a fine man to be willing to give up a situation that was going so well for him and start over just to please his wife. What a lucky person [Susan] was indeed to have had someone like him step in and take responsibility of a large family after the untimely death of her first husband."

The Lindops accepted the offer and arranged to move in at once. Once the deal was agreed upon, Hassell asked the Lindops if he could remain in the rear bedroom (the same room in which he had murdered Alton). Then he would be ready to move out permanently and join his family in Oklahoma. He also informed them that if they wished, they could move in right away. N. A. told Hassell that "he could set his things back to one side and [he] would board him free of charge until he had his sale and got away. He had groceries there and everything and furnished his part."[6]

The Lindops moved in on December 20, just two days before the auction, and later testified that they didn't notice anything amiss or unusual about Hassell's behavior. He "talked naturally about his family" when they asked him, and he said something about his family deciding to move because they "didn't like it here." Hassell sold some of the furnishings to them and stored the rest in the rear bedroom and the barn to await the auction. All went well with the move until the oldest Lindop son, Mervin, driving the family's mules and freight wagon, came perilously close to the planking over the fresh earth covering the cellar pit at the end of the house. His mother, Tinnie May, scolded the big eighteen-year-old for not being more careful, telling him to listen to Mr. Hassell and do as he said.

After the bloody family massacre several weeks earlier, one might have expected some tangible evidence of the struggles inside the house, at least some drops of blood. But when asked about evidence of fresh scrubbing during the subsequent trial, Lindop testified that he "did not see any signs of blood stains on the floor; not a bit. I did not notice a thing unusual or out of the ordinary in his conduct." Lindop admitted that he had never known anyone that had murdered someone and saw nothing to make him think Hassell had killed nine people.

As agreed upon, Hassell stayed in the easternmost of the three back rooms. To put the house in perspective, it is helpful to picture it as being "three rooms long behind, and two rooms in front, and a little porch on the south side." His room was rather spartan, as might be expected. He slept on a bed with an iron bedstead, but planned to sell it the day of the auction (after the sale he slept on the floor on a feather bed loaned to him by Lindop). During the several days he lived with the Lindops, Hassell shared dinners with the family at the dining table or sometimes drove into town.[7] All seemed well in the home in the days leading up to the farm sale.

According to Hassell family descendants, the Lindops enjoyed his company. They were glad to be able to rent such a well-developed farm to live on. Each day Hassell, according to Hassell family lore, would go down into the root cellar and bring up food to eat.[8] Susan "had a reputation for her ability to capture the best flavors of the food she canned; she even knew how to preserve 'heavy dough cakes and bread' that tasted as fresh as if it had just come out of the oven and cooled. Each evening was a fine meal around the big round table, with Hassell telling stories of all his travels and the things he had seen and done"—that is, except for his thirteen murders in California and Texas.[9]

Hassell gleefully told the Lindops that he was not going to sell the contents of the root cellar but was instead giving it all to them because of the kindness they had shown to a lonely man who was missing his family very much in this holiday season. They could hardly believe their good fortune and told each other, in what proved to be an understatement of the highest order, that they were not likely to meet another like Hassell in their lifetimes.[10]

Chapter 10

Auction Day

"George was just a good old boy."

So far, Hassell had covered his tracks without a hitch. He had hidden the bodies, and his neighbors had taken over his lease. He could have fled any time he wanted and probably could have disappeared under one of his aliases, but apparently his avaricious nature would not let him leave before banking the profits from his auction. He was methodical in organizing the sale of his property and went to great lengths to get the word out. The auction was well advertised through newspaper notices and the local grapevine as scheduled for Wednesday, December 22, 1926. The auction notice printed in the local newspaper directed prospective customers to the property on the Hamlin farm, known locally as "the old John Coley place," located three and one-half miles northeast of Farwell.

A young E. Paul Crume (1912–1975), who would go on to become a distinguished journalist in Dallas, recounted in 1948, more than twenty years after the sale, how he had worked "as a printer's devil" to Hop Graham "in the Panhandle country" during his Christmas vacation when his family lived in Farwell. At the time, he recalled "wearing high laced boots to school, with boot pants, which flared at the thighs and were laced tight along the calfs to accommodate the boots." In addition, he wore "loosely knit wool socks which extended above them and were folded neatly above the tops of the boots."[1] On the face of it, the description of his sartorial choice would seem insignificant. That is, until Crume recounted the appearance in the printer's office of "a big red-faced jovial man named George Hassell." The ever-gregarious Hassell, as usual, made a grand entrance and informed the young Crume that he wanted some bills printed, "advertising a public sale of his farm possession." The loquacious farmer explained that his family "had gone back home to the folks and he was winding up his affairs."[2]

Hassell was a talker, probably more so now that he was trying to blend in with the community the best he could. Crume said that while Hassell was in the shop they "ran off his sale bills." In retrospect more than two decades later, he still couldn't believe that he had been so close to a mass murderer and had no clue. Even more jarring was the fact that he was alone with Hassell as he "fed the sheets into the old Chandler and Price jobber" as Hassell looked on, "making a pleasant joke now and then."[3]

The young man would not find out about the killings at Hassell's farm until the next day, when all hell broke loose. He admitted that when he found out what had transpired on the small farm, he couldn't sleep for weeks and "kept dreaming of the heavy iron poker beside the pot-bellied stove where George Hassell had warmed himself while waiting for me to print his sale bills." As for Crume's future sartorial preferences, "after [Hassell] was electrocuted [he] said goodbye to high-laced boots,"[4] He explained that whenever he thought of his first meeting with the killer, he could not get over the fact that they wore the same boots, it brought up too many bad memories.

Once Hassell had printed and distributed his auction handbills, he went over to the local school to turn in his children's textbooks. The school superintendent, F. M. Sawyer, received Hassell in his office, recounting at the murder trial the following month that "I think he returned all of their books but three. He returned, I guess, twenty books." This was his first meeting with Hassell, and they chatted briefly. In his estimation, Hassell "appeared perfectly normal and showed no signs of excitement."[5] As he had during his meeting with the young Crume, Hassell was able to put Sawyer at ease with his superficial jocularity and gift for mimicry. But that is what many psychopaths do.

On his way out of the school, Hassell handed out auction handbills to many of the local children, telling them to "Get your daddy to bring you cause there will be a fine Shetland pony and saddle for sale."[6] Recently enrolled student, Albert "Blackie" Smith, ended up receiving Virgil Hassell's schoolbooks, with the teacher expressing his hope that he would be as good a student as Virgil, who had been, "a favorite of hers."[7] Almost seventy-five years later in 2001, Smith could vividly recall moving to Farwell in early December 1926, not far from the Hassell place. A nephew of the Lindops, he remembered going to the school superintendent's office to get his books the first day of school. He was sitting in the office waiting to collect his books, when Hassell brought the books back. He remembered "a man walked in carrying a bunch of books" and overheard him saying "his wife and kids had all gone back to Oklahoma and he was returning their schoolbooks."[8] Later that month, Albert would witness the beginning of the exhumation of Hassell's victims on December 23. By the late 1980s, he would be the last living witness to the removal of the bodies.

***

On a frigid December afternoon, according to the local *State Line Tribune*, "the Hassell place was a center of activity ... In spite of the nasty weather more than 150 men, women and children milled around the little five room stucco house. The sale items had been arranged to the right of the house around a ten-foot square area of freshly turned earth where an old dugout had been filled in."[9] Mrs. Hamlin remembered that the recently dug pit near the house was packed and tamped down evenly "so that a great many of the people at the sale didn't know there was ever a dugout there. It was filled in as level as a table. The sale took place 20–30 feet south of the pit, 'very close.'" Attendees would not realize until the next day that they were actually standing on the temporary sepulcher of the Hassell family.

In the Texas Panhandle, a farm sale was considered a big event. One crime writer who chronicled the murder case in 1935 noted that "everybody in the country—big, little, old, and young—goes to the sale, where they visit with neighbors, eat a big dinner at noon, and bid on what they want."[10] It snowed sporadically in the days leading to the auction, followed by "a slow, soaking rain." However, as the sale began, the sun greeted the crowd coming together: "Women, with long coats buttoned tight around them, and men wearing fleece-lined jackets and high-topped boots stomped around the place in the heavy mud."[11]

Meanwhile, Hassell worked in tandem with the auctioneer. As soon as Hassell handed an item to him, the auctioneer began "praising the benefit of each item as he put it up for sale." As the bidding continued, Hassell stayed busy assisting buyers, loading larger items, and making sure everyone was comfortable. At noon, women from a Farwell church served a hot meal. According to one observer, people sat and ate wherever they found it convenient, and several times Hassell had to caution them not to step into the filled-in cellar," warning them that it was awfully muddy due to the "water-soaked dirt." As the others ate, Hassell sat on a nail keg "some four feet from the cellar and wolfed his lunch."[12]

Hassell made it clear to any potential customers that this was a moving sale "as I am leaving the country," making sure they knew he was selling "without by-bid or reserve" all his material possessions and livestock. His terms for purchase, introduced at his trial, were as follows: cash for anything under $20 ($292 in 2020); for items over $20, a 10 percent discount for cash; ten months' time on bankable notes bearing 10 percent interest on all sums over $20.[13] He had already sold the wheat crop to Lindop, reaping about $600, as well as "the row crop," which his landlord estimated to be worth more than $1,200.

Mrs. Hamlin remembered seeing the handbills in circulation advertising the sale. In fact, her tenant brought some over to her house the week before. She remembered being present for most of the auction, until 4:30 or 5:00 p.m., and that by the time she left she believed most everything on the handbill had been sold. She was impressed by the size of the crowd. Everything was for sale, including farm implements, livestock, household goods, and "other things too numerous to mention." Once the farm machinery and livestock were sold, the crowd began to move closer to the house, hoping more merchandise would be auctioned off. The 1951 chronicler of Hassell's mass murder reported that "item after item was sold as the auctioneer's gavel fell, the cook stove, washing machine, sewing machine, cases of canned vegetables and fruit."[14]

As the auction continued, Mrs. Hamlin and Mrs. J. O. Ford, who Hassell would later refer to as the "gossiping women," began to wonder between them why all of these farm home essentials were being sold. Ford told Hamlin something to the effect of, "I can't understand why Mr. Hassell is selling all that good food, sewing machine, the washing machine and those fine quilts."[15]

Most of the women who attended the auction visited with each other while their husbands bid on the farm equipment and livestock. Other women also thought it odd that Hassell was selling so many family items. But when they witnessed the sale of a baby's drinking cup, it really "struck them as strange" that Susan would have left these easy-to-transport items behind.[16] Mrs. Hamlin apparently agreed with Mrs. Ford, and they wandered into the house, looking through rooms for things they might like to purchase. Hamlin noticed that she "didn't see any lady's clothes."[17]

Another woman asked Mrs. J. O. Ford if she had noticed that there were some suitcases and trunks in the back room of the house. Ford said that she had not and was going to look for herself. She walked to the rear of the house and found three trunks and several suitcases. She tried to lift one trunk, but it was too heavy for her. The suitcases were full as well. Ford noticed a new pair of boys' boots and some children's overshoes under a bed. The discovery of these articles, which to her mind, "would not be left behind under [any] circumstances," made her suspicious as to the fate of the family. They opened one suitcase and found it full of children clothing neatly packed. When they came upon Susan Hassell's collection of religious books, the women remarked on how odd it was that Susan would leave such things behind. Gradually, the "whisperings of the ladies reached the ears of their husbands and as days passed a mounting suspicion pulsed under the serene surface of the little cattle town. Some scoffed: George was just a good old boy."[18]

Further discussion among the women turned to the odd circumstances, and their suspicions grew as to what took place on the Hassell farm that had led the family to move out with little notice. One of the women at the trial said, "something was queer about the whole affair." The women, having raised many children between them, found the series of events just "too queer."[19]

Another variation of the above sequence of events puts Mrs. N. A. Lindop, better known as Tinnie, in the thick of the investigation. With Hassell now living with the Lindops on the farm the day of the auction, Tinnie took a quick look in the rear bedroom of their house to see if Hassell might have missed anything else that could be sold. She found several boxes. Some were still open at the top, enough so that she could see some baby clothes, diapers, and bottles in one. In another was Susan's open purse still, containing her wallet, a coin purse, and some money. Susan wouldn't have left this behind, Tinnie must have thought. Worried, Tinnie went outside and shared her discovery with her neighbors, Mrs. Ford and Mrs. White.[20] They all went back inside together to have a look before reporting what they found to their husbands.

Hassell relished managing the sale being conducted by Mr. V. Tate. He assured customers that they had made a good buy on this item or that one. J. O. Ford witnessed the sale of Hassell's shotgun, a twelve-gauge single-barreled gun "that carried two shells." He watched Hassell proudly showing it to potential bidders, explaining how to use it and chambering two shells to demonstrate. Hassell told R. F. Lloyd, that the shotgun "don't look all that much but it'll get the job done."[21] The twenty-one-year-old Lloyd lived with his father in Bovina about four and one-half miles southeast of the Hassells. He was at the auction for most of the day, and his bid of $9.50 was enough to purchase the gun.[22]

J. O. Ford remembered watching the large crowd as various goods were sold and carried off, while his wife snooped around the Hassell home. Ford witnessed the sale of numerous sundry items, such as dishes, clothing, and ordinary knickknacks. He also mentioned that he had seen some quilts "piled up out there but not the actual sale of them." He observed Hassell conducting the sale like an impresario, bringing out more goods for the auctioneer. Ford "didn't observe anything about him especially out of the ordinary at that time."[23]

***

Hassell had previously mentioned to Mrs. Hamlin that he would not be able to finish the new cellar. He explained that he had filled it in and laid out the planks on the freshly turned earth so that it would settle properly. The conniving killer had figured out another way to keep the law off his tracks: suggesting to Mr. Lindop and Mrs. Hamlin that the planks should stay in position till after the spring thaw to assure a smooth surface. They agreed.

To be sure it would not be disturbed during the auction, with so many folks wandering around, Hassell asked the members of the Ladies Aid, who were serving noon lunch, to set up their tables on the planking. They were pleased that he had made such a nice place for them, where they wouldn't get muddy, and all agreed that Hassell was such a nice man it was no wonder that Sheriff James H. Martin called him a real likable fellow. Like most serial killers, Hassell was adept at image control, with an ability to blend comfortably into any community. The dinner was laid out on tables toward the front of the house, "north of the pit." Perhaps Hassell got a thrill out of the fact that these benevolent women would be serving meals just above his family's burial site.

Mrs. Hamlin later admitted to sensing some cracks beneath his usually impenetrable happy-go-lucky veneer at the time of the auction, remembering "he appeared to be nervous." In the morning, at the time the fruit was being sold, she offered to lend a hand. He was selling it so fast that "he couldn't hand it to the clerk fast enough, and he had told me he had two boys hired and they were in the crowd talking and not attending to their business, and that he couldn't get it done by himself. It was at this time I noticed he was upset and seemed to be very nervous. And at the time he told me that, I noticed his eyes filled with tears."[24] This was notable, for Hassell was not prone to showing emotion. In fact, one contemporary newspaper described him in the aftermath of the killings and auction as demonstrating "absolute control of his nerves," as indicated by the fact that "at [the] public sale of his farm equipment shortly after the murder, he ate a hearty dinner in his home within twenty feet of the crypt in which victims lay."²⁵ In days to come, newspapers around the country would add layers to the Hassell mystique, contributing to his profile as a stone-cold killer without a shred of remorse.

The evening following the auction, Mrs. Ford shared her fears with her husband, who decided to drive over to Farwell and have a talk with Sheriff Martin. No one was home when J. O. Ford stopped by, so he put it off until the next morning.²⁶

Chapter 11

The Noose Tightens

"If he was that bad a man, he better get another man to go with him."

The day following the auction, J. O. Ford barged into Sheriff James Martin's office to discuss the suspicions brewing among the womenfolk about Hassell. James Henry Martin had been elected Parmer County Sheriff every term between 1922 and 1931. Born in nearby Bovina, on February 18, 1888, the same year as Hassell, he was described as tall and stout with blue eyes and black hair.[1] The sheriff went over to the office of Parmer County attorney J. D. Thomas to share the local fears about the Hassell family disappearance, later testifying that "other parties were suspicious about his family, and we ought to make some investigation." Thomas and the sheriff purportedly concocted a plan to bring in Hassell without arousing his curiosity.

There are several versions of this story. According to the 1935 account by the attorney J. D. Thomas, it was decided to ask the bank clerk who conducted the auction, Hamlin Overstreet, to come up with a ruse to lure Hassell back into town. Overstreet asked Hassell to meet him at the bank in order to fix up some notes that he had accepted in payment of property the day before.² This account, however, conflicts somewhat with Hassell family lore, which suggests that Hassell had already decided to come into town to the bank so he could finish settling the last of his accounts with Overstreet.³ Whether he was lured into town or came on his own volition, it didn't really matter because Hassell did come to town, seemingly unconcerned about the storm of suspicion gathering around him.

After Hassell finished his meeting with the bank clerk, the sheriff brought Hassell over to the county attorney's office. By some accounts, Thomas "cautioned [the sheriff] that if he was that bad a man, he better get another man to go with him and I believe he did."⁴ The sheriff brought along Deputy R. A. Hawkins, and both accompanied Hassell over to the attorney's office. When the sheriff initially confronted Hassell at the bank, he shared some of the concerns of several neighbors, who were rather flabbergasted that Susan left town without a word to anyone. Moreover, he told Hassell that it was curious that no one had heard whether or not the family had made it to Oklahoma safely. Hassell, in his inimitable way, assured the sheriff all was well.

Sheriff Martin was not easily convinced and pointed out to Hassell that his wife was "after all a Russellite, a follower of a home-based religion that called for strong family ties with other members."⁵ The ladies in her circle told the sheriff that they held services in each other's homes, and it seemed odd that Susie would up and leave without a word or even a note to let them know that the family had arrived at their destination. What's more, when they heard that she left all of her religious books behind, this only heightened their doubts. To put the ladies at ease, the sheriff asked Hassell to confirm the Oklahoma address of Susie's destination so that he could send a telegram to confirm the family's whereabouts.

As they entered the attorney's office, Thomas assured Hassell he was not under arrest at this point but told him he just wanted to ask him some questions. Hassell was under the impression he was "just there for a talk" and really "didn't know what he was coming there for."⁶ Having never met the burly farmer before, the attorney no doubt studied him closely, the same way he would take the measure of a defendant he was prosecuting in court.

He started with some basic questions, along the lines of "where he came from, to this country." Hassell responded: "Oklahoma."[7] It didn't take long for Thomas to get to the point, telling him he was under an investigation related to the disappearance of his family. Thomas thought Hassell "looked rather excited, but I expected that of course. Coming to the County Attorney's office; whether guilty or not."

Hassell assumed that the suspicions had been first raised by Mrs. Hamlin, who did her share of interrogating him at his farm. He told the attorney "that he considered his business is his business and her business was her business."[8] He also assured the lawyer that he had given pertinent answers to her questions and was not happy with her inquiring about his personal affairs. Thomas was in no mood to beat around the bush and "asked him pointblank where his family was."[9] Apparently, he was taken aback by this question and "momentarily lost his composure," a rarity for Hassell. But just as quickly, he recovered his poise and was back on his game, launching into his story about where his family went. He betrayed little if any nervousness at this point, and the more he talked the more convincing he became.[10]

He repeated his much-practiced yarn, telling the attorney that Susan's brother, J. D. Ferguson, lived in Perryton, Texas, and had come down to the Farwell farm in a Chevrolet truck. The Hassells had been expecting a forthcoming visit, but the brother arrived unexpectedly. After spending the night, Hassell said Ferguson took the family back to Blair, Oklahoma, with him. On the face of it, the story seemed "plausible."[11] Thomas even conceded to Hassell that his story might indeed be true, but this still did not stamp out growing suspicions and rumors surrounding their actual whereabouts, due in no small part to his conflicting explanations about where they were. He had told some people it was Shallowater, Texas, and others Blair, Oklahoma.

Thomas remained curious in the extreme. Hassell sensed that he might not be in control of the narrative for once and might have met his match with the county attorney. Recognizing he was on the proverbial hot seat, Hassell told the lawyer he could verify his statement about his wife's whereabouts by wiring a Jack Scroggins in Blair, Oklahoma."[12]

He then reached into his pocket for a letter that he claimed he had received from his wife the previous day.[13] He handed it to Thomas and waited for him to read it. Thomas responded, "You've handed me the wrong letter, Mr. Hassell ... This letter is from a person who wanted to know something about your farm sale." Hassell apologized and went through the motions of looking for the letter on his person, telling Thomas "I have the letter from the family on me someplace." He looked in each pocket carefully, knowing full well there was no letter, and when he came up empty said he left it at the farm. He was going through the charade with great theatrical skill and told the men, "Let's run out and get it." Thomas told him to never mind, "we'll be out to get it later."[14]

As Hassell was stepping out the door, Thomas asked him if he would provide him a reference that would verify his claims, and Hassell told him to go ahead and wire Jack Scroggins in Blair, Oklahoma, to verify his statement. Hassell must have known he was slowly painting himself into a corner. Thomas told him that he would follow up and be in touch and that he was free to go. After Hassell left the office, Thomas and Martin "went into a huddle." Neither one of them was wholly satisfied with his story. Thomas would soon wire the address that Hassell gave him. The peace officer and the attorney discussed whether or not they should hold him until they found out. But Martin, a veteran lawman, pointed out that "it was a serious matter to arrest a man on such little evidence as we had," so they let him go for the time being.[15]

The conundrum of whether to let Hassell go or not reminded Thomas and Martin of a recent incident that had turned into a wild goose chase. In this incident, they needed to "run down a rumor" concerning the murder of a local child. A farmer's son had missed school for several days and when the teacher asked his little sister why he was absent, she replied, "Papa took him down in the fields and killed him." Shocked, the teacher sent for the sheriff, and the next day the girl repeated her statement. However, as it turned out, they found the boy hale and hearty, helping his father harvest his crop.[16] If there was any moral to this story, it's that when it came to law enforcement, it was better to act on facts rather than rumor.

The way he remembered it in 1935, he and Sheriff Martin "tailed" Hassell around town once he left the office and until he left town heading for his farm. While following the farmer, they popped into the bank and found out that he had almost $2,000 in his bank account. Fearful he might use it to flee, they asked the bank cashier to contact them immediately if he withdrew a large amount of his deposit. They picked up another bit of tantalizing information when they found out that Hassell had ordered an automobile "which would be delivered in a few days."[17]

Further confounding Hassell's litany of explanations, according to research conducted by the Hassell family, was a conversation he had with Alton's employer that same day (December 23). Hassell had picked up Alton's last check from N. M. Crawford and told him that the family left for Oklahoma the same day Alton got back from work. In this version of events, Hassell related that Alton had to drive the car to Oklahoma, since his wife, Susan, didn't drive. However, when Tinnie Lindop got wind of this story back at the house, she wondered, "What car?" as the family only had one car and the Ford automobile that Hassell used every day was still sitting at home. But for the time being, Tinnie decided she would be better off not bringing it up.[18]

As night drew near, Hassell pulled his car toward the house and drained the radiator before going in to join the Lindops.[19] When he returned from town, the Lindops noticed he was in "a kind of daze."[20] He usually shared supper with the Lindop family at the dining table and sometimes went into town. Lindop was curious why Hassell, usually a hearty eater, didn't eat much of a supper. Moreover, usually a talker, he hardly uttered a word. After dinner, Hassell "did a lot of figuring on slips of paper" at the dining table.[21] He went out and put his car in the shed and returned to the house. Afterwards they all sat around a spell before turning in between 9:00 and 10:00 p.m. By the time Hassell retired to the rear bedroom, his mood had become increasingly sullen.[22]

As they readied for bed, the Lindops had an uneasy feeling. With all the suspicions and rumors floating around and Hassell's odd behavior since returning from town, the Lindops had become anxious if not frightened and were having a hard time falling asleep that night. To feel more secure, N. A. made sure his gun was near at hand, reachable from his bed.[23] Another unsubstantiated account suggests that N. A. "sat up in a chair with his shotgun across his knees."[24] In any case, when they retreated to the back two bedrooms, they kept the doors between the bedrooms open. Moreover, the Lindops remained clothed as they lay in bed, just in case they had to make a speedy escape.

By the time December 23 ended, the authorities still had not heard back from Blair, Oklahoma.

George Hassell and his first family victims, c. 1917.
Macfadden Communications Group.

George Hassell as oil field worker, c. 1918.
Whittier Daily News/Southern California News Group.

George Hassell as Merchant Marine cook, c. 1926.
Shamokin News Dispatch.

George Hassell and his last victims, c. 1926.
Macfadden Communications Group.

Susan Hassell, 1926. *Clovis Journal.*

George Hassell with stepson Alton, 1926. *Shamokin News Dispatch.*

TWO OF HIS VICTIMS

Two of George Hassell's step-children, slain by the Farwell murderer a year ago last week.

Two of Hassell's stepchildren playing, 1926.
Amarillo Sunday News-Globe.

Legend

- ○ = Town
- ● = Residence
- ▬ = Roadway
- ┊ = State Line

to Amarillo

Hassell Home

Ford Home

Texico, NM

Clovis, NM

Farwell, TX

New Mexico | Texas

to Muleshoe

Hassell Farm

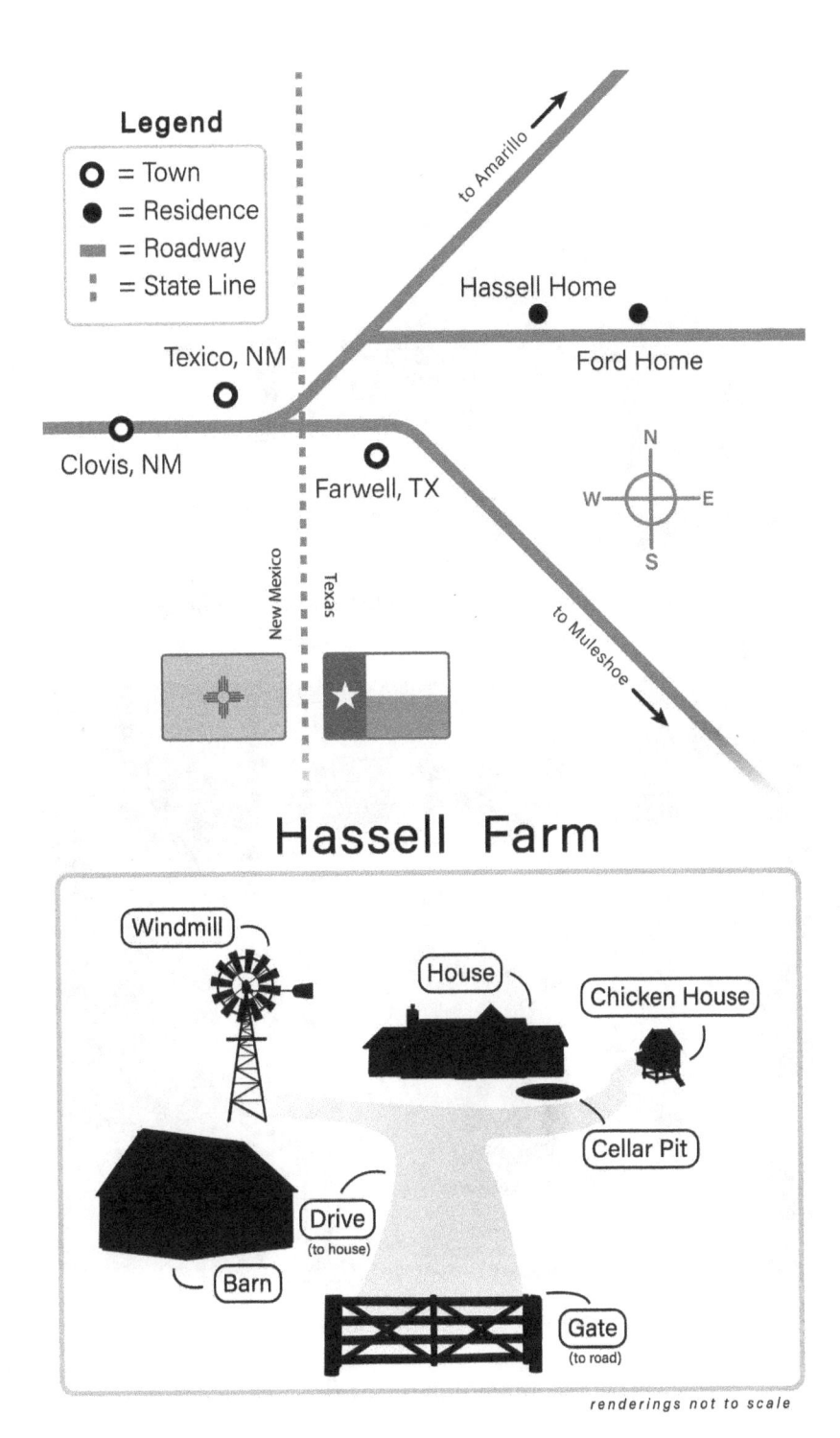

- Windmill
- House
- Chicken House
- Cellar Pit
- Drive (to house)
- Barn
- Gate (to road)

renderings not to scale

Map of Hassell property, 1926. *Sam Kuzel.*

Hassell farmhouse. *Astro Distributing Group*.

Clovis Baptist sanitarium today. *Photo by author*.

Operating room where Hassell received treatment, 1926.
H. Wayne Martin Jr..

J. O. Ford and his wife, c. 1935. *Macfadden Communications Group*.

Attorney J. D. Thomas, c. 1935, standing over burial pit and in front of room where Hassell stabbed himself.
Macfadden Communications Group.

George Hassell standing with Sheriff J. H. Martin, 1927.
Astro Distributing Group.

Parmer County Jail in Farwell, Texas today (with second story added). *Photo by author.*

Parmer County Courthouse in Farwell, Texas today. *Photo by author.*

Parmer County Courthouse (interior) in Farwell, Texas today. *Photo by author.*

Staring straight ahead in the middle is George Hassell with his lawyers reviewing his case on either side of him. This picture was taken at the trial Jan. 10, 1927 at Farwell.

George Hassell on trial, 1927. *State Line Tribune.*

Sheriff J. H. Martin, c. 1935. *Macfadden Communications Group.*

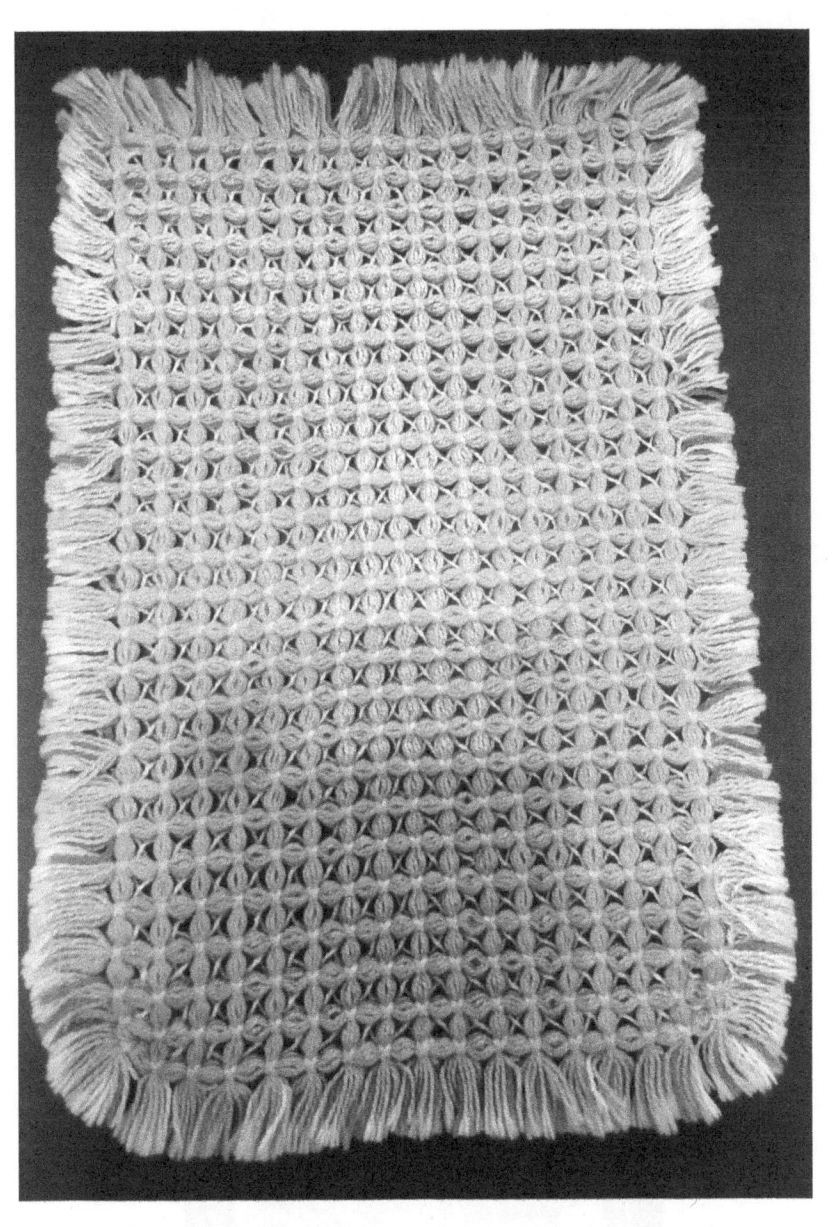

Doily made by Hassell behind bars while awaiting trial.
Parmer County Museum in Friona.

Two views of George Hassell, 1927.
Macfadden Communications Group and Fort Worth Record-Telegram.

Original tombstone of Hassell family in Farwell, 1926.
Astro Distributing Group.

Huntsville Prison façade, c. 1920s. *Texas Prison Museum.*

Original death row at Huntsville Prison, c. 1924.
Texas Prison Museum.

Death row mugshot, 1927.
Texas State Library and Archives Commission.

Ghastly Find Confirms Texas Murderer's Tale

California victims found, 1927. *Los Angeles Times.*

Map to location of California victims, drawn by
George Hassell, 1927. *Los Angeles Times*.

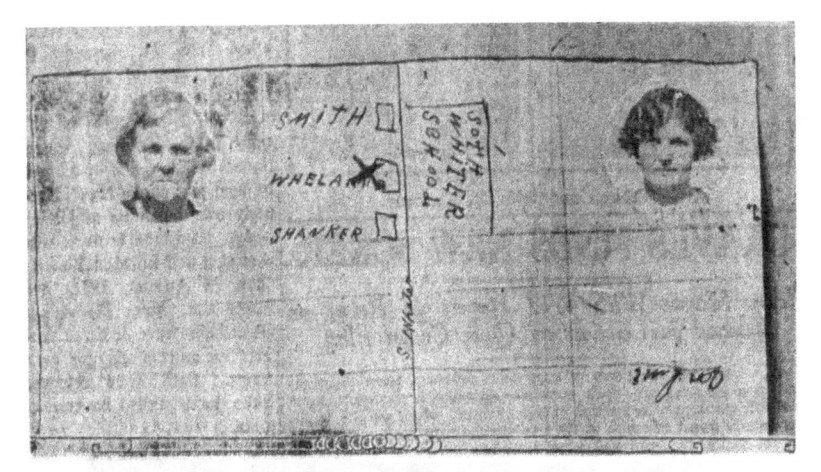

Huntsville Warden N. L. Speer, c. 1924. *Texas Prison Museum*.

Electric chair at Huntsville Prison, c. 1924. *Texas Prison Museum.*

Dr. E. L. Angier, prison doctor, c. 1920s.
James Patton/Texas Prison Museum.

Last picture of George Hassell before execution, c. 1928.
Clovis Journal.

George Hassell's tombstone in Huntsville Texas Prison
cemetery today. *Franklin T. Wilson.*

Modern tombstone of nine Hassell victims in Farwell.
Photo by author.

Chapter 12

Suicide

"Mr. Lindop, it is that old whiskey."

Lingering suspicions about Hassell's behavior remained as the Lindops turned in for the evening. There were a number of reasons for their fears, not just Hassell's out-of-character behavior but the continuing mystery of where his large family was and "the way they left here."[1] At this point, having already sold his bedstand and mattress, he needed to borrow a mattress and feather bed from the Lindops.

The night of the auction turned out to be uneventful. Nonetheless, the Lindops rested fitfully that night. N. A. mostly tossed and turned, maybe shut his eyes for a few minutes, but then "for some reason I woke up."[2] He would later testify that he had been awake maybe two hours before getting up when he heard some noise. He assumed that Hassell was up making a fire, but his wife knew better and told him to get up and make the fire himself, since Hassell had no clue how to operate the stove. Lindop, whose clock was not working, yelled out to Hassell for the time. He responded, "5 a.m.," from inside his bedroom.[3] Lindop got up and lit the stove. The stove was now heated and the room was warming up, when Hassell "called me in the room to him."⁴ As soon as N. A. got to the bedroom door, Hassell excitedly told him to fetch a doctor.

Lindop told his older boys, Mervyn and Lester, to go get the doctor in town. Hassell called him back again a few minutes later and asked if the boys had left yet and said to hurry with the doctor. He called back a third time and whispered, "Mr. Lindop, it is this old whiskey; Don't excite your wife. Get the doctor and bring [Sheriff] Jim Martin." As soon as he heard that, Lindop closed the door separating them, "reached for the baby and the blanket, got the wife, and children and everybody in the car and left that place" right away. Lindop claimed he stopped at Judge Hamlin's house first, around 4:30 a.m., but no one answered the door.⁵ If this is true, it conflicts with his testimony that Hassell told him it was 5:00 a.m. when he was asked for the time.

They then left the Hamlin's and went looking for Sheriff Martin. Martin later told Parmer County Attorney J. D. Thomas that early on Christmas Eve morning, "Lindop and his wife came to my house ... They were scared to death. Lindop was carrying his baby wrapped in a blanket and, from the looks of his clothes, he left the farm in a hurry—his teeth were chattering so he could hardly talk." In his conversation with Thomas, the sheriff told him that the Lindops were "staying in town the rest of the night."⁶

In the early hours of Christmas Eve 1926, a blue norther "swept down on the town of Farwell. Sheets of powdery snow were whipped through the air by the fury of the storm." J. D. Thomas remembered the storm well years later. He recounted how his frame "shivered and groaned under the blasting wind." He was attempting restlessly to sleep when he heard several knocks at his door, followed by the familiar voice of Sheriff Martin calling out his name "Thomas—Thomas!" Being disturbed by the sheriff at this ungodly hour could only mean one thing—trouble.⁷

It took Thomas only a few seconds to dress himself and open the front door. A "swirl of snow" followed the Sheriff through the front door. Answering the attorney's puzzled look, all he had to say was, "It's Hassell."⁸

The sheriff, his deputy, R. A. Hawkins, and Thomas were soon on their way to the farm just northeast of Farwell. They made good time, considering they had to drive through a blizzard. They were informed that they would find Hassell "awful sick" and requesting a doctor and sheriff as soon as possible.[9]

They turned off the road to the Hassell property. Thomas later remembered that "as we entered the gate the little five room stucco house loomed darkly to our right about a hundred yards." More than a decade later, he could still hear the wind in his memory as it had "wailed through the stunted leafless trees about the place and the rusty groans of the windmill added to the eerie impressions of the scene."[10]

When the men arrived at the farm before sunrise on Christmas Eve, they exited the car, stamping their feet on the frozen ground "to restore circulation." There was no sign of life in the house, which was "cloaked by eerie darkness [between 4:30 and 5:00 a.m.]. The ground had a light coating of snow, and it was very cold." All they knew was that "in the darkened house, awaited Hassell, the man of mystery."[11]

The Sheriff shouted "Hassell! Hassell!" at the entrance while they attempted to enter the house. But nobody answered immediately. Fortunately, Deputy Hawkins had once owned the house and was familiar with its layout. He walked around the house, came in a back door, and walked through the house to let in Thomas and Martin. Thomas would later admit that, being "a man of small stature and unarmed," he cautiously "brought up the extreme rear" in case they were walking into trouble.[12]

Finally, Hassell answered Hawkins, and the three men went into his room. One of them shined a flashlight on him and almost simultaneously the bleeding farmer said something to the effect of, "here is what they [have] done to me and this [the knife] and this what they done it with," as he handed over the knife. Under dim lighting and the silhouettes cast by the flashlight, the shocking scene was a lot to take in so quickly. The next words out of Hassell's mouth were, "Let's go to a sanitarium and get there quick." The men tried to dress him but struggled getting his clothes on him. It was plain to see he was in a very weakened state and in quite a bit of pain. His wrist was cut and bleeding as well. At the time, they were unable to ascertain the nature of all of his wounds, but from the look of his bloody clothes the damage seemed significant. Once they dressed him and got him into the car, they headed to the Baptist sanitarium in Clovis, New Mexico.[13]

Sheriff Martin pulled his car around to the front of the house. Thomas and Hawkins braced Hassell as they walked him out, and when they got him into the car he fell between the seats and rode in that condition to Clovis. Initially it was unclear how serious his wounds were; indeed, it wasn't for certain whether Hassell would recover. However, one of the doctors assured them he had a chance to recover, thanks to the fact that his deepest stab wound had not punctured the intestines, and if no infection occurred, he would be out of danger.

The Parmer County attorney Thomas was queried during the January 1927 trial as to whether he asked the defendant who did it, after he handed over the knife to him. He said he did not but did ask him on the way to the Baptist Sanitarium. He said Hassell "gave an unintelligible answer that sounded like Lindop."

Thomas and Martin stayed at the hospital while Hassell was operated on by a Dr. [Clyn] E. L. Smith. Hassell's suicide attempt would be widely chronicled in the days to come, with reports of his injuries ranging from minor to mortal wounds. The best report of his actual injuries was given by his attending doctor and surgeon, who was tied professionally to the Baptist Sanitarium. A graduate of the accredited St. Louis University School of Medicine and Surgery, Smith regarded himself as a regular practitioner. He had been practicing his profession for twenty-five years.

Dr. Smith remembered Hassell being brought into the hospital on the morning of December 24, still bleeding from his left wrist and from three stab wounds to the chest and stomach. Two of the stomach wounds were about one inch deep. However, the other penetrated Hassell's abdominal cavity just below his ribs. As Smith later described at the murder trial, he had first to tend to what seemed the most serious wound, which was to the omentum. From the witness stand Smith described the omentum as "an apron shape arrangement that sort of covers over the intestines," and was protruding from his deepest stab wound. Smith made an incision of about four inches, taking off part of the omentum. He then sewed the wound up, putting the rest of the organ back in and prepping the rest of Hassell's wounds so that he could be safely taken away that night and locked up in the local jail.[14]

Smith would check up on him each night between December 24 and 28 at the Farwell Jail and then once more in Muleshoe on January 6, 1927. The doctor was impressed by Hassell's jocularity, both under surgery and sitting behind bars for his murders. During Hassell's trial, Smith "observed his demeanor during that time and noted his method of talking and expressing himself, and his reasoning. I have some experience in observing and studying the mental activities of people." At trial, Hassell's attorney immediately objected and challenged his acumen related to diagnosing mental illness. Smith admitted that, while he was not professionally trained to diagnose the defendant, he had taken some social science courses in college and had observed many people during his twenty-five years in general practice.[15]

One incident in particular stood out to Dr. Smith as showing the alleged killer's state of mind in the week before his trial. Dr. Smith was dressing his wounds while he was locked up in the Muleshoe Jail. Hassell mentioned that it seemed like a doctor in the previous jail in Plainview was "trying to embalm him, by pouring some fluid on the wounds." Hassell chuckled as he told his yarn, seeming like a man "that didn't have a care in the world."[16] Sitting in the Farwell Jail soon after his trial, he explained away his false Lindop accusation and recounted how he plunged a three-inch knife blade into his own stomach to commit suicide. He told how he "pushed the knife with the palm of his hand until only a small portion of the hilt was visible. He withdrew the knife with his fingers and plunged it into his stomach again."[17]

***

Shortly before his execution in 1928, Hassell offered one last perspective on his attempt to take his own life. He recounted that he couldn't sleep that night and "got to thinking things over. If I hadn't sold my guns, I would have shot myself. Instead, I stuck my knife between my ribs here, and nothing happened. Then I stuck it between the ribs a little lower and twisted first one way and then the other trying to find my heart—the district attorney, at my trial, said my heart was so hard that a knife couldn't pierce it. Maybe he was right."[18] One modern expert on psychopathy found that, although most psychopaths are "not suicidal," many "may feign it" in order to comport with their deceptive behavior.[19]

Following his successful surgery, Hassell made a recommendation: "Get a doctor and examine that girl [Maudie]." Obviously, his abuse of his murdered thirteen-year-old stepdaughter, Maudie, was still occupying his mind. Then he said that "one of the brothers—boys—had had intercourse with the girl." He followed this self-serving statement with a claim "that the boy had intercourse with the mother, and that is how the row [with Susie] started." Thomas asked Hassell whether his wife had accused him of having had sex with the girl, and he replied, "no."

The sheriff and his deputy stopped in Farwell after dropping Hassell off at the hospital, each going their separate ways for breakfast, with plans to meet up later at the Hassell farm. In Farwell they ran into J. O. Ford and several other residents who were out on the streets. All attention was now focused on searching the Hassell property for the bodies of the nine missing family members. It was generally agreed by all involved that the logical place to start was the recently filled-in dugout close by the house.

Chapter 13

Exhumation

"God shall wipe away all tears from their eyes."

Once Parmer County Attorney Thomas heard about the cellar pit dug out by the Hassell boys at their stepfather's behest, it seemed the best place to start the search for the missing family. Like several of his neighbors, Thomas was curious as to why Hassell went to so much trouble to fill the cellar up just two months after it was dug out, if he didn't have something to hide. Even though Hassell had already explained to others that he "wanted to leave everything just like he found it when he moved in a year earlier," it still didn't make sense no matter how he tried to spin it.[1]

Christmas Eve morning, Sheriff Martin caught up with J. O. Ford in Farwell. Martin told him to "get up a crew of men with shovels" and "dig out that cellar that morning."[2] According to Ford, he rounded up "some men that was on my place" and waited for the county attorney and sheriff to arrive. Attorney Thomas, Deputy Hawkins, and Sheriff Martin had been awake since 4:00 a.m. The men had gone in different directions, probably checking in with family, maybe changing clothes and having a quick breakfast, before meeting back up six hours later. According to an interview with Thomas in 1935, newspaper reporter W. H. Graham[3] would join the three men in their car in Farwell and, together with another carload of local residents, they headed to the farm, where Ford was waiting for them.

N. A. Lindop, the person most familiar with the property, directed them to the cellar. Reportedly, "noticing the plants and dirt were piled high over the dugout beside the house, lawmen began digging."[4] Ford remembered having to "dig for a while" before they finally located it. A crowd had begun to gather around this time. First, they removed some planks and then began digging in the southeast corner. The planks were laid side by side and would later be used to support the undertaker's wicker baskets.[5] They dug about two feet down before finding some quilts.[6] Ford later testified,

> We shoveled off a little dirt, about one foot square, about these quilts, and I got my knife out to cut thru the quilt to see what was under there, and one man told me not to cut through it but to wait until the officers came. About that time Mr. Martin came up to the place, and I asked him if he cared for me cutting through there, and he said 'no,' so I did. I cut right through the quilt and on top of something—I don't know what until I pulled it out. But it exposed a baby's hand and arm to the elbow. I pulled that much through the slit in the quilt, and it afterwards developed to be a baby—a small baby about two years old, I suppose.

It was at this point that "everyone's worst fears" were confirmed. By the time the bodies were being disinterred, C. V. Sneed, the undertaker, was on the scene. It was decided, once contact was made with the bodies, to put the shovels aside.

In 2001, Albert "Blackie" Smith could still recall going with his father to help with the exhumation of the Hassell family from the dugout crypt. He only watched for a short time, before his father told him "he didn't need to see" this and should go back home.[7] Unfortunately, once something is seen, it can't be unseen. He remembered clearly seeing the victims uncovered from beneath "a bedspread or sheet that had been laid on top of them" and the removal of the little two-year-old, Sammie, "with nothing on but a diaper lying on his stomach. His two little hands were gripping handfuls of dirt." In fact all the victims were found lying on their stomachs, including the oldest child, twenty-one-year-old Alton, who still "had all of his clothes on." But Smith added that he didn't find out why he was fully dressed until the murder was described at Hassell's trial in 1927. In the late 1980s, when Blackie's memories from that day were perhaps a little clearer, he told Hassell family chroniclers that when each body was removed it was shrouded in white sheets and put in "long narrow baskets."[8]

Also on hand at the exhumation was Hassell's neighbor, J. O. Ford, who watched as each body was carefully lifted out of the pit and "placed on some boards beside the house for an hour or so, then put in the ambulance and brought into town." He said he "didn't see the bodies after that time ... didn't see them no more."[9]

When the bodies were exhumed, Sheriff Martin, who admitted he wasn't familiar with the family at all, left it to others to identify the bodies. In his 1935 interview, County Attorney Thomas could still remember the scene clearly. It is probable that his interviewer added some dramatic flourishes to his account, including such details as how "snow lingered in the ditches around the roots of stunted trees planted about the house. As they started digging a crowd gathered. The silence told the story, no conversation. Mute testimony for what many feared they were about to find ... An awesome silence enveloped everyone as we worked. Only the thud and clink of pick and spade broke the silence."[10]

Sheriff Martin was asked at Hassell's January 1927 trial to describe the positions of the deceased. Like Albert Smith, who remembered the bodies all laying on their stomachs, Martin described how, "Some of them [were] lying on their faces. Eight of them on the west side of the dug out; some on their faces some on their backs. They are all piled up; laid there in kind of systematic order, side by side, with quilts or bed clothing spread over them." On the west side of the cellar "covered by quilts" lay Susie and the youngest children, teenaged Maudie, and twenty-one-year-old Alton. The baby and some smaller children were on the north side of the pit. A bit removed from the others was "one [victim] ... lying on the west side of the cellar covered by quilts."[11]

The bodies had been in the ground for close to three weeks but were still identifiable to the women standing around the cellar, "women who knew the children by sight, for the Hassells had no close friends."[12] All the bodies were dressed in their nightclothes. The younger children still had "stockings knotted around their necks." It also seemed that Hassell's rush to bury the lot so soon after the killings left some of them still breathing when they were entombed. According to Martin, "The sprawled position of the bodies showed they had been thrown in the pit while still warm. One of the bodies still had his arm thrown up across his face as if to ward off a blow."[13] Hassell would later brag while in jail that after killing his Whittier family almost ten years earlier "he buried them under the floor of the house before their bodies were cold."[14] The patterns between the two mass killings were unmistakable. In one of his last interviews, Hassell recounted that after each of his mass murders, "when he disposed of the bodies, he calmly returned to the bed that he had butchered them in a few minutes ago and slept as sound as any man."[15]

***

Probably due to the horrific nature of his injuries, Alton received the most newspaper coverage and local interest. Deputy Hawkins admitted that Alton was the only one he recognized, since he knew him better than the others: "He was lying on the east side of the pit, with his feet in the southeast corner. I judged his body was a little higher than the rest of them. There were some on the other side, but Alton higher in the pit, not more than eight to ten inches from the surface." Hawkins said that, as Alton was taken out, "I noticed his head wound. I could see a hole in the side of his head. His head seemed flattened and out of shape; but the skin wasn't broken anywhere except where there seemed to be a gunshot wound."[16]

Sheriff Martin also remembered that Alton seemed to be in the southeast corner and didn't appear to be "on the same level with others, at any rate he wasn't covered quite so deep, but it looked like he was lying on the bottom of the dugout—out where it hadn't been dug quite as deep."[17] Of course, this was because, as the last victim to be buried, there was limited room for his body in the pit. Martin evaluated the gunshot head wound as Alton was taken out and laid out: "The wound was in his head, in the side of his head, and his forehead seemed to be smashed in." Like his deputy, Hawkins, Martin too noted that "the skin wasn't broken, as I remember. The skin wasn't broken on the front part, but his head was kind of mashed out this way. I said there was a hole in the side of his head, but not positive which side (I believe left). I will say that it appeared to be result of gunshot wound."[18]

Several other observers also commented on the condition of Alton. J. O. Ford, who knew the family, was one of the few who could immediately recognize some of the bodies as they were exhumed, including Mrs. Hassell, Alton, Virgil, and Maudie. He was later asked if he noticed the "nature of the wounds on Alton's head." In court he testified "that his head was crushed, but I don't know just where the wounds were that did it, or what it was. I remember his forehead being crushed in."[19] He hadn't yet learned that the young man had been murdered by a shotgun blast to the head.

Alton was found on the east side of the dugout, with his feet pointing south. He had been placed "laying parallel with the east wall of the cellar, right against the wall."[20] County Attorney Thomas, who witnessed the exhumations, remembered seeing him, along with his bedding, mattress, and pillow, "bloody as can be." This conflicts with most other accounts, which claim he was found in a sitting position. However, there was no mistaking who it was, with family chroniclers mentioning that, due to cold weather, there had been very little decomposition" and that the "gun blast ... ripped away much of the skull at the exit."[21] Similarly, the attorney, Thomas, "noticed that his skull seemed to have been crushed," adding, "of course I couldn't tell what caused it, but there was a big hole in the forehead."[22]

Once all the bodies were recovered, they were laid out neatly so that they would be ready for the undertaker, C.V. Sneed, to take back to town. One witness remembered in the 1980s that Sneed had arrived "with an open truck and a stack of long narrow heavy wicker baskets."[23] They were put into this impromptu ambulance and brought to town. Sheriff Martin recounted at trial that after the bodies were taken to town, they were kept in a warehouse until they could be buried the following day, which Martin said, "I did not attend."[24]

At the funeral held at Farwell Cemetery, Rev. Crouch of the Baptist Church read the seventh chapter of Revelation, beginning with the ninth verse, and concluded with the words, "For the Lamb which is in the midst of the throne shall feed them and shall lead them unto living fountains of waters: and God shall wipe away all tears from their eyes."[25] The funeral was attended by farmers and ranchers from all parts of the county.

It was 3:00 p.m. on Christmas Day when the nine victims were placed in five caskets and lowered into a mass grave at the old Farwell cemetery. Many of the local townsfolk who had participated in lifting the bodies out of the dugout helped wrap them in white sheet shroud, placed them in the undertaker's long narrow wicker baskets, and now paid their respects at the old cemetery. Carefully, one after another, they were placed side by side in a single grave, a simple pit, dug long and deep enough for five caskets.[26] A few days after the funeral, Rev. J. F. Nix from the First Baptist Church of Clovis passed on a request to have it announced that the following Sunday "he will use as his subject, 'Hassell—His Life and the Cause of His Crimes.'"[27]

Chapter 14

The Jig Is Up

"I've killed people before."

Although there was initially some doubt whether he would survive his self-inflicted wounds, Hassell was soon on the mend. As he recovered at the Baptist Sanitarium hospital in Clovis and then the Farwell jail, news that bodies had been found on the Hassell farm "spread with the swiftness of a Texas wind." In the hospital, the news was passed from patient to patient, "precipitating a panic," leading a desperate hospital administrator to call Sheriff Martin to "come and rid them of his fiendish prisoner." Martin transferred Hassell over to the Farwell jail, where the sheriff prepared a cell for him and made sure a guard was posted nearby at all times. Evidently the hospital grapevine never reached the prisoner, and by the time he was put behind bars he did not yet realize that the bodies had been found in the cellar on his property.[1]

The day after the bodies were exhumed, the nine Hassell family members were interred in a Christmas burial in the Farwell Cemetery. But before the bodies were buried, a funeral procession was due to pass by the jail where the stepfather was currently lodged. Hassell was still under the impression that his story about his family moving to Oklahoma held water. But his charade was about to end.

County Attorney Thomas and Sheriff Martin decided they would pay Hassell a visit before the funeral procession passed by. Thomas wasted no time in calling his bluff, informing Hassell as he lay in his cell that he had received a wire back from Jack Scroggins in Oklahoma. Hassell feigned interest, replying laconically, "You have," to which Thomas responded, "Yes Sir," to which Hassell asked, "What did he say?" Thomas told him, "Well, your family wasn't in Blair and hadn't been there." With a perplexed look on his face, the alleged family annihilator said, "That is strange. I have a letter from my wife written since she left. I do not understand why you have not heard from them."[2] Hassell was determined to play out his string, but the lawmen were having none of it. None of the three men spoke for a few minutes, until Thomas "looked directly at Hassell straight in the eye" and told him, "Your family has been found—was found in the cellar where you placed them after you knocked them in the head with an axe."[3]

Then silence, as Hassell processed the information for several minutes, no doubt lamenting that he did not get away with his latest mass murder by departing when he could have. Hassell's facial expression changed, becoming increasingly mottled, with "drops of perspiration." The only thing he seemed to be concerned with at the time was if they had found out whether "the girl," Maudie, was carrying his child or not.[4]

As Christmas was drawing to a close, Thomas and Martin both left the lockup, probably trying to spend time with their families as Christmas faded away. Hassell likely tried to process the latest turn of events. Sometime later in the evening, his guard heard him whisper in a soft moan, "I did it, I did it."[5] The prisoner asked if he could wait until he was stronger to make a statement. As one observer put it, George Hassell had come "to the end of his trail where the westbound Santa Fe trains say goodbye to Texas and Hello to New Mexico," a trail that could be summed up as one that "led him over 37 states, into countless jails and prisons, including the disciplinary barracks of Leavenworth, the army, Texas state, onto the sea and into the Gulf of Mexico with the merchant marine."[6]

As the suspected killer sat stewing in the jail, tensions were running high in Farwell and there was a growing undercurrent of potential mob violence. At least some residents thought so.[7] The consensus among the townsfolk was that the Hassell should be tried, convicted, and executed as quickly as possible. One local resident and representative for a large coffee company in the region, E. Frank Congrove, sent a telegram to Texas Governor Miriam A. Ferguson. From Fort Smith, Arkansas, Congrove wrote the lame-duck governor, "Should there be courage enough left in the manhood of Texas to convict George Hassell, colossal slayer of his wife and eight children, as a native son I beg you in the name of Bowie, Crockett, and Hogg not to pardon him as the last and crowning act of your administration."[8]

***

Deputy Hawkins spent several nights guarding Hassell while he recovered from his injuries in his cell. Initially Hassell was quiet, almost "speechless," and just "sat staring at the wall." Hawkins managed to earn his confidence through his "kindness and consideration." Late one night, probably December 26, Hawkins heard Hassell calling for him in his "husky voice ... Hawkins, Hawkins." He rushed to his cell, where the accused killer was grasping the steel bars of his cell so hard "his knuckles showed white." Hawkins was evidently tired of his shenanigans that night and irritably asked him, "What's the matter with you?" According to an interview with attorney J. D. Thomas in 1935, "Hassell's face was working with some powerful inner emotion. His eyes were popping, and he was breathing hard." Hassell asked Hawkins in a gruff voice to come inside his cell because he wanted to speak with him. Hawkins was unsure what was on his mind. His "eyes narrowed" as he studied the burly prisoner closely, seemingly taking his measure from head to foot.[9]

Hawkins asked him what it was he wanted to tell him. Hassell "turned away from the front of the cell and threw himself down on his cot." The deputy hesitated for a minute before letting himself into the cell, bolting the door behind him. Hassell was at this point sitting up on his cot, "his head in his hands," when he suddenly burst out, "I've killed people before ... I've got to tell someone about it."[10] According to Thomas, Hassell proceeded to recount the Whittier murders of his common-law wife and three children in June 1917. Hawkins listened but was not altogether believing of what he heard. Hassell didn't help matters, refusing to offer any information beyond the fact that he had killed four people in California as the country entered the First World War.

By Monday, December 27, Hassell had regained some of his vaunted vitality, and seemed calm and in good spirits and ready to tell his life story. Hawkins had evidently notified County Attorney Thomas and Sheriff Martin about these latest revelations, and preparations were made to take Hassell's formal confession, which had grown to include thirteen victims in two states and two mass murders committed almost a decade apart. The county attorney, Thomas, had warned the prisoner before he began speaking that he did not have to make a statement and whatever he said could be used as evidence against him. But apparently Hassell wanted to talk.

His confession was recorded in his jail cell. Present were Thomas, Martin, Sheriff Kennedy from Clovis, a court stenographer, and W. H. Holmes, who was also a Clovis resident and the court reporter for the 9th Judicial District of the State of New Mexico. Hassell dictated his statement in narrative form as the stenographer took it down in shorthand. However, during the subsequent trial this protocol would be challenged by Hassell's defense attorney. The court reporter explained that he had "reduced the statement to shorthand in the jail." Moreover, he "did not take notes to Clovis to transcribe—took them to Judge Thomas's office and did it there." Once this was finished, Thomas returned with it to the jail, accompanied by the court reporter, who served as witness as the prisoner signed the statement, which had been transcribed by typewriter. It would become State Exhibit Number 1 during the January 10, 1927, trial.[11]

Hassell spared few details as he described his tawdry life. He confessed to the family murders and to killing Alton, as well as to his suicide attempt at the Lindop place. Recovering from wounds in the Farwell jail, he made his statement as he lay in bed and signed it shortly after 6:00 p.m., Monday night, December 27. Some of his story was considered inappropriate for popular consumption and would be left out of the newspaper versions of his confession, especially topics pertaining to his incestuous relationships with his nieces and stepdaughters, Nora and Maudie.

As he disclosed "a catalogue of crime mingled with generous impulses in caring for the children of his dead brother," he not only confessed to the killings of his nine family members but also the murders of a common-law-wife and three children in California in 1917. This surely threw authorities a curve, especially since Hassell remained silent after this admission, refusing to give their names and where exactly the killings took place.

Forced to dig up information on their own, lawmen scoured the Hassell farmhouse for clues. The investigators were intrigued by the mysterious photos they found. On the back of one of them was written the name "Maggie."[12] This would be the only clue police had to work with as far as the Whittier murders for the time being, and as 1926 ended, Hassell had still not divulged the names of the victims nor the location of the crime. Since there was little argument over who he killed in Farwell and the only mystery that remained was why he did it, the California killings would become the center of the ongoing investigation into his pattern of murderous activity over the past decade. Meanwhile, authorities had already begun working on a theory that his brother, Tom, probably "did not die a natural death" either.[13]

Although there were no tangible signs of potential crowd violence, throngs of people had been gathering in Farwell all day and into Tuesday night, trading rumors and sharing insights about the nine murder victims. Among the crowd were most of Susie's Ferguson relatives, who had traveled from Colorado and other parts of Texas to watch justice be served.

Once word was out about the four potential murders in California and Hassell's possible involvement in his brother's untimely death, many began questioning whether he was responsible for even more deaths. This must have been on Sheriff Martin's mind on Tuesday night, December 28, shortly before Hassell was transferred to a more secure jail in Plainview. Since nothing had been heard from his first wife, Minnie Laughlin, and his son, James Delbert, it might have crossed Martin's mind that he could also have killed them. He couldn't help but ask Hassell, seemingly out of the blue, "One of the women you married was Miss Minnie Laughlin, so I am advised. Is that right?" Hassell responded, "That's right, I married her at Ovalo Texas." Martin asked him, "Did you harm her in anyway?" Hassell responded in a cryptic manner, commenting, "No sir, so far as I know, she is still alive." He told Martin that he thought she had married again but didn't know the name of her husband, though "he was pretty sure they lived in Jarrell, Texas."[14]

As noted earlier, Minnie went to extraordinary measures so that she and her young son could escape into anonymity from her past and beyond the clutches of her first husband. This was years before his first mass murder. But the scant evidence she left in her wake surely would have made it near impossible for her ex-husband to track her down. The names of Tom and Minnie Laughlin Hodge turn up in the 1910 US Federal Census. They were married in 1910, which would have been the same year Hassell claimed to have left her. Presumably, Hassell and Minnie were legally divorced, after which Minnie could have married Tom in 1910 and adopted the new last name. Genealogy records, however, indicate that she changed James Delbert's name to John Benjamin Laughlin, but without him ever formally adopting the Hodge surname.

Marriage records and census reports match up with the ages and birthdates of both Minnie and her son. In 1938 the son she produced with Hassell married Frances Uecker in Toledo, Ohio. The marriage record notes he was born in Fort Worth and that his parents were Minnie Hodge and one Hassel Laughlin. Moreover, the 1910 census lists both Hodges and a son. The one-year-old son is listed without a name, just as "Baby Hodge," which suggests an attempt at obfuscation on the part of the mother. Both Minnie and her son lived long lives and were most certainly not murdered by Hassell.[15]

On December 28, the Hassell murders made front-page headlines across the country, and most of his detailed confession was reprinted in newspapers. The December 28, 1926, issue of the *Los Angeles Times* offered a succinct summary of the overall perception of his crime spree: "Hassell told a story of crime ranging in degree, from drunkenness to murder, including desertions from the army and navy, draft evasions, skin game operations and illicit relations with members of his own family."[16]

Restive crowds continued to gather as Hassell prepared to be moved between jails on Tuesday night. Meanwhile, local law enforcement remained on alert in case of any mob activity. A "double guard" of armed officers spirited Hassell out of Farwell. His escort included Sheriff Martin and his entire force of deputies, along with Bailey County Sheriff Douglas. All lights in the Farwell jail had been extinguished when they carried Hassell to a "big auto in which a litter was placed in back." As the car moved down the street, it was followed by another "jammed with heavily armed men. Two blocks from the courthouse both cars picked up speed and whirled south to Hale County at rapid speed."[17]

The following morning Hassell was lodged safely at the Hale County Jail in Plainview. The alleged mass murderer was not kept in solitary confinement as one would expect but was held in a "run around" with other prisoners.[18] Hassell was still weak from his wounds, and Plainview Sheriff Sam Faith therefore viewed him as "harmless" in his current condition. Indeed, the Hale County Jail was regarded as one of the strongest lock-ups in "plains country and no extra precautions against mob violence have been taken." Hassell's wounds were administered to by a Plainview doctor named C. A. Cantrell, who pronounced his wrist wound as the most serious injury, and declared that his overall condition was not life-threatening. The normally loquacious patient refused to speak about any subject and completely disregarded questions from the doctor when he tried to make small talk with his patient.[19]

Hassell would gradually get over his reticence, eventually chatting amiably with the doctor and the other inmates. One observer noted that he had shown an inclination to talk during the twenty-four hours since he had been arrested. He regaled the other inmates with his exploits, talking extensively of his life and crimes. As Dr. Cantrell dressed his wounds, Hassell attempted to add some levity by telling him, "I want to be in shape to go to the electric chair when my time comes. That is why I want a doctor. I do not want a long jail sentence, nor do I want to fall into the hands of a mob."[20]

On Wednesday, December 29, Judge Reese Tatum issued an order calling for a special session of the District Court for Parmer County. Parmer County court sessions were traditionally held each spring and fall. But due to the overwhelming public outrage over the murders on the Hassell farm, local officials set a special session of the District Court to begin on Monday, January 3, 1927, in order to dispose of the case as soon as possible. An early trial was expected to begin soon after a grand jury would be convened to rule on whether to take the case to trial. Meanwhile, the alleged killer waited in the Hale County jail in Plainview, the county seat. It was thought best to keep Hassell out of Farwell for as long as possible.[21]

While waiting for resentencing, Hassell was asked to pose for a photo. It would turn out to be the most widely circulated photograph of the mass killer. The photo session produced two photos, offering both sides of the man who would be compared to Dr. Jekyll and Mr. Hyde. In the first, he wore a serious expression. A reporter for the *Amarillo News-Globe* was present and, struck by this out-of-character pose, said, "George, you say you aren't worried about what is going to happen to you. Let's see you laugh," which he did, just as the photographer took his picture.[22] Many who saw the smiling killer noted his ability to charm with his healthy set of teeth and broad smile.

Chapter 15

Picking a Jury

"... just doing my duty under the law."

On January 4, 1927, nine original bills of indictment were levied against George J. Hassell. Each one described the manner of death of each victim, noting the specifics of each murder: how Hassell allegedly killed his wife Susie with a hammer and choked her with his bare hands before killing the rest of the family with an assortment of techniques ranging from choking and strangling the littlest ones to killing the older boys and girls with a combination of axe, shotgun, and strangulation. Each method of murder for each victim was noted on their separate bills of indictment.[1]

Approving the indictments was mostly a formality, required in order to proceed with the trial and the selection of jurors as well as to determine whether the defendant should live or die. It was decided to move ahead, beginning with the murder of his last victim, his twenty-one-year-old stepson and nephew Alton, for whom Hassell had patiently waited before "unlawfully with malice and aforethought" adding the oldest child to his list of victims. Of all nine capital cases, its specifics were the most applicable for proving that the killing was planned.[2]

Judge Reese Tatum would serve as the presiding judge, with B. N. Richards of the Dalhart District Attorney's office conducting the prosecution's case: "District judges and district courts served judicial districts that included several counties, so a sheriff's most fateful and intimate relationship was with his county judge" and "most brought their criminal cases in county court."[3]

On January 5, Hassell was assigned a defense attorney to represent him, William H. Russell (1878-1950) of Hereford, Texas. Born in Dixon County, Tennessee, Russell's family moved to Texas in 1890 after a brief respite in Indian country. Russell attended school in Paris, Texas, before matriculating at the University of Texas School of Law in 1901. While in Austin, he worked for a few months for Governor Hogg, who talked him into opening a law practice in Hereford, Texas, the following year. He was one of the city's first practicing lawyers and served as a Deaf Smith County judge between 1904 and 1910. His US World War One draft card described him as of medium height and weight with blue eyes and brown hair.[4] Tatum, Richards, and Russell would be the three main actors representing the criminal justice system.

Shortly before the trial and jury selection, Hassell's attorney moved for a change of venue outside Parmer County, arguing that "on account of the high state of public feeling in this county against the defendant [it] is and will be impossible for him to obtain a fair trial."[5] For any chance of obtaining a change of venue, the defense had to produce affidavits from at least three Parmer County residents attesting to the fact that Hassell would not receive a fair trial in Farwell. Unsurprisingly, other than George Hassell himself, no other residents were willing to sign a supporting affidavit, leaving him two affidavits short.

The focus of the argument in favor of seeking a change of venue was predicated on the understanding that there was such a "dangerous feeling among the citizens of this county against the defendant." Hassell confided to others that he had been informed by credible citizens that if the outcome of the trial was not to their liking, they "would attend to the defendant themselves." Such an atmosphere of potential vigilantism, it was argued, would likely "invade the jury and the jurors and the jury box." Thus, the defendant should be "entitled to a trial in an atmosphere where such feelings does not exist."[6] In any case, this strategy was quickly overruled by Judge Tatum, and his decision was accepted by the defendant in open court. Throughout the proceedings, the prisoner sat under personal guard.

A covey of officers from the surrounding counties had been deputized to assist Sheriff Martin in case any mob violence broke out. As mentioned previously, sheriffs tended to have good relationships with their counterparts in neighboring counties, usually cemented through sporadic personal meetings or telephone conversations. In some cases, sheriffs transported convicted criminals to the state penitentiary in Huntsville, requiring a long, arduous drive through a number of counties. It was common for sheriffs to let their counterparts house prisoners in their local jails for a night or two while they waited for weather to clear or for messages from Austin.

Before a jury could be selected and a trial commenced, it was necessary to present the facts of the case to a grand jury to determine whether there was enough evidence to move forward with a formal trial. To be clear, the grand jury does not determine guilt or innocence; rather, it determines if there are grounds to move the case to a courtroom before twelve jurors. It was common for grand juries made up of citizens to serve a district court for six-month terms. They were expected to decide whether to indict and hold a jury trial in district court, and they also determined whether, if convicted, to sentence the accused to state prison. According to one Texas historian, "Sheriffs paid close attention when they joined the district judge in choosing the five grand jury commissioners who then met up with the secret names of the 'good, honest, homegrown, hard-working God-fearing people' who served on the grand jury."[7]

***

On January 3, F. W. McElroy, E. T. Caldwell, and J. W. Farr were summoned to serve as jury commissioners, tasked with selecting a grand jury and then a petit jury, which listens to evidence presented by both parties and returns a verdict. Once the jury commissioners were approved, they were sworn in and instructed on the duties expected of them by law. After they retired to another room, they began the process of selecting petit jurors from sealed envelopes for the special January term.⁸ Each of the grand jurors was paid three dollars and given certificates of their service.

The following day, twelve grand jurors were selected for the special term of the district court. They were a representative cross section of the male residents of Farwell and its neighboring towns. Willie E. Williams, for example, had returned home to Springtown, Texas, some 350 miles east of the Farwell area, after serving in the Great War. Faced with few job prospects, he moved to Bovina in 1920 and worked on a farm and in a general store. Within two years, he had saved enough to start his own business, which was located in a shop he built himself from handmade adobe bricks. His store sold groceries, harnesses, drugs, hardware and dry goods and even had a barber chair in the back, where the school superintendent, John Belew, gave haircuts on his off hours.⁹

Juryman J. F. Foster moved there from Oklahoma in 1920, bringing with him "some fine Percheon horses" and setting to raise some hogs. He had five kids to help him and was known for his "productive fruit trees," considered a rarity for the area.¹⁰ Ben T. Galloway moved from Coleman to Friona in 1917, driving his Model T. However, his first two years on the prairie were tough ones for raising cattle, and he soon found farming unprofitable. He found more steady employment at the Kinsley Hardware Store (in 1929 he was able to open his own business).¹¹ Other grand jurors included H. D. Ellison, J. J. DeOliviera, J. O. Ford, Jack Carr, R. L. Hightower, N. E. Wines, E. M Sherieb, W. S. McDaniel and W. C. Crowell.¹²

On Friday, January 7, petit jury selection was set to begin at 10:00 a.m. Hassell had arrived in Farwell from the Bailey County Jail in Muleshoe the previous night. In his first court appearance, Hassell was described as "neatly dressed and apparently unconcerned, glancing seriously over the large audience."¹³

Picking a jury in a large town is challenging and time-consuming, even under the best of circumstances, but in trying a high-profile crime in a small burg like Farwell the challenges were multiplied. The *Dallas News Almanac* for 1927 stated that there had been a little over four hundred votes cast in the county in 1926. According to Hassell's appeal, there was an assumption that the four hundred voters were split fairly evenly by gender. In the 1920s, Texan women were allowed to vote and hold political office "but were not yet permitted to serve as jurors in criminal and civil trials."[14] Since women were barred from jury duty, there were only about two hundred qualified jurors in the county. Therefore, the order issued for 188 special veniremen meant it would take "nearly every qualified juror in the county." Because of the small size of the jury pool, representing a town where everyone is familiar with the crime at hand, especially the alleged murder of the Hassell family by its patriarch, it was quite a challenge to find jurors acceptable to both sides. It was important that they get it right, following judicial process to the tee. This was made particularly clear when the state announced it was seeking the death penalty.[15]

Every juror had to be "qualified," which meant that he had to demonstrate his willingness to sentence someone to death, that "he had no moral scruples against the assessment of the death penalty in a proper case."[16] In the selection of the Hassell jury, this would become abundantly clear as several jurors admitted they could not sentence a man to death. According to Texas legal historian and former attorney Bill Neal, "One of the most persuasive arguments of those who oppose the death penalty is that when the prosecution is permitted to 'qualify' potential jurors on the death penalty, any panelist who ... expresses any scruples against the death penalty is excluded." This process "tends to skew the final jury in favor of prosecution—in effect turning it into a 'hanging jury' that is more likely to convict than a true cross-section of the defendant's peers."[17]

The court reopened for the afternoon session with only one juror selected, local farmer E. W. McGuire. Eleven of the original 108 veniremen summoned for jury service had already been examined. One of the biggest challenges in selecting a jury was that so many people already had "fixed opinions and conscientious scruples against the death penalty."[18] Few expected the entire jury to be selected by the end of that afternoon. Judge Tatum stated that if required, he would conduct a night session so that the trial could be held on time. But with only five jurors selected and impaneled in the case, it seemed that the special venire pool of 108 had been exhausted by Saturday, January 8.

In order to reach the requisite number of twelve jurors, another eighty men were summoned. The Court instructed the Sheriff to summon all "such men as have legal qualification to serve on juries, informing him of what those qualifications are and also directing Sheriff and instructed him to summon as far as he may be able to do, men of good character, who can read and write and such men as are not prejudiced against defendant, or biased in his favor."[19]

Each prospective juror was interviewed, first by the prosecution and then the defense. Like the members of the grand jury, the petit jury comprised mostly local farmers from the towns of Bovina, Friona (five from there), and Farwell. F. W. Reeve had moved to Parmer County from Indiana eighteen years earlier and had never met Hassell but said he had some impression of the case from newspapers and everyday conversation.[20] Marvin Whaley, his wife, and their two sons had moved from New Mexico to Friona in 1920, reasoning that the roads were better and there were "no draws to cross."[21] G. W. Atchley lived in Farwell, just seven miles east of the courthouse and about six miles from the Hassell farm. He was born in Alabama and had been in Texas for twenty-three years at the time of the trial. Atchley recalled meeting Hassell a couple of times but claimed he didn't know him by name. Carl Fowler, a bachelor, had been farming eight miles east of Farwell over the past ten years and remembered seeing the defendant a couple of times.[22]

First and foremost, jurors were asked if they had any reservations about sentencing someone to death. Unsurprisingly, several prospective jurors did indeed feel conflicted about consigning someone to the electric chair. Dud Read, for example, a lifelong Texan married with two kids, had been a farmer in Parmer County for just over a year. He took a pretty strong stance against capital punishment but said he was sure he could sentence someone to death "if it was a proper case ... I guess, if the man ain't insane, I suppose I could. It is owing to what he done. If he is proved to be sane I could."[23]

Another important question focused on how familiar a prospective juror was with the case and whether he had already made up his mind on guilt or innocence. G. W. Atchley from Farwell claimed not to have any fixed opinion. While he had "heard something about the case, both from hearing people talking, and from the newspapers," he claimed to have "formed what I would call an impression in my mind, instead of a fixed opinion. An impression is what I would call it ... I could lay the impression aside ... leave my mind free to hear evidence and make up my verdict from what I hear on the witness stand."[24]

J. L. Landrum had resided in Friona for about two years. Originally from Floyd County, he had lived in Texas all his life except for four years. A lumberman, he was married and expressed no fixed opinion on the case, nor was he an opponent of the death penalty. On cross-examination by Russell for the defense, Landrum admitted he had "heard and read" about the case, but he said that he had never met Hassell, although he was aware of the defendant's confession and the heinous nature of the crime. But he had not reached any conclusions as to guilt or innocence in the lead-up to the trial.[25]

One would think it was impossible for any potential jurors to be unfamiliar with the case before them, especially since it was the most notorious event in the short history of Parmer County. W. R. Scheihagen had been farming in the area for four years, and like the rest of the juror pool, he had an impression gained mostly from the newspapers, but he claimed that he could judge the case according to the testimony he would be hearing.[26] T. E. Lovelace had spent seven of his forty-eight years in Parmer County and had seen Hassell once but had no fixed opinion.[27] Likewise, T. J. Crawford, the proprietor of a thriving mercantile business and a native of Tennessee who had moved to Texas in 1892 and had lived in Friona since 1908, had heard of the defendant but "didn't know him," and nor did his wife and four kids.[28]

Of all the petit jurors, none dominated the historical memory of the George Hassell trial more than Clyde V. Goodwine. In the late 1980s, he was still granting interviews as the last living member of the jury.[29] The best-known of the jurors, Goodwine was a native of Indiana who had settled in Friona with his family back in 1909. Goodwine was an unmarried farmer at the time of the trial. One of nine children, six of whom would become teachers, Goodwine had been a member of the first graduating class of Friona High School. Clyde had taken over the family farm after his father died in 1923 and, thanks to several years of wheat farming, he was able to expand his property.[30] He was a favorite of researchers documenting life in Parmer County in general and his involvement in the notorious trial in particular. Over the years he shared his thoughts and experiences with journalists, historians, and investigators. He recounted being the eleventh juror selected from the second group of veniremen. He had neither a fixed opinion on, nor any knowledge of, Hassell. He once mentioned that he had been no stranger to juries prior to the Hassell trial, commenting, "I probably averaged serving on one jury per year ... They used to have a court session every spring and fall, but due to the public feelings about the case a special session was called in January [1927]."[31]

More than half a century after the trial, Goodwine could look back and remember the trial and its goings on like it was yesterday and seemed to enjoy entertaining interviewers with his recollections. One of his most oft-repeated stories, an "amusing anecdote," revolved around the lawmen assigned to guard Hassell during the trial. Most of the jurors had never met Hassell in person before the trial. But Clyde remembered noticing a "big man, with rough features, [who] looked like he might be capable of anything." He and several jurors were under the impression that this "big man" was the alleged murderer and that the "well-dressed good-looking man sitting next to him was a lawyer." When they found out the "well-dressed" man was actually Hassell, Goodwine said, it proved that they "sure didn't lie when we said we didn't know Hassell."[32]

Goodwine also recounted how he was vetted for the jury by Hassell's court-appointed defender, W. H. Russell, who he said put him through the "most tedious ordeal during his examining period." It appeared that Russell was exasperated by the time he got to Goodwine, who had figured out that "the only way I would be disqualified would have been to disqualify myself— and Russell asked me everything in the book."

Several prospective jurors had already been excused because they claimed they could not sentence someone to death. In fact, one of Clyde's acquaintances told him that if he voted for the death penalty, he "would be just as bad as Hassell." But the pragmatic Goodwine didn't see it that way, recognizing he was "just doing my duty under the law." Moreover, he added, "If Hassell did not qualify for the chair no one ever did."[33]

Ultimately, it took longer to select a jury than to hear the case, with the selection process lasing three days and the trial two (including two night sessions).

Chapter 16

Life or Death: The Trial of George J. Hassell

"Anyhow I done what I did, and I am here to pay my penalty like a man, whatever it may be."

Under heavy guard at the Bailey County jail in Muleshoe, twenty-five miles southeast of Farwell, Hassell was expected to be delivered to the Parmer County Courthouse on January 7, which was also when the selection of the jury was scheduled to begin. Officers from all sections of the Texas Panhandle were called in to be on hand to control the anticipated arrival of hundreds of spectators. One estimate predicted that "there will be 2000 people" attempting to hear the trial.[1] One observer described the "Hundreds of farmers" that "flivvered [sic] or drove buckboards or road horseback to Farwell" early that day to attend the trial.[2] No one could remember a bigger event in the history of the small farming community. More than sixty years later, Wendell Pettee, who lived in the town until 1940, fondly recounted helping his grandfather sell hamburgers "to all the people who came to view" the trial. In an interview with the *State Line Tribune* in 1988, he noted how awed he was "as a little boy" when he saw the Parmer County Courthouse for the first time, describing it as "the biggest building I had ever seen."[3]

When Hassell was arraigned before the judge, he listened to the indictments, and when it came time to enter a plea of guilty or not guilty, he refused to plead. Pursuant to courtroom protocol, the judge ordered that a plea of not guilty be entered for him. It was now the burden of the state to prove that Hassell had committed murder.

By 3:30 p.m., Monday, January 10, 1927, all the trial preliminaries had been completed and the jury selected, and the attorneys were ready to do battle. Once the jury selection, indictments, and other miscellaneous paperwork were completed, the attorneys were ready to face the jurors and give them the evidence. Judging by the work of one Texas legal historian, the jurors deciding Hassell's fate would have fit a similar profile to those in other overwhelmingly agricultural areas of the state: "rural, provincial, poorly educated ... highly susceptible to emotional appeals and hyperbole."[4]

Despite objections from Hassell's court-appointed attorney, W. H. Russell, the prosecution began its case by introducing Hassell's chilling confession of how he killed his nine family members, and the prosecutor was ready to read the three-thousand-word document. He began by assuring the jurors that the statement had been given voluntarily and that the defendant had been read his constitutional rights. Seated and accompanied by an armed guard, Hassell listened as his confession was read to the courtroom by the prosecutor, Richards. "A deathlike stillness fell over the court" as Richards introduced "the grewsome detail" of Hassell's crimes. Observers would later recount that the alleged killer appeared "smiling and unconcerned."[5]

Hassell's initial confession had chronicled his life from birth to the present time, beginning with his early life with his parents, his crimes, and his fondness for whiskey ... meanwhile, the defense counsel, Russell, continued to object "to all the contents of this instrument except for reference to the particular homicide in question."[6] The court sustained this objection and noted the exception, and began instead with Hassell's well-worn account of his year in Farwell and relations with family members, including his incestuous conduct with his underage nieces Maudie and Nora.

The confession included his decision to kill his family. Here again we see his talent for misdirection, such as when he asserted that he had intended to

> go to the oil fields when we got our crop gathered up to get the money to start another crop on, and of course I believe my wife thought my idea of going to the oil fields was to get the chance to hike off, which if she would have let me go to the oil fields no doubt that I never would have come back—I would probably have kept on going, and she fussed around me going to the oil fields, she said if I went that she was going to too and so forth, so any how we fussed I guess until about 12 p.m. and I got up and dressed and went in and sat down in the other room, and she gets up and comes on in there an tells me to come back to bed.[7]

He then described how he went out to the barn to drink some whiskey. He claimed that almost as soon as he got in bed, Susan got "roused again" when she smelled liquor on his breath and he attacked her "with a ballteen [sic] hammer and killed the rest of the family ... waited for Alton for several days ... anyhow I done what I did and I am here to pay my penalty like a man, whatever it may be. I tried to make it a death penalty."[8]

Once he admitted to having had "sexual intercourse with the girl [Maudie]" and described how he had tried to get her to blame her pregnancy on her cousins, the wheels for the looming tragedy were set in motion.

Hassell introduced one other facet of his relationship with his wife in his confession, noting that "just awhile before this happened, we had a chance to have sexual intercourse and she refused me and wouldn't give me no cause for it. I asked her then if she figured on staying with me and keeping our secret or going to turn me down, and she wouldn't give me no answer ... If my wife had let me gone, I would have gone and I wouldn't have left a disgrace on the girl."[9] As in other cases of familicide, Hassell's reaction to his wife turning him down for sex is a familiar excuse for other mass killings of family members by the father.

As Parmer County Attorney J. D. Thomas, the first witness, took the stand, Susan's family, including her elderly father and mother, her three brothers, her daughter Nora, and her current husband, filed into the courtroom. Nora burst into tears when she saw her stepfather and "turned her back on him."[10]

Thomas would later state that Hassell had "preferred not to read [the confession] on account of his feelings."[11] Hassell's attorney jumped on the fact that the defendant had never read his own confession, or heard it read to him, before he signed it. But the prosecution reminded Russell that Hassell had been offered multiple chances to have it read to him but "preferred not to read it on account of his feelings."[12] Russell also objected to the reading of the confession in its entirety, because "it contains a lot of other matters about various things" besides the homicide at the center of the trial.

Thomas, who had been present when Hassell confessed to his crimes of the previous month,[13] recounted that he had warned Hassell at that time that he did not have to make a statement and that whatever he said could be used as evidence against him. Evidently, no one could stop the narcissist from talking once he got started, even if his life depended on it. The first witness, attorney J. D. Thomas, "swept the courtroom spectators into tears in opening the state's case to the jury shortly after supper" that January 10, when "in a masterful recital of the details of the tragedy, he rose to the heights of oratory as he painted a word picture of events of the tragic night, sobbing was heard throughout the room, and the defense counsel W. H. Russell wept as he left the counsel table."[14]

Russell returned following the conclusion of Thomas's pleading. Addressing the jury, he asked them to give the evidence and testimony careful consideration and sought to impress upon the jury that "only a man of unbalanced mind could have perpetrated the crime and sustain an attitude of utter indifference to it and its consequence."[15]

Thomas was recalled for one more question by Russell, who asked him whether "there was considerable talk of mob violence at that time?"[16] Thomas said, "I don't know that I can say there was. I have heard of mob violence, but I never have known of any mob violence around here from any authentic sources," but had heard the rumors. Russell asked Thomas whether Sheriff Martin had told Hassell that "he wouldn't take the time to read it because he was afraid a mob might form and he was"—Thomas interrupted him: "I never heard the Sheriff make a remark like that."[17]

Following the reading of the confession and the testimony by Thomas, Hassell's landlord, Mrs. "Kate" J. D. Hamlin, took the stand.[18] She recounted that the defendant "lived and worked a place of ours last," having moved there in December 1925. Mrs. Hamlin, who oversaw tenants on family properties, claimed to have known the Hassell family "pretty well." She described Mrs. Hassell as a "splendid woman." When queried about when she last saw the family members, Hamlin said that she noticed they were missing right after Thanksgiving, around December 1. There were few revelations from her testimony. Shedding some light on Hassell's relationship with Maudie, Hamlin described Maudie and Hassell working in the field together, commenting, "Well, I saw them go to the field once, I think about the time they finished up their crop. I remember I was there, and Maudie just finished washing the dishes and Mrs. Hassell called her and I think they went together."[19]

A hush fell over the courtroom as Mrs. Hamlin testified that she had seen the "frail" boys, Russell and Virgil, digging the pit the previous fall season. Both "toiled with spade and shovel for days digging the hole where they were [later] buried." She described the pit as being "a square hole in the ground about four or five feet deep ... about ten by fifteen feet square."[20] As one reporter wrote, little could they have realized that "the pit would soon wrap its silent folds about them and seven others, and again unfold to yield the nation's greatest crime of the decade."[21]

When asked to describe any other specifics of the dugout, Hamlin noted that it was located close to the back door of the house, less than ten feet away. She added that she "never knew or understood what it was being dug for. You ask me if there was any other pit or dugout there, on the premises. Yes, there was a dug-out in which Mrs. Hassell had used for canned fruits and preserves. That was already on the place."[22]

The landlord went on to describe the December 22 auction and how Hassell showed her the handbills printed up for it.[23] She went on to mention that the dugout was filled in flat, like a tabletop. Her initial suspicions about her tenant were aroused, as mentioned previously, when she noticed the scratch marks on his hands while sitting at the Hamlin dinner table shortly after the family's disappearance. Conversely, on cross-examination from the defense attorney, Hamlin described the family as getting along, nothing to arouse suspicions. Following her testimony, the court took a break for dinner, and it was announced that the trial would be adjourned at 7:30 p.m.

***

The night session on January 10 kicked off with the testimony of J. O. Ford at 7:50 p.m.

Ford described his interactions with Hassell, particularly his curiosity about the fire on his property one morning and how Hassell had walked down the driveway to meet him, seemingly to stop him from going any further. On cross-examination by Russell, he remembered that Hassell had "seemed bothered by something; didn't appear quite as jovial as ordinarily."[24] He recounted the auction and the discovery of the bodies on Christmas Eve, as well as an odd incident where he and his wife stopped at the Hassell house the previous summer. He described how Maudie "came and called me and asked if we were going to Clovis any time that week, and I told her I thought we would, and she said if we did, Mrs. Hassell wanted to go along to Clovis."[25] He added, "Perhaps I better not say what I figured."[26]

On cross, Russell asked Ford if he "figured that or anything else looked funny until you heard about this occurrence [murders]."[27] Ford admitted he wasn't well acquainted with the family and had only been neighbors about six months, but, he said, "It is not a fact that I didn't think about that until after I heard about the occurrence; I thought that was suspicious at the time." Ford recounted watching Hassell deliver a sales pitch on the day of the auction, when he "saw something that created some suspicion in my mind ... What I thought about it was that him and his family had some trouble and they had gone for some cause, and he was selling out. I thought he was selling out to get away with the money, is what I thought."[28] Russell objected to this response, and it was sustained, and the jurors were told not to consider the comments about the auction. Almost every witness had held some suspicions as to the fate of the Hassell family.

Next up was N. A. Lindop, who mostly testified to his interactions with Hassell while moving onto the Hassell property and during his disagreement with Hassell over the purchase of Hassell's crops. He described how

Hassell had stayed on with the Lindops until after the auction and how he had observed Hassell scrubbing and mopping floors and preventing anyone from going into his room, "the middle room on the backside."[29] Lindop said that they had broken bread together a number of times and engaged in sporadic conversations. But, Lindop stated, it was the day after the auction that probably stood out most to him, which was when Hassell returned from town after being questioned by authorities about the disappearance of his family. That same night, uncharacteristically, Hassell didn't eat much, just sat at the dinner table "figuring in a little book or something." Lindop said that he had just assumed he was figuring up his sales accounts and paid no attention to him.[30] He also testified about the sequence of events that finally brought Hassell to justice: the hours leading to his suicide attempt and the subsequent call for the sheriff and the county attorney.

Lindop had been present throughout the exhumation process, but he had not seen them take the bodies out, nor had he attended the funeral.[31] On cross-examination Russell asked him if he saw anything unusual in the area that Hassell had scrubbed prior to the Lindops moving in. Lindop replied, "I did not see any blood stains on the floor, not a bit. I did not notice anything unusual or out of the ordinary in his conduct."[32]

When it came to the whereabouts of the Hassell family, Lindop had mixed feelings. Initially Hassell had told him that his family moved to Oklahoma, she "didn't like it here–dissatisfied." Lindop testified that he had discussed this with his wife, who told him that it seemed suspicious to her because Susan had always told her that she was satisfied. It was at this point that N. A. Lindop "knew something was wrong ... In other words, I didn't believe the family had moved away voluntarily, my wife agreed with me."[33] However, as Lindop explained, Hassell convinced Lindop that "there wasn't anything wrong." Nonetheless, Lindop said that he had known Mrs. Hassell "tolerably well. She was not a grouchy or quarrelsome woman, but she seemed like an awfully fine woman. She was a pleasant woman—just as pleasant when she was around my home and place as could be."[34]

On redirect from the prosecutor, Richards, Lindop said that the house had recently been repapered and painted inside, just after Christmas. It was at this time, he said, that he "observed some bloody fingerprints on the door on the house in one place."³⁵

Following his father on the stand, sixteen-year-old Lester Lindop described how his father had told him, his brother, and another boy to get the sheriff and doctor to come to their house, arriving around 4:30 a.m. When it came to establishing a timeframe for the digging of the dugout, Lester was able to narrow it down to October, "during the Dallas [State] Fair." On cross-examination from the defense, he told the courtroom that he had known the Hassell boys and had occasionally eaten dinner with the family. As far as he was concerned, the "family seemed to get along well, and I never heard any fusses; all seemed to be happy ... Didn't know names of all the children, they were all pleasant."

After Lester stepped down from the witness stand, it was time for J. D. Thomas, one of the main actors in this saga, to testify again. Most of his testimony was related to the activities that began on December 23, the morning J. O. Ford came to his office to voice his concerns about the Hassells. Much of Thomas's commentary was devoted to the meeting he had with Hassell in his office later that day regarding the suspicions swirling around him. He remembered Hassell telling him that he was none too pleased about Mrs. Hamlin's inquiries into his personal affairs. The courtroom was probably hanging on his every word when he explained how he had sent a telegram to Oklahoma and found out that the family never arrived. As Thomas explained, this was kept a secret until he ended Hassell's weeks-long subterfuge by confronting him in the Farwell jail with what he already knew: "Mr. Hassell your family has been found ... in the cellar where you placed them."³⁶

Thomas said that it was he and Sheriff Martin who had ordered the cellar dug up immediately. He described how he had watched the exhumation of the bodies and seen the bloody fingerprints that Lindop discovered on one of the house doors. What Thomas could never understand, he explained to the court, was why Hassell stayed just ten feet from where the bodies were buried for several weeks: "He had every opportunity to climb in that Ford car, draw all the money out of the bank and go as far as the car would take him." It's worth speculating that he might have been more inclined to try and get away if he was ten years younger, but now on the cusp of forty, well into middle age for the 1920s, he might have figured that he lacked the vitality and fortitude to flee once his charade was exposed. Or perhaps he was too overconfident since he had gotten away with a similar murder in the past.

Thomas then informed the court that he had thought Hassell's account of his family moving to Oklahoma with the help of Susie's brother seemed plausible at the time. But, Thomas continued, Hassell's explanations for building the cellar never convinced him. When Thomas interrogated him about it, Hassell told him that he had thought "he needed it and later found he didn't need it, and that he wanted to leave premises in same shape he got it,"[37] an odd response to say the least. In light of all Hassell's inconsistencies, the attorney was convinced the answer to the mystery of the missing family would be solved once the cellar was searched.[38]

Sheriff J. H. Martin followed Thomas on the stand and began his testimony about responding to the predawn phone call from the Lindop boys that summoned him, Hawkins, and Thomas to the Hassell farm. Much of his testimony has been covered in previous chapters. However, he did admit in court that he was not present for the entire encounter because he was out in the car. According to Martin, when he ran into Hassell in town the previous evening, he followed him around, but he wasn't convinced he was guilty of murdering his family. But after the encounter at his residence that morning he had changed his mind. He told the court that up until then, "all his actions, talk and conduct appeared to be absolutely normal, and there was nothing about it to arouse my suspicion." But by the time he left for home after getting Hassell to the hospital, "all [his] suspicions were allayed—didn't ask him because he figured he did it."[39] In retrospect, Martin can be forgiven for misjudging Hassell as so many others had, for after all, he had probably never interacted with a psychopath before.

On recross from Russell, the sheriff said that once Hassell regained his strength, he had talked freely with him, and "from there on out he didn't do anything but talk and tell the history of his life and everybody else's; at least part of it; he told us considerable of his history. Every time he gets an audience, he talks and seems to enjoy it; and his words and attitude in all of his conversations—he would tell about these various things he has been into with as little concern as you and I would talk about duck hunting."[40]

After Martin's testimony, court was adjourned for the day of January 10, 1927.

***

At nine fifty-five the following morning, the day's first witness took the stand. Deputy Sheriff R. A. Hawkins repeated the same story recounted by Thomas and Martin about their visit to the Hassell farm on December 24. He described how he assisted in dressing Hassell following his suicide attempt and how he had then left him at the sanitarium. After breakfast, he had returned to the farmhouse to help identify the bodies being exhumed from the cellar. He described the burial locations of each of the bodies in the pit. Among the more shocking details of Hawkins's testimony was his description of Alton's injuries, including his head, which was "flattened out of shape and the skull was crushed."[41]

Hawkins claimed that he knew Hassell fairly well, having done business with him through his feed and grain business in town. During these occasions, Hawkins said that "he appeared to be like any other normal man,"[42] adding that he "never noticed anything abnormal" about Hassell's conduct.[43] But, asked if Hassell seemed nervous at the time of the questioning about suspicions surrounding his missing family, he stated that while talking to the county attorney and the sheriff in Thomas's Farwell office, Hassell had seemed a little bit nervous.[44] Hawkins had chalked it up to the fact that these circumstances "would naturally make a man feel a little bit bad, or a little nervous. It would be calculated to make the ordinary man feel nervous to accuse him of something like we did; even if he had been guilty, it would ordinarily 'shoot' an ordinary man all to pieces."[45]

Hawkins had looked after the bodies until the undertaker received them the next day, and he also stated that he had decided not to attend the funeral. When asked about a ring that had been taken off Hassell's hand while he was in the Farwell jail, Hawkins replied that Hassell had told him it was likely to swell his finger and wished for him to take it and put aside, so Hawkins had laid it in a window in the jail. He then submitted the gold ring to the district attorney to be placed in evidence.

Hawkins introduced some levity into the macabre proceedings by describing how the defendant had asked the doctor while locked up in the Plainview jail if "he was trying to embalm him when he poured some fluid into his wounds."[46] By Hawkins's account, Hassell had laughed and talked about the same matter to everybody that he could, and he had kept that up the entire time he had been under arrest. Hawkins also added that Hassell laughed and talked with the press photographers "and suggested he get between a couple of sheriffs and give them a reputation for having handled the biggest criminal in the state of Texas. He made that remark and laughed and joked about it."[47]

Hawkins left the stand. The next witness was Mrs. Nora Guidry,[48] the eldest daughter of Mrs. Hassell and the mother of Hassell's daughter, Georgia. As she sat down, "a dramatic silence settled over the courtroom," and one reporter noted how her stepfather and uncle "dropped his eyes and the girl diverted her gaze from his direction as she faced the audience."[49] Tears sprang to her eyes," the sensationalizing journalist continued, as the district attorney handed her the ring that had been introduced by Hawkins: "Sobbing and with a voice choked with emotion she identified the ring as one she had given her slain brother, Alton, on his last birthday [August 25, 1926]."[50] Nora was allowed to step down as the proverbial noose began to tighten around Hassell's neck.

Taking the stand next, G. W. Crawford, Alton's former employer and one of the last people to see him alive, testified about Alton's sleepover with his sons and dropping him off at the farm on Sunday, December 5, 1926. He explained that never saw him again after that. But, he said, in Texico the next day, he did run into Hassell, who informed him that he "would have to get another hand" since Alton had left for Oklahoma. Crawford left Alton's wages with Hassell, who assured him he would mail the check to Oklahoma. Following Crawford, twenty-one-year old R. F. Lloyd recounted buying a shotgun at the auction, and this was placed in evidence.

The courtroom was probably most touched by the testimony of Susan Hassell's father and older brother. Both contributed to the growing revulsion for their former son-in-law, now on trial for his life. The Fergusons had traveled more than five hundred miles, from Colorado, Texas, in Bastrop County, to reach Farwell for the trial. Susie's father, P. M. Ferguson, recounted what he knew of Susan's life with Tom Hassell, her first husband, as well as his untimely death, and her marriage to her brother-in-law, George Hassell.

The grieving father told the jury that since arriving in town he had gone out to the Hassell farm three different times to "see if I could find any mark or anything by which I could identify my daughter."[51] Seeking evidence that might have been overlooked by investigators, he managed to find "some pearl buttons and hair pins." These must have come from the fire pit where J. O. Ford saw Hassell managing a large fire earlier in December 1926. Ferguson lamented the fact that "the pearl buttons had been in such a hot fire you couldn't pick them up because they would crumple to nothing."[52] He also found, he said, "a little hole in the ground where the fire didn't reach very much," where "I found a little piece of goods with a big button on it, and it has a small piece of a brown cloak."[53]

However, the most troubling evidence he found was "a small piece of quilt with blood on it, and under there was a tick and some feathers and you could see where some oil had been poured on it. The larger piece I mentioned had some blood on it; it didn't hardly look like blood, but evidently it was. But it was all in ashes, and I wouldn't have even found this if it hadn't been for that little hole in the ground, so the fire didn't reach it."[54] Ferguson said that he only went into the house the first time he visited the farm. It was so traumatic for him, he noted, that "I was hurt so bad that I couldn't make much of an examination."[55]

J. V. Hassell, Susan's brother, had been in Farwell for almost two weeks but only went out to the farmhouse once. He told the jury about the late Tom Hassell's prosperous farm and informed the courtroom that Susie had collected $1,100 in life insurance from his death. Tom's insurance had been used to pay for his funeral expenses, including the hospital bill and the undertaker. He also described a family reunion, which Hassell had been asked to leave after he began "raving" about something that was said that bothered him and then forced his family to sleep in the yard.[56]

The Clovis doctor, E. L. Smith, who had operated on Hassell at the Baptist Sanitarium, followed the Fergusons onto the witness stand. Smith shared his credentials with the courtroom, explained the extent of Hassell's wounds in lay terms, and chronicled his visits to the defendant at the jails in Farwell and Muleshoe. He had seen him at the local lock-up each day between December 24 and 28 and then once more in Muleshoe on January 6, 1927.

Smith was one of the first members of the medical fraternity to question Hassell's state of mind. As he began to describe Hassell's demeanor and reasoning ability, he was interrupted by the defense counsel, Russell, who objected to Smith's observations because he was not an expert on mental illness. Smith responded that he can only claim the "ordinary experience that comes to the average doctor" over a twenty-five-year career. The prosecutor, Richards, chimed in, asking Smith whether he was "capable of passing credible judgment in that respect."[57] Russell's objection was sustained.[58]

Dr. Smith shed light on Hassell's formative years, sharing information gleaned from his numerous conversations with Hassell while tending to his wounds. Under cross-examination from the defense, Smith described Hassell as normally "cheerful."[59] Smith said, "he talked like an ordinary man that didn't have any particular troubles at all."[60] One of Hassell's habits, Smith explained, was to speak about his "checkered career … in a casual way, as an ordinary man would talk about ordinary experience." Smith also revealed that the alleged killer sometimes showed feelings, giving an example in which "tears came to his eyes and his lips quivered the last time I talked with him in jail."[61] The prosecution jumped in, unwilling to permit any attempt to humanize Hassell, and asked the doctor about this observation. He challenged Dr. Smith: "As a matter of fact, the time you say you saw tears coming into his eyes was when you were pulling some adhesive tape off his wounds, wasn't it?" Smith remained unshaken, responding to Richards, "No sir, it was as I said a while ago."[62]

The attorneys allowed Smith to give more insight into his ability to judge an individual's mental state. He noted that during his quarter century of practice he had occasion "to observe the ordinary human conduct, conduct of people who are sick and in trouble and distress, and as a matter of fact, mental conditions will effect a person physically to a considerable extent."[63] Moreover, he commented that "people who are worried and troubled about things will usually largely make up the doctor's bunch of patients, to some extent at least." After finishing his thoughts on the subject, the doctor was excused.[64]

Anyone hoping to hear any new revelations about Hassell and his Farwell murders would have been sorely disappointed as the state presented its last witnesses. A handful of witnesses took the stand following Dr. Smith. F. A. McCutcheon, a banker with the Security State Bank of Farwell, had interacted with Hassell over the past year, including making some of the arrangements in connection with the auction on December 22, 1926. He noted that the burly farmer had close to $1,800 (about $26,000 in 2020) in the bank at the time of the crimes, and that he always paid his debts, commenting, "He was the first man who paid me his notes this year … We considered him a very reliable farmer, and a very attentive man to business."[65] Likewise, up until December 23, 1926, he "never noticed anything abnormal about his methods or conduct."[66]

Following the banker, Mrs. J. D. Hamlin, who had testified earlier, was recalled as a witness for the state. Under direct examination from prosecutor Richards, she recounted her conversations with her tenant about how his family was and his intentions of possibly continuing to farm there. At one point, it seemed, she had seen through his evasiveness, for she stated that she had "looked at him sharply and asked him if he had been having trouble with his family."[67] She described how he had seemed taken by surprise by her pointed question and accusatory demeanor and that he "hesitated" before answering.[68] She remembered, he "didn't look me in the face for a little bit. He looked off—rather down—before he answered me. He made no reply, but he looked back and rather gave me the impression that he had (trouble with the family) … I won't say he quite said 'yes' … He was nervous at that time."[69]

Hamlin had clear memories of several other incidents that were germane to the case. She recalled his nervous behavior on the day of the auction, especially when he complained to her that the two boys who were hired to help him were just in the crowd chitchatting. At this point, she had "noticed he was upset and seemed to be very nervous. And at the time he told me that, I noticed that his eyes filled with tears."[70] She went on to recount how his scratches had been on display at her dinner table, and she repeated his unconvincing explanation as to where they had come from. He had seemed disturbed and fidgety, she said, especially when she had asked him how his wife would feel about him "selling all the stuff." This seemed to have caught him off guard as well, she said, but he recovered and told her: "Oh nothing; she told me to."[71]

D. O. Fayville, the owner of a drugstore in Texico, only testified for a few minutes, telling the jury about how Hassell had returned some medicine for a refund around the time of the auction. His testimony offered little else. The state rested its case.

***

A recess was called between noon and 1:30 p.m. on January 11. Following the break, witnesses called by the defense took the stand, beginning with Farwell School Superintendent F. M. Sawyer. The schoolteacher and superintendent was described as "qualified as an expert in psychology."[72] He remembered several of the Hassell children and was able to locate records that indicated that the first day of December 1926 was the last day David had attended school. This was crucial, because it gave credence to the probability that the family was slaughtered no later than December 2. Sawyer also stated that Hassell had returned his children's schoolbooks and given the explanation that they had left the state. This was the first time their paths crossed. Like all the other witnesses, Sawyer didn't notice "anything extraordinary in his demeanor that morning. He appeared normal and showed no signs of excitement."[73]

Additionally, Sawyer said that he had visited Hassell at the Hereford jail on January 9, intending to "make a study of him, sociological, psychological and physiological."[74] Hassell was quite cooperative, and they spent five hours discussing his history and background. Sawyer, unsurprisingly, found Hassell's philosophy on life "a bit peculiar."[75] Russell ended his questioning of Sawyer, asking him if he had any insight into Hassell that might explain his crimes. Sawyer said, "I could not tell."[76] On cross examination by the prosecutor, Richards, Sawyer was asked whether Hassell's actions were the actions of a sane man. The school superintendent asserted that he thought him sane, which was probably useful for the prosecuting lawyers trying to establish the defendant's sanity. Sawyer agreed with the state attorney's suggestion that "a man may commit so many crimes that he become inured or hardened and criminal acts do not react upon his conscience."[77] Sawyer's questions suggest that the defense was angling for an insanity plea. In his last comments, Sawyer said that he believed Hassell was "the type of man who could commit crimes and show no signs of emotion."[78]

With only a handful of remaining witnesses set to take the stand for the defense, Mrs. N. A. Lindop was called to testify next. Her testimony made many observers question the exact day of the murders, since she claimed that she had seen the children at the farm on December 4. This ran counter to the timeline established by the investigators, which was that the family, except for Alton, was slain no later than December 2. She claimed that her oldest boy had been with her in the car when they saw the family as they drove past their house. She thought she had seen Alton unharnessing a team of mules in the barn. However, it had already been established that Alton had not returned by December 4. Most probably, Mrs. Lindop had the dates confused, since it had been almost six weeks since this occurred.[79]

The next to be questioned was V. Tate, who helped conduct the auction on December 22. Hassell's attorney asked Tate whether Hassell had acted "like a man that killed nine people and had them buried there on the premises walking over their graves all the time, did he?" The best answer he could muster was: "I don't know as I could say that."[80]

Claude Benton, sheriff of Deaf Smith County, testified next to last. He said that he had gotten to know Hassell a bit while he was held in the Hereford jail at Muleshoe. Like the other witnesses, he thought Hassell acted as if he didn't have a care in the world. He had bragged to the sheriff about wearing "the next to the oldest boy's shoes ... he apparently thought that perfectly alright." And he said, "Well, about all the clothes ... he had none of his own clothes, except his underwear. He said the suit belonged to his dead brother."[81]

On cross-examination by Richards, Benton recalled that Hassell had told many stories about his exploits spanning a twenty-year period and had been talking about being married three times. He even went as far as talking about the offenses he was now charged with, even mentioning the interval between the killing of his eight family members and Alton.

The final witness was R. E. Maddux, who had a retail hardware business in Texico, New Mexico. There wasn't much for him to add. He mainly talked about his business dealings with the accused and suggested that when Hassell came into the store in the middle of December, "he seemed to be a little nervous at that time."[82] And with that, the trial testimony was over and all that remained was to issue a verdict and punishment.[83]

At 2:40 p.m., the state and defense both rested their cases. The attorney for the State of Texas, B. N. Richards, opened by presenting the facts of the case and the "high spots of the crime and maintaining that there was no defense of the man who committed the slayings." Hassell's attorney, W. H. Russell, followed Richards for the defense, doing his best to present his client as mentally ill, arguing emphatically to the jury "that only a man who was unbalanced in some way could have perpetrated the crime and sustain a perfectly calm manner and joking mood in the face of it." Throughout the short trial, it had been clear that the defense was laying the groundwork for an insanity plea, as Russell had repeatedly raised "questions as to Hassell's sanity."[84]

According to an interview with jury member Clyde Goodwine in the late 1980s, the defense counsel closed with a theatrical flourish. In Goodwine's telling, the defense attorney "burst into tears and left the courtroom" as the prosecution made its closing remarks. B. N. Richards offered a scathing indictment of Hassell, characterizing him as an "arch criminal who killed, not through an insane rage, but to protect himself against his crimes." Once Russell had composed himself and returned to the courtroom, "he made no plea on George's behalf" and was ready to hear sentence read.[85]

The case was finally submitted to the jury at 9:35 p.m.

Chapter 17

Verdict

"On his last earthly journey ..."

The Farwell courtroom emptied out. Hassell's fate now rested in the hands of the jury. No more grandstanding before the gathered witnesses and gawkers. No more demonstrating his expectorating skills at the cuspidor. Now it was just twelve men who stood between him and the electric chair. The jury was out for two and a half hours at the most, although many suspected that a guilty verdict had been reached much sooner[1]—and withheld until the overcrowded courtroom could be cleared out as "the late hour drew on."[2] Sometime in the 1980s, the last surviving juror, Clyde Goodwine, told an interviewer that, as he remembered it, the jury "reached their verdict in five minutes but waited a couple hours to tell the judge so the crowd around the courthouse [would] thin out."[3] When all was said and done, it took longer to select a jury (three days) than to hear the case (two days, including two night sessions). Hassell, along with his attorney, was brought back into open court to hear the sentence and the verdict imposed by the jury.

Hassell scanned the faces of the jurors as they filed back into the jury box, then took a quick glance at the audience returning to the courtroom for the verdict. This was his first chance to face the spectators, since he had been seated with his back to the audience throughout the trial. As Hassell waited to hear the verdict, "His face was set and ashen in color as if he sensed the fateful words."[4] Shortly after midnight January 12 (some say closer to 1:00 a.m.), foreman F. W. Reeve delivered the jury's decision: guilty of murder in the first count of the indictment, for the murder of Alton Hassell. The verdict was death in the electric chair at the state penitentiary in Huntsville on Friday, February 25, 1927, where "in a room arranged for that purpose," the defendant would be "executed by the warden of the State Pen at any time before the hour of sunrise ... causing to pass through the body a current of electricity of sufficient intensity to cause his death, and the application of such current through the body until he is dead."[5]

After the verdict, Hassell was asked by Judge Reese Tatum to stand up. The judge asked him "if he had anything to say why such sentence should not be pronounced against him," to which he responded with a brusque "no." According to one reporter, the judge then gave the defendant "one of the most serious upbraidings ever administered to a prisoner before the bar of justice."[6] The judge wasted few words in describing Hassell's horrific family annihilation but reserved his greatest loathing for Hassell's incestuous abuse of Maudie, telling the courtroom: "in my mind the most despicable was his alleged familiarity with his niece and stepdaughter, his own flesh and blood."[7]

A large crowd had gathered outside the courthouse over the past four days but had dispersed by that late hour, and only a few, including his stepdaughter Nora and Susie's aged parents, were present when the jury reported its verdict. One surviving jury member later remembered that "spectators in the courtroom were so pleased with the outcome they 'passed the hat' and raised $113 for the attorney, who was performing in an official duty and received no extra pay."[8]

A reporter asked Hassell after the verdict if he would make a statement, to which the Texas Bluebeard said, "I have nothing to say. I have perhaps talked too much already. But I am still not afraid to die." He kept his stoic countenance, and as he left the courtroom "took a long distance shot at the cuspidor and grinned."[9] Claiming to have begun the habit of chewing before he was six, he apparently could not resist one more chance to be the center of attention.[10] Once the punishment was announced as death, he was "hurriedly removed from the courtroom."[11]

Hassell would have more surprises in store for reporters in the days to come. Behind the scenes of the trial, other criminal investigations were being considered against Hassell. Authorities reopened an investigation into the death of his brother, whom Hassell had alleged was kicked to death by a mule. In addition, on December 27, he had confessed to slaying "a woman and her three children" in California several years earlier but refused to give names or location.[12] During his trial Hassell stated that he would not reveal the location of his first mass murder victims until he was in the electric chair. Of course, most figured that this was just Hassell mouthing off. No one in the United States, let alone the world, had heard of anyone murdering two of their *own* families. Hassell was returned to the Hale County Jail in Plainview to await a transfer date to the state penitentiary in Huntsville.[13]

Hassell, as usual, showed no emotion when the judge read the jury's verdict, and by the time the decision was announced, his attorney had already left the courthouse. As a result, no appeal was filed by the defense at that time. Little did anyone suspect that the appeals process would take up much of the following year.

***

By most measures, Hassell's background and the sentence accorded him conformed with other death penalty sentences handed down in Texas between 1923 and 1972. A majority of those convicted of murder were, like Hassell, "from a non-urban setting."[14] Moreover, their employment histories indicated that they tended to be "unskilled laborers with lengthy histories of job instability."[15] However, Hassell was a little older than the typical killer, who was usually less than thirty years old. Another distinction was that he was white. By contrast, most inhabitants of death row who eventually sat in the electric chair were Black. Many of these offenders, Black and white, were described as "functionally illiterate," with "marginal intelligence."[16]

Although Hassell did have a rap sheet dating back to his teens for embezzlement and, later, military desertion, he did not fit the mold of other death-sentenced murderers from the era. Almost two-thirds of the other killers were single or divorced at the time of their murders, but Hassell was married at the time he slaughtered his Farwell family. In addition, having served two years in prison for stealing from his employer, Hassell differed from other prisoners on death row, most of whom had no recorded convictions for property crimes prior to their first murders. Those that did had records that reflected their rural backgrounds and generally poor economic conditions: convictions for stealing cattle, turkey, hogs, or chickens.[17]

While it will never be fully understood why he committed his mass murders, there is enough evidence to categorize his actions by motive within the homicidal milieu. Approximately one-third of the death-sentenced killers in Texas between 1923 and 1972 were "subjectively labeled" as being the result of arguments predicated on issues of jealousy or lust. Of these, almost 90 percent were considered "passion homicides," which are often in the heat of the moment and involve "family members, friends, or acquaintances in arguments over debt, spite or jealousy."[18] So, while Hassell could never adequately explain his motivation for his murders, he does insinuate that the killing spree he began on December 2, 1926, revolved around arguments with his wife over issues regarding his sexual abuse of two of his stepdaughters/nieces. Moreover, he offered a secondary reason, which was that his wife had refused to have sexual relations with him once she found out Maudie was pregnant.[19]

Finally, like a majority of his fellow killers, Hassell committed his murders at home and knew his victims. But what separated him from his peers was his preference for strangulation and bludgeoning over the much more common use of guns.[20] What is more, while 75 percent of the murderers did not confess, Hassell did, and he never denied his crimes. Moreover, it seemed he took pride in discussing his heinous handiwork with anyone who would listen.

Hassell's itinerary from Farwell to Abilene and from there to Cameron is well documented. However, it remains unclear where else he might have stopped along the way to Huntsville and when exactly he arrived. It was about a two-and-a-half-day trip to Huntsville from Cameron by train. His first stop from Farwell on the way to Huntsville was the Taylor

County jail in Abilene. Built in 1896, the facility was described as a "three story rusticated stone lock-up with a central tower on Pecan Street."[21] On January 14, a physician dressed his knife wounds in preparation for his long trip to the Texas big house.

Hassell consumed a substantial breakfast, talking almost continually between bites whenever an audience was within range. On this occasion, he went on about his physical health, commenting, "I don't want you all to think I am boasting but I have never had a toothache, earache, or been sick a day in my life." He also couldn't resist adding, "I have a four-inch chest expansion."[22] It's unknown if anyone was impressed.

Late on Saturday night, January 15, Hassell once more recounted his life story, this time from his Abilene jail cell.[23] One reporter described stepping "on the run around that led to his dark cell," where he found the mass murderer in bed, "raised on his elbow."[24] After the prison keepers introduced the scribes to the killer, Hassell "complained he was too tired to talk."[25] However, all who had experienced a conversation with Hassell knew that he never tired of hearing his own voice and so, with little persuasion, "he began chatting of the day's incidents."[26]

Among the coterie of reporters that night was one from the *Abilene Morning News*, Edward E. Anderson (1905–1969). It is fortunate for posterity that this future novelist chronicled Hassell's three-hour soliloquy in his own lyrical prose. Best known for his only two novels, *Hungry Men* (1935) and *Thieves Like Us* (1937), he "left few tracks" in Abilene and "half a century had obliterated most of those."[27] While Anderson stayed active as a reporter, he spent most of his later life in obscurity. Anderson brought Hassell to life like no other journalist, and there was usually a scrum ready to jot down anything Hassell said. When he spotted Hassell for the first time in the Taylor County jail, he noted: "With features ghastly under the reflection of a moon that streamed its dim light through the steel bars of the prison cell, George Hassell, super-slayer and condemned by a man-made law to pay the supreme penalty, lay on a cot." It was from the Taylor County jail that Hassell would recount "the sordid pages of his life story."[28]

There were probably only two things Hassell liked as much as talking—eating, and abusing women. Once he had decided to tell his story to the reporters, he launched into complaints about his hunger, lamenting that the "officers had promised to feed him but had neglected it" since his arrival in Abilene earlier in the evening.[29] He suggested that they "bring him something and throw a cigar in with it." He apologized for "not raising from his bunk," and gladly accepted "a chew of tobacco." The nicotine seemed to energize him, and he began speaking in "sing-song fashion," which suggested to Edward Anderson, the reporter from Abilene, that Hassell "was accustomed to audiences." Hassell boasted of his ability once again to "out pray every man in Washita County, but one old brother who was longwinded." It is doubtful that the irascible storyteller saw the irony in this last comment.[30]

Anderson was struck by the way Hassell "spoke of God and religion; romances, gruesome killings and blasted ambitions and wasted opportunities" while at the same he "awed listeners in laughter nearly as often as horror."[31] Hassell chronicled his life from his first school days in Tarrant County to his murders in Farwell, hitting all of the highlights and lowlights of his roustabout past. He spoke of his travels and the failure of his first marriage. Once more he claimed that he had been in New Orleans and nowhere near the Oklahoma ranch when his brother was felled by a mule kick in 1924, and that he married his brother's widow and tried to step into his shoes and raise his large brood of youngsters. But like his previous versions of his story, he was never able, or perhaps willing, to explain why he killed, telling reporters, "I may be wrong up here," gesturing to his head, "but I don't know why I killed." with his fingers." The reporter Anderson described him "tapping his forehead" with a "gnarled, toil-worn hand."[32]

Hassell was somewhat aware of the dual nature of his personality. Just a year after the interview with Anderson, Hassell explained his quirks to another reporter, telling John L. McCarthy shortly before his execution, "The way I see it is that there is an old cell back up in my head here, now this may be a crude way of putting it, but you understand, I believe that old cell which directs a person to murder is dormant back in there and all of a sudden wakes up and gets into action and makes me kill."[33]

Within the confines of his prison cell in Abilene, Hassell told the reporter Anderson that "they [the justice system] get things wrong, sometimes," returning again to a "sing-song voice," he moved "steadily from one subject to another." Hassell laughed as he explained that he was particularly disappointed in the way he was portrayed at the trial, because "down at Farwell when the trial was going on one said I broke down and cried. That's a lie, I just blew my nose in a handkerchief."[34]

Anderson couldn't take his eyes off the man, diverted by "his glassy, steel grey eyes," which "never registered emotion," and the way his "hearty laugh echoed often through the murky county jail" as "other prisoners within hearing distance—mischievous boys in comparison with this man's criminal record—listened in awe."[35]

Hassell offered little that was new to the now oft-told saga of his life as newspapers throughout the country picked up the story. As Anderson described, he had an affinity for describing his wanderings as "globe-trotting," although there is no evidence that, except for a couple short stints at sea, he traveled outside the United States. He took pride in his wide-ranging job history, "everything from digging ditches, tending a furnace on an ocean steamer to pulling the throttle on a locomotive."[36]

With time remaining short, a reporter asked him, "what do you think of God?" According to Anderson, he took a chew of tobacco, and as if warning his audience, said "I could talk on that a long time, if you folks have much time." He delivered a short dissertation on the topic, explaining, "I don't believe in hell and this fire and brimstone stuff. I believe that men all will die and that there will be a resurrection. I believe I will live again and in the same world that men who have observed God's laws and lived a religious life shall live ... But the devil will work hard on me in the next world. He will not pay any attention to the fellow that lived straight here. I will be tempted and if I fail in the next world I will have to suffer." It is easy to imagine the assembled journalists, perhaps nodding their heads or raising their eyebrows as he rambled on. Anderson, the reporter, was convinced that Hassell's references to biblical scripture indicated "he has given it earnest study."[37]

As the interview concluded, Hassell once more returned to his pet peeve about jails, commenting, "Let me say one more thing. I can't say any more. If there is one thing that prisoners in Texas jails need it is more food."[38] He had little to say about his looming execution, but he would be damned if he was going to the chair without a full stomach. Sounding like a nascent prison reformer, Hassell declared that "when a man is in jail and is given only two meals a day and is forced to go hungry, it makes him envious of those on the outside. It makes him want to commit crime. I know because I have had that experience."[39] His hunger pangs would be a familiar refrain of Hassell's until his dying day.

As the handful of reporters filed out, one of them told him, "Hope you sleep well Hassell," to which he responded "flippantly" that he had "so far."[40] Anderson ended his version of the interview with the following, "And Hassell, the super-slayer, returned to his bunk 'to get some rest'" and "sleepily murmured, for tomorrow's ride to where they're going to push the button on me."[41]

On the morning of January 16, "smiling and apparently unperturbed over his fate," a "heavily manacled" George Jefferson Hassell was back on his trek to the state prison in Huntsville. Under heavy guard, officers from the sheriff's office in Farwell and lawmen from Muleshoe and Hereford "started the pilgrimage to the death chamber."[42] Included in the assemblage were Deputy Sheriff Sam Hoffman of Muleshoe, Deputy Sheriff Bill Massey from Farwell, and Sheriff J. H. Martin from Parmer County. They reached Cameron, the last stop before Huntsville, by nightfall on Sunday, January 16. Hassell was placed safely behind bars at the Milam County jail by Sheriff Blaylock. "In another dimly lit cell" once more, Hassell spoke freely of his life, "[keeping] up a running conversation" as he "joked with prisoners, boast[ing] that he would walk to his death to show them how a brave man can die, if you please to call it brave."[43]

This would be his last interview with reporters before reaching Huntsville in the next few days. Like his previously chronicled statements to the press, there were few revelations, mainly a recital of the best-known high points of his life, along with a seeming unwillingness to revisit the Farwell murders for which he was arrested. He met with a much smaller retinue of newspapermen this time, at least compared to Abilene the previous night. He seemed more subdued and "in bad humor," perhaps from the long trip to Abilene and the fact he was one step closer to Old Sparky in Huntsville. Although he swore a bit, "on the whole he was cheerful about his fate."

Once more he took the Fourth Estate to task for "some things they have printed." However, he "showed deep interest in the public mind," always asking for the latest newspaper accounts of his case "so he could read what they were saying about him."[44]

Of course, Hassell could not speak to the press without the family annihilator broaching the subjects of smoking and eating. In his bid for more smokes, he told the reporters, "I'll not tell you anything. You are just like other newspaper men. You smoke only cigarettes. Not one of them has yet given me a cigar. Come back after supper and bring some cigars and I will tell you something."[45]

When the newsmen returned from dinner, they found Hassell sitting on the cell floor with his shoes off. He told them, "Well, I've cooled down some," and thanked one of the reporters for some cigars. He quickly lit it and "continued to smoke one after another throughout the hour and a half in which he told much of his life," but still he resisted speaking about the murders. His meeting with reporters was only half as long as in Abilene. Perhaps he had at last grown tired of hearing his own voice, or maybe the jail officers decided to cut the press meeting short. One reporter, J. B. White, was struck by Hassell's "piercing blue eyes and light brown hair growing loosely over his head" as the prisoner recounted his colorful life, the crimes he committed (except for the murders), and the five years he had done in at least three different prisons for embezzlement, military desertion, and fraud.

Hassell promised, "I'll tell everything before the end," which was only forty-one days away. "Before they put me in the big chair, I'll make a complete statement," he said. Probably disappointing his latest audience, who were hoping Hassell might be more forthcoming before he left Cameron, he said that he "was going to tell the answers to all those questions you are asking me when the time comes. I don't want any misunderstanding."[46]

When he wasn't spouting off about food, cigars, and his conquest of women, Hassell could wax philosophical on occasion. The reporter J. B. White noted that "Hassell looks upon his fate with a buoyant philosophy, takes it as a matter of course and scoffs at the idea of being scared." The convicted killer expressed his take on his looming fate by commenting,

"Why, when I get in the big chair it will be all over ... You see I am not a bit nervous. They felt my pulse before the verdict and the sentence and afterward and there was no difference."[47]

While he loved to hold court, he especially loved to boast, trying to impress whoever was in the audience, perhaps to elevate his self-esteem. Whenever he was presented as being weak or empathetic, he took this as a challenge to his notions of manhood. Over and over again, he would assure his listeners that he was not afraid of death. When confronted with questions about his sentence and its omnipresence during his journey to death row, he would go on about how he "could lay down and sleep as sound as I ever could." In order to back this up, he evoked a false equivalency between his own impending death and his actions after the Farwell murders: "This may not sound human to you, but I slept for nearly 20 days while these bodies were there, and it didn't bother me."[48] His sitting in the electric chair would be another matter, however.

His final act of braggadocio focused on his suicide attempt, showing those assembled "an ugly scar on his left wrist" where he tried to slit an artery. He admitted to trying to kill himself and became so "engrossed with the story that he got to his knees" and theatrically demonstrated how he went about stabbing himself five times before he "cut away some flesh so I could get the knife inside. I tried to stick my heart but couldn't locate it." It is doubtful that Hassell noticed the humor so implicit in his last comment.[49]

Toward the end of the interview, he bragged once more that he had been married three times "and lived with seven women to whom I was not married. I lived in 27 states and Old Mexico part of the time." Hassell was once more asked if "he had ever made any profession of faith," to which he replied: "A long time ago my mother had a book, and that book had a picture in it that stayed with me. It was a picture of angels standing near the lake of fire, and some little children playing around. In the background was the devil. The angels were keeping the little children from falling in." Once more he commented that he didn't believe in hellfire and brimstone but admitted that the picture of the angels "worried me more than the big electric chair does. A fellow sometimes prays when he is in trouble, but he ought to think about that beforehand. As far as I am concerned now, I don't intend to ask God for any mercy. I believe I'll have another chance after this life." Then he launched back into his focus on food and cigars, concluding: "Anyway, they ought to feed a fellow good when he's in prison and he wouldn't be hungry. He could then spend some time thinking about those things. Well, I'm much obliged for the cigars."[50]

Hassell's trial and conviction "were among the speediest recorded in Texas courts." He was allowed to bid farewell to friends in the lock-up and was "hurriedly put on the early morning train which is carrying Hassell on his last earthly journey."[51] As he expected, he got his one-way ticket punched to the Huntsville death chamber. But there was at least one last saga still playing out. Since he admitted on December 27, 1926, to killing a woman and her three small children in California in 1917, investigators were still unable to come up with any names or even a location for the crime, but that was all about to change.

Chapter 18

It Was a Good Job

"The strangest of all Texas killers."

If Marie Vogel and her kids had still been alive in 1927, her only biological child, Gerald, would have been seventeen and her adopted kids, Anthony and Rita, on the cusp of being teenagers. But no one in Marie's family or anyone else had heard from them in more than a decade. Of course, Hassell had told Marie's mom she had gone off to Australia and the neighbors that she had either eloped with another fella or moved to San Francisco to help her sister. Back in the 1920s, it had been easy to disappear, either on purpose or by misadventure. But as the decade moved into its final years, one of its mysteries was about to be solved.

Just after Christmas 1926, Mrs. Gertrude Hoffman was sitting at home in Pittsburgh, reading the Sunday newspaper. Her focus was drawn to headlines pertaining to an axe murderer in Farwell, Texas. She did a double take when she saw a photo of George J. Hassell, the alleged perpetrator. The first likeness of him to reach the public pictured him working an oil pump in Kern County, California.[1] The more she studied the picture, the more it resembled the man she had known as "G. Baker." As discussed in chapter 3, Hoffman and her mother were introduced to "Baker" around 1916 when he was living with her sister, Marie Vogel, on a ranch near Whittier, California.

Sometime in June 1917, Marie Vogel and her three young children had disappeared from the cottage they shared with her common-law husband on 236 South Whittier Street. Although shortly after she returned to Pittsburgh from her visit to California, Marie's mother had received a note from Hassell alerting her that Marie had moved to Australia, the family had not heard from Marie since 1917. From the get-go, this seemed strange, but as time would tell, Marie was somewhat estranged from her family and had maintained less and less contact with its members over the decade prior to her vanishing.[2]

Gertrude Hoffman, Marie's sister, had written the Whittier, California police sporadically over the years, attempting to ascertain the whereabouts of her sister and the three children. As explained in chapter 3, not long after Marie was first reported missing, Whittier Constable R. B. ("Bob") Way received a letter from Pittsburgh asking him to search the property, but Way later noted that the "information was so meager ... no trace of her could be found." However, as recently as November 12, 1925, Whittier police had received another letter, which remained in its files, stating that Hoffman had not heard from her sister in over eleven years. But if she was certain of one thing, the letter continued, this photo of the so-called axe-slayer was the very same man Marie had been living with before she disappeared. She sent the police a copy of a family photo of Marie and Hassell with one of their children in order to help the search.[3]

Frustrated by the attempts of the Whittier authorities to search for her sister after she identified the photograph as Hassell, and once she realized he was in a Texas prison, she decided to contact the Texas authorities. In a letter to Walker County Sheriff L. L Leaward, she insisted that Hassell was actually the same person as G. Baker and was probably responsible for the disappearance of Marie and her three kids. When Hassell was apprised of this communication, he vehemently denied "all knowledge of Mrs. George Hoffman ... who in a letter to Texas officers said her sister disappeared from Whittier ten years ago."[4]

***

In general, Hassell remained tight-lipped about his purported Whittier slayings, but he offered the cryptic comment that "it was a good job."[5] He might have confessed to the four California murders, but many things still remained unclear. Did he really kill another family? If so, where did it take place? And most importantly, where were the bodies?[6] Initially, authorities were dubious about his claim. Of course, it didn't help that Hassell "could not remember the exact location of the house."[7] Officials contacted the Whittier constable's office to determine whether he had ever heard of George Hassell or of the unsolved murders of four people in the jurisdiction at that time. Constable Bob Way responded that in his twenty-six years as a peace officer in Whittier "there was never a report of a similar crime being committed or of four persons disappearing as described."[8]

The case became even more confusing when Hassell's niece and oldest stepchild, now Mrs. Nora Guidry, muddied the waters on Sunday, January 2, 1927, by informing authorities that as far as she knew, Hassell had never lived in Whittier but had resided in Santa Ana.[9] She explained that "for a while he had his mail sent to Whittier and then had it transferred to Santa Ana."[10] But authorities still had no idea where exactly the killings occurred.

To Parmer County Attorney J. D. Thomas, who played such an important role in bringing Hassell to justice for the Farwell familicide, it seemed that Hassell might never divulge the names of his Whittier victims, preferring to "carry that secret with him to the end, after partially relieving his conscience by recounting the details of his crime."[11] He thought he knew Hassell pretty well by 1927 and recognized that his client enjoyed having the upper hand with the authorities and was not one to provide information unless it bolstered his ego. Thomas claimed that after "hearing of this new twist," he contacted California authorities, who then made an "exhaustive search of their files of unsolved crimes, with special reference to those persons reported missing." Ultimately, Thomas's account does not quite match the actual sequence of events leading to the location of the Whittier burial pit. Soon the location was narrowed down to Whittier, near Los Angeles. Former neighbors recalled that a family living in a cabin at 236 South Whittier had "mysteriously disappeared" some years earlier and that the woman's surname was Vogel.[12]

Perhaps, Thomas's memory was already fading eight years after the Farwell trial, when he recalled that "immediately a crew was sent to excavate the ground under the floor of the house ... Then bit by bit, pieces of bones were dug up. When they had finished four skeletons had been recovered ... Hassell offered no comment when informed of the results of the search. He lapsed again into his dull stupor and took no interest in anything."[13]

In reality, while Thomas seemed to regard himself as an important source in locating the crime site, most of the credit to the discovery should go to Hassell's former neighbors and to Marie Vogel's sister, Gertrude Hoffman. The Parmer County attorney's account suggests that the bodies were quickly located and exhumed once they knew which house to look under, but it actually took several days and some help from the killer to finally bring the search to conclusion.

Hassell had confessed to the killing of four family members back on December 27, 1926, but the remains were not discovered until the beginning of February 1927, some six weeks later. In between, Hassell had gone to trial for the Farwell murders and was convicted and sentenced to death. Taking this into consideration, it is quite probable that Thomas, in his 1935 interview, claimed that he was much more involved in this part of the Hassell saga than he actually was. Likewise, his supposed observations of Hassell in his Huntsville prison cell may also have been based on secondhand information, since there are neither any reports of him being present when Hassell was informed that the case had been solved nor any record of him being in Huntsville at that time.

***

When Hassell first notified authorities that he had committed another mass murder in California in 1917, investigators searched Hassell's Farwell farmhouse for any evidence that might shed more light on his purported Whittier years. The closest they came to connecting him to California were some letters that indicated that around the time of the Whittier murders, he was indeed working for the Southern Pacific Railway in California, as well as the Associated Pipe Company in Fresno, and that he later worked as a chef in the Merchant Marine on the West Coast. This evidence of his proximity to Whittier was tantalizing, since it placed Hassell in California at the time when he claimed to have committed his first mass murder.

Until his arrest for the nine Farwell murders, his 1917 California familicide was neither a cold case nor even on police radar at all. For almost a decade, the bodies of his four victims had lain decaying under the small cottage in Whittier, California. No one knows why Hassell decided to come clean about these unknown murders when he did. Maybe he thought, "well they can only execute me once." More likely, it was another example of his extreme self-importance and his desire to up his body count. In any case, the first inkling of his Whittier familicide only became public once he signed a confession in Farwell in 1926, several days after the nine bodies of his Farwell family were uncovered.

Though he confessed to the 1917 murders, he remained mum on any other details pertaining to the killings beyond his admission that he had been living in Whittier and other California oil towns in 1915. However, when prison officials went to check out his story, they were unable to find any record of him living in California under his given name. Likewise, the local Whittier police were unaware of any missing family of four. So perhaps, it must have seemed, this was after all just another embellishment by the self-absorbed braggart, an attempt to increase his list of victims to garner even more notoriety.

In actuality, the authorities were correct in concluding that there were no records of a "George Hassell" in the Whittier area at the time in question. But this was easily explained once it become known that he lived under the pseudonym G. Baker then. Indeed, "it was the hunch of Mrs. Myrtle Lark of Huntington Beach that led to the location of the cottage where the bodies were buried."[14] As mentioned in chapter 3, she had been living next door to Hassell, Marie, and the three kids at the time of the murders. She remembered a family named Baker disappearing at that time. In fact, she was among the neighbors whose suspicions were aroused in the days following their disappearance. She was also the neighbor that first called Whittier Constable Bob Way to notify him of her suspicions. To his credit, as discussed in chapter 3, the constable did respond at the time, but only conducted a cursory examination of the premises and came up empty.

Fast-forwarding to ten years after the disappearance of the family, Lark's husband, like Mrs. Hoffman in Pittsburgh, saw the picture of George Hassell in a local newspaper in conjunction with his 1926 murders in the Texas Panhandle. The newspaper photo did not identify Hassell as "Baker," but to his former neighbor this Hassell fellow was unmistakably the same person. He showed his wife the picture from the newspaper, covering up the name under it, and asked her who it looked like. She immediately responded that it looked like Baker, "who lived next door and whom she suspected" of nefarious deeds all along.[15] Her husband informed her that it was undeniably the same man held in Texas for a familicide with chilling echoes of the events that had taken place next door all those years ago.

Feeling that her 1917 hunch had been confirmed, Myrtle Lark called the local Whittier authorities and once again had Constable Way on the phone, telling him to "get busy and dig under the house"—the same house, no doubt to Way's chagrin, that he had inspected too briefly ten years earlier. But first, she asked him what "he thought of the chances the Texas killer was the same man whom she reported to him years earlier." Way "scoffed at the idea."[16]

Once the search began in earnest, Myrtle Lark couldn't wait to share the news with her mother, Mrs. S. C. Shanker, who still lived next to the Hassell "death house."[17] Lark had lived with her mother in the house at the time of the family disappearance and wasted no time rushing over to tell her about recent developments.

The pieces of the Whittier puzzle began to fit together soon after Hassell arrived in Huntsville to serve his sentence for the murder of his nephew. Initially reluctant to give any more information beyond the fact he killed a woman and her three children in Whittier, California, in 1917, the only tidbit he offered to authorities was that he had strangled the baby boy with a stocking. According to the Huntsville warden, when Hassell mentioned this, it was the first time they saw him show signs of emotion; reportedly, he teared up when he mentioned that his victim "reminded him of his own little son by his first wife." The warden reported that the only other time he noticed any emotions from the mass murderer was when he exhibited "an evident excitement when asked to describe the murders."[18]

Since authorities were unable to find the location of his purported murders almost a decade earlier, Hassell became intent on leading them to the bodies, lest they suspect it was just another of his fabricated stories. Among Hassell's many gripes was the notion that someone thought he might be playing loose with the truth. He never denied he was a murderer and in fact rather relished his sinister celebrity, but he took umbrage with anyone who suggested that he was also a liar or that he was low enough to allow someone else to be charged for his crimes.[19]

Once the house was located, the digging began. There was only room for one man at a time to get into the space that supposedly held the bodies, so the spade work was done in relays. Diggers had to crawl in on all fours to start the recovery operation that began on Monday, January 31. The excavation team consisted of Constable Way, Police Chief Easley, Officer Ackles, and Motorcycle Officer Vandemark. But by the time "darkness intervened," they had only established that some of the earth beneath the purported location of the bodies had been disturbed.[20]

One explanation for their initial lack of success was the fact that they concentrated their search on a concrete basement under the rear of the house. However, Hassell was unaware that since he had lived in the house a cement cellar had been added beneath it. The officers began digging from this location in order to get to the spot where the Texas slayer said he buried the bodies four feet underground.[21] Unsurprisingly, their first efforts "were to no avail."[22]

Officers told reporters that the work was "of a difficult nature, the clay being hard, and the earth settled by concussion of heavy traffic."[23] That Monday night, Constable Way wired Texas authorities for more specific directions to aid the search. Walker County Sheriff L. L. Leaward told Hassell that the searchers needed more "explicit instructions."[24] During his Farwell trial the previous month, he had stated that he would not reveal the location of the bodies until he was in the electric chair.[25] But now, just weeks away from his scheduled execution date on February 25, he had a change of heart and agreed to draw a diagram to send from his cell on death row. He told the sheriff, "I want that cleared before I swing," although the operative term here should have been "fried."

He might not have remembered the precise address in Whittier, but he was able to provide descriptions of three houses in Whittier and declared his cottage was the middle one.[26] Hassell's rough illustration of the location of the house also indicated the names of his neighbors on either side of the house. The crude map showed the "scuttle hole through which he claimed to have crawled to dig the grave." Prominent in the sketch, which was published in the *Los Angeles Times*, were the names of his neighbors, "Shanker" on one side of his house and "Smith" on the other. In between the two houses he marked his house with the name of the owner of the cottage. Constable Way, Police Chief Essley, and other investigating officers checked carefully using the information supplied by Hassell and located the house where he had lived under the pseudonym G. G. Baker in 1917.[27]

Hassell's instructions indicated he had gone through the "trapdoor in the rear porch and tunneled beneath the foundation to reach the other side of the house," taking three days and nights to bury his four victims.[28] Hassell instructed the diggers, who got back to work at 8:00 a.m. the following morning, to "start digging at a point about five feet toward the front of the house from where the basement portion left off and about six feet to left of center of house."[29] From there, he instructed them to "go three feet straight from a scuttle hole. Turn to left, go halfway between scuttle hole and outside wall." The diggers wisely dug a trench "a little to one side in order not to disturb bodies." Soon enough, "soft earth told them they were on the right track."[30] During the two days of digging, "crowds of neighbors who gathered around the diggers corroborated many details given by Hassell regarding the 'Baker' family that lived there in 1917."[31]

Constable Way dug through the hard clay for several hours before uncovering an adult thigh bone. The removal of just a few more spades of dirt revealed the rest of the bones of the four victims, which corresponded with the descriptions given to the police by their killer. Officers identified a woman, an eight-year-old boy, a five-year-old girl, and an infant in short order.

At about 7:00 p.m., the remains were taken out by the coroner. The victims had been placed face down, with "two stockings and a piece of rope tied in square knots around the necks of each victim."[32] The coroner determined that

Hassell had either choked his victims to death or "used a rope to drag their bodies under the floor of the house."[33] His analysis was based on his observations that fragments of knotted rope were still intact, bound around the necks of three of the victims.

As the investigation proceeded, several initial claims were contradicted. It was originally reported incorrectly that the bodies had been dismembered and the skulls had been crushed. This misinformation was dispelled when the bodies were found intact. One rumor had the children being "thrown in first" and the mother buried on top.[34] However, this was proven inaccurate, with Marie buried first and the children above her.[35] The fourth victim, the smallest child on top, was distinctive for having "a bit of rotten cloth ... adhering to the neck."[36] The boy's skull was "wrapped in a heavy cloth, indicating he had been smothered and strangled."[37]

The skeletal remains were found under the dining room floor, "piled on one another with" the bones of Marie, the mother, on the bottom. The officers of the law began assembling the pile of bones in preparation for the coroner's inquest. Further examination of the crawl space indicated that Hassell had crawled fifteen feet to a point under the dining room five feet deep.[38]

Sitting in his death-house cell in Huntsville, Texas, the convicted killer heard that the bodies had been found the previous day. He told the warden, N. L. Speer, that he was "pleased that they have found the bodies, so they wouldn't think I was lying."[39] Moreover, he emphasized that he had told the unvarnished truth "about everything that has happened in my whole life."

***

Los Angeles Homicide Captain William J. Bright[40] ordered a report submitted by Deputy Sheriffs Allen and Arnstein chronicling the Whittier case from the first time a neighbor reported to Constable Bob Way her suspicions of Hassell's actions "until at the behest of the neighbor" Way ordered the preliminary search of the basement. Allen and Arnstein also made a report to the chief of the constabulary, W. T. Osterholt, "touching on the handling of the entire case by Way."[41]

A correspondent from the United Press was allowed to visit Hassell, who he described as "the strangest of all Texas killers,"[42] shortly after the

Whittier murders were confirmed. During his interview, Hassell gave "his only detailed account of the killing of his common-law wife and their three foster children."[43] The reporter was caught off guard by his demeanor and noted an entire absence of any regret or sorrow, writing, "A vulgar jest where there might have been an expression of remorse, a smirk where there might have been a tear, he talked for two hours of his wholesale slaughters, his impulses rather than motives for his crimes, his roustabout life that has blunted any fine sensibilities he might have had." Hassell was almost boastful, displaying not a shred of conscience as he told the correspondent how he had choked the three babies and "buried them under the floor of the house before their bodies were cold." As Hassell bid the reporter farewell, he gestured to the adjoining death room, where the reporter was heading to inspect the electric chair, telling him laughingly, "If you see any spooks in there tell them I'll soon be with them." The reporter was mystified by the strange murderer, writing, "Death holds no fear for this man who has dealt it to two women and eleven children."[44]

Hassell enjoyed talking freely about his murders whenever he had an audience: "To the amusement of condemned prisoners in adjoining cells he described obscenities with a housekeeper in the very house that hid the grave of his murdered victims."[45] He was quick to ascribe his murderous urges to two events that had purportedly "[warped] his character." He blamed it on his two years' incarceration in Texas as a teenager for embezzlement charges and on his estrangement from his first wife, thanks to the intervention of her parents—his usual go-to excuses.

Hassell confessed to choking and clubbing to death his common-law wife, Marie Vogel, before killing the sleeping children while living under the alias G. Baker. If he was to be believed, he claimed it had all begun over an argument over whether he should join the army, shortly after the United States entered the First World War. What was indisputable was that he had buried the victims under the house shortly after the killings and continued living in the house afterwards, much like he did with his Farwell victims.[46]

He would always claim that neither of his familicides were premeditated.[47] However, this doesn't jibe with his actions: having dugouts prepared to hold the bodies in the days and weeks preceding each of the mass murders. Hassell said that in Whittier he had dug the hole two weeks before the murders to please his wife (as he referred to Marie Vogel). He claimed that she had received spiritualistic visions of a treasure buried in the very spot where the bodies were later found. One reporter noted, "She little dreamed her own body would constitute the only 'treasure' the hole was to disclose."[48] Similarly, the purpose of the pit he dug on the Texas farm two months before his second family annihilation, Hassell had explained, was to provide his family a storm shelter.[49]

Hassell's behavior since his arrest indicated that he seemed to enjoy hinting that he might have had even more victims than the thirteen already attributed to him.[50] Meanwhile, in Whittier, the head of the homicide unit "placed little credence in reports to the effect that Hassell may have murdered other women who kept house for him." His reasoning was understandable: "In the first place the chances that if he killed anyone else, he would have told of it when he confessed to this murder [in Whittier]."[51] Moreover, the officer continued, "there is no reason why he should hold it back, he is going to hang anyhow. And in the second place the basement of the house has been so thoroughly dug up that there is little possibility of any other bodies being buried there."[52]

In order to determine the final disposition of the remains, a wire was dispatched to Marie's sister, Mrs. Gertrude Hoffman, after it was established that she was next of kin. That night, the bodies were transported to the coroner's morgue, where they would be held pending investigations of Hassell's confessions. A coroner's inquest was scheduled for the following day, but the coroner ended up deciding it would not be necessary and notified reporters that the undertaking firm of White & Emerson at Whittier had taken charge of the remains.[53]

Chapter 19

Appeals and Reprieve

"Do what you can, the time is growing short."

❝❝ Once a fixture in American society,"[1] public executions on the square were designed for maximum deterrence value. It was not uncommon for parents to bring their children, hoping that, before it was too late, they might benefit from the "awful and effecting demonstration of the dangers of sin."[2] In an era with little entertainment outside the home, particularly in rural areas, crowds flocked to these events, sometimes in the thousands. In the more than one hundred years following the American Revolution, hanging predominated as the only state sanctioned form of capital punishment in America.[3] But a sea change was on the horizon as the country entered a new industrial era.

Between the late 1870s and early 1880s, hanging became increasingly vilified as a method of execution.[4] According to death penalty historian Austin Sarat, as newspapers lavished more attention on sensational and gruesome executions, reportage highlighted "one unavoidable truth about hangings: a huge percentage of them were botched."[5] When one occurred, it was widely publicized.[6] No hanging earned more opprobrium than the bungled execution of "Black Jack" Tom Ketchum on April 26, 1901, in New Mexico. In this incident, the rope severed his head and the body fell "doubled over, and horrified spectators watched blood spurt intermittently."[7] Photos of the beheaded corpse under the gallows were widely disseminated, further exposing the brutality of this mode of execution.[8]

Since the era of the Texas Republic, hangings had been the purview of county sheriffs.[9] During those years their death-dealing tool was "a well-oiled length of pliable five strand manila rope approximately [three-quarters] to [seven-eighths] of an inch in diameter employed for almost instant death by Hangman's fracture."[10] By most accounts, the correct protocol was to locate the knot "high up under the left jaw,"[11] where it could produce a violent snapping back of the chin when the malefactor was released through the gallows trap door. If done correctly, it resulted in rupturing the spinal cord, which prevents oxygen from reaching the brain, causing instant paralysis in the rest of the body.[12]

At the time of the Hassell murder case, capital offenses in Texas included robbery, rape, and murder.[13] After witnessing a particularly appalling public hanging in 1922, John William "J. W." Thomas Sr. (1884–1971) purportedly decided to run for the Texas Senate as a Democrat out of Bell County. Central to his platform was the replacement of hanging with electrocution as well as centralizing all executions at the Texas State Penitentiary in Huntsville. During the 2nd Called Session of the 38th Legislature in June 1923, he introduced a bill that would replace hanging with electrocution. Once the bill was passed, the three-member Board of Prison Commissioners issued instructions to immediately start preparing the Huntsville Walls Unit for the centralization of the Texas death penalty.[14]

Legal public hangings had been the mainstay of capital punishment in Texas until they were officially replaced by the electric chair in 1923.[15] Of the state's 254 counties, according to West Gilbreath, a historian of hanging, executions were only performed in 122 of them.[16] Some were reconfigured to other uses.[17] The scaffold at Travis County Jail, one of the better-known gallows in Texas, for example, was converted into a "sleeping porch" for prisoners.[18] But according to one Texas reporter, "the prisoners held by some perverse fascination were loath to see the Travis County Jail gallows done away with and so obtained permission to use it for sleeping quarters." Once permission was given, the convicts who wanted to sleep on the gallows "arranged their bedding pallets in the square above the trap door, avoiding with respectful circumspection the trap of the gallows" in order to avoid "desecrating this spot."[19]

Lynchings occurred regularly in the Jim Crow period.[20] In 1922, the year before hanging was abolished as a state-sanctioned form of capital punishment, there were at least sixteen in Texas. In May alone that year, "white Texans carried out at least 10 lynchings, more than any other state but Georgia for the entire year."[21]

In 1923, Governor Pat Neff was so enraged by Texas lynchings he proposed a new method of execution: electrocution. Along with this new form of capital punishment, Neff ordered the centralization of executions, which would be carried out only in Huntsville. Previously, capital offenders in Texas had been executed in the county of conviction, under the supervision of the local sheriff.[22] As one Texas prison historian put it, "Progressives hoped that by sequestering such events at the Walls, they would discourage mob sentiment and encourage reverence for the 'majesty of the law.'"[23]

Between 1924 and 1927, with "delocalization" of executions, Texas went from having the greatest number of lynchings in the nation to having none.[24] The centralization (or delocalization) of executions began in Vermont and Maine after the Civil War, when several states mandated that executions be carried out under state authority in one specific location. But by the 1950s, there were still states, such as Delaware and Montana, that continued to conduct executions under local authority. Once Texas made the transition to the new execution regime, "Neff wasted little time in authorizing its use," and five Black men convicted of murders were electrocuted on February 8, 1924."[25] Between 1924 and 1964, men, mostly men of color, were put to death using this method.

***

The adoption of electrocution in America followed in the wake of a decade-long "battle of the currents" between the inventors Thomas A. Edison and George Westinghouse Jr. Their competition was over whose type of electrical current would be utilized in homes and businesses.

As one popular history of executions pointed out, each current had its advocates and "each group fought tooth and nail, determined to drive [the other] out of the marketplace."[26]

Edison developed the first electric power in 1882.[27] He spent a fortune on its development and marketing, certain the future of electricity would be dominated by his invention, direct current (DC). Meanwhile, Westinghouse countered Edison's invention with his own: alternating current (AC). AC seemed to offer more advantages. Operating at a higher voltage that could be transmitted at a cheaper price over longer distances, it was the most economical of the two.[28] Despite his crusade to light up America, Edison would never be able to overcome the benefits of the competing current. Never one to give up easily, Edison devised a plan to win the battle.

Initially, Edison sought to discredit AC, going as far as to attempting to have it banned, because it was so dangerous. The inventor made a great show of demonstrating AC current's dangerous capacity by using it publicly in various cities to electrocute a range of animals, including an elephant. Ultimately, his strategy was "short-circuited," so to speak, when his campaign had the unintended consequence of convincing New York to adopt AC current in homes and businesses.

Thirty-eight years before Texas adopted the electric chair, a movement began in New York to adopt electrocution as a more humane form of capital punishment, when the newly inaugurated New York governor, Davis Bennett-Hill, called for the creation of a commission to explore more modern methods of execution. As a result, the Gerry Commission was inaugurated in 1888. Electrocution was selected as the new method of execution. Dr. Alfred Southwick, a prominent dentist in the Buffalo area, recommended the technique after hearing about the death of a local citizen who was killed by accidental contact with the brushes on an electric generator, making him "one of the first deaths associated with electricity."[29] The Gerry Commission offered several other recommendations, some of which would be adopted in other states, including taking executions out of the hands of county sheriffs and centralizing them at three state prisons (Auburn, Sing Sing, and Clinton).

Once death by electricity had been approved in New York, no one was quite sure what the new technique should be called. Although AC was selected as the state's current, as the inventor of electricity, Edison hoped he could dub it "electromort," "dynamort," or "electrocide." Others suggested "electrolethe," "electronirvano," electrorevoir," "electrosiesta," and "*vimort*" (Latin for "man and death").[30] Some Ivy League scholars offered a litany of choices that were described as "etymologically impeccable but thoroughly impracticable words," running the gamut from "electrophony," "electricize," "joltacuss," "galvanation," "superelectrication," and so forth. At first, "electricide" had a number of proponents, following in the pattern of making other forms of unnatural death, such as suicide and parricide. But in the end, the term "electrocution" won the day.[31] On January 1, 1889, the New York Electric Execution Act took effect.

In 1890 at Sing Sing Prison, the Buffalo axe-murderer William Kemmler became the first American to die in the chair. Its introduction as a method of execution in America was supposed to begin a new phase in the country's continuing quest for a more civilized means of execution. As for Kemmler, shortly before sitting in the chair he had appealed his sentence to the US Supreme Court, citing the Eighth Amendment protection against cruel and unusual punishment.[32] The Court responded, "we think that the evidence is clearly in favor of the conclusion that it is within easy reach of electrical science at this day to so generate and apply to the person of the convict a current of electricity ... to produce instantaneous, and therefore painless death."[33]

Death in the chair was, theoretically, instantaneous. However, the reality of electrocution was another matter. In the axe murderer's case, after a seventeen-second surge of current, the attending physician approached the chair. He observed the body and face and, convinced Kemmler was dead, told the switchboard room to cut the current. The head electrode was removed, and the other doctors gathered around also assumed Kemmler was dead, pressing fingers against his face and "noting the play of white and red when the fingers were removed."[34] One doctor, however, noticed that a cut on Kemmler's hand was dripping "rhythmic pulses of blood," as one of the onlookers yelled out, "Great God! He is alive." Kemmler's chest suddenly began heaving and "from his mouth came a rasping sound, growing quicker and harsher with each suck of breath. A purplish foam from his lips splattered onto the leather mask ... he groaned an animal cry." Someone shouted to turn the current back on while another roughly placed the electrode back on his head. The electricity had been off for over two minutes. Once current started flowing again, Kemmler's muscles contracted, "his body rising up, rigid as a statue."[35] Nothing would be left to chance this time and the current was left on for a full two minutes. In the confusion of the moment it seemed no one remembered to keep track of time. By the time the current was shut off, one of the electrode sponges had "dried out and burned away, allowing the bare metal disc to press sizzling against Kemmler's skin." Meanwhile, "the stench of burning hair and flesh filled the room" and "the smell of urine and feces mingled with the acrid smoke in the air."[36] Onlookers were horrified; some were crying, and one even vomited. It would seem that Kemmler had been prescient in his plea for protection against cruel and unusual punishment.

Once the execution was finished, witnesses couldn't leave the prison fast enough. Barred from covering the electrocution, reporters descended on the eyewitnesses for testimony like a plague of locusts. They interviewed anyone who could be persuaded to talk, most of whom clearly expressed their revulsion. One doctor told reporters that he "would rather see ten hangings."[37]

The day after Kemmler's execution, the *New York Times* reported that one of the electricians responsible for handling the apparatus had headed straight for the Western Union office across the street, where he dispatched a telegram to the Westinghouse office informing them that the "Execution was an awful botch ... Kemmler was literally roasted to death."[38] Following this first usage of electrocution, one New York attorney suggested that being "westinghoused" would be a more appropriate verb for describing the process.[39]

Reporters who queried Westinghouse about the execution debacle found him unwilling to say much beyond referring to it as "a brutal affair" that could have been "done better with an axe."[40] In the days after the first electrocution, newspapers offered every grisly detail of the Kemmler execution, and the *New York Times* reported on its front page that it was "Far Worse Than Hanging."[41] It would be a year later, on July 7, 1891, before it was used again in New York, when four convicts went to the chair at Sing Sing.[42]

After Kemmler's execution, other states soon adopted electrocution as well, including Ohio (1897), Massachusetts (1901), Kentucky and New Jersey (1907), Virginia (1908), Tennessee (1909), North Carolina (1910), South Carolina (1912), Arkansas (1913), and Pennsylvania (1915). By the end of the 1920s, over half the death penalty states utilized the electric chair. It's worth noting here that in 1924 Nevada's pursuit of a more humane form of execution led to the introduction of lethal gas (hydrocyanic acid), arguing that it was more humane than the firing squad, the electric chair, or hanging.[43] But it never gained the same acceptance as electrocution. Between 1924 and 1934, Nevada was the only state to use it. Eventually, eleven western and southern states began using some version of the gas chamber (eight of these had not yet adopted the electric chair). It was the potential for death or injury among those participating in the execution protocol that kept most states from adopting lethal gas.

***

The Texas Electrocution Bill in 1923 specified a number of provisions, including a limit on the number of relatives or friends that could be present (no more than five), a specific time of execution (after midnight and before sunrise), and a prohibition against any inmate attending the execution.[44] Five thousand dollars in legislative appropriations were directed toward the construction at Hunstville of the electric chair and a death row that contained nine single cells and a shower, giving convicts a separate prison unit in which to await their executions.

The work of erecting a death house and installing an electric chair at Huntsville's Walls unit began in June 1923. Prior to purchasing the equipment for the electric chair, several experts traveled from Texas to the Oklahoma Penitentiary: Prison Commissioner H. Walker Sayle, Warden R. F. Coleman, and the prison system's master mechanic (in charge of all mechanical and electrical systems) and a consulting mechanical engineer for the state, Robert T. Storm.[45] The purpose of their visit was to witness the execution of two men on January 13, 1924, and "acquaint themselves with the electrical method of execution."[46] Before they returned to Texas, they also visited Arkansas, where there was another penitentiary already using the chair, for further research.[47]

Before joining the prison system on June 10, 1920, the Louisiana-born master mechanic Bob Storm had served in the Army after being mentored in technical skills by his father, who was a mechanical engineer by profession. He began working at the Huntsville Walls Unit for $200 a month in 1920 and resigned in November 1923 to work in the petrochemical industry along the Gulf Coast.[48] Before leaving Huntsville, he played a major role in the researching and building of the state's first electric chair.

Storm was especially taken with the electric chair in the state penitentiary at McAlester, Oklahoma. It had been designed and installed by the governor of Oklahoma, J. C. Walton, who was a professional engineer (though Walton banned execution, including by electrocution, while serving as governor).[49] Storm would later claim that Walton's plans "embodied the Texas death house and electric chair in the best and most modern features obtainable," and that he believed that Storm had "succeeded in improving the electric chair in a way those condemned to die may be disposed of in a humane manner."[50] He made it clear, probably referring to the Kemmler execution, that he had "given much thought to the elimination of the burning of the body after the subject has been strapped in the chair and the current turned on." When Storm retired, he was replaced by N. L. Boudreaux, who was tasked with electrifying the chair that Storm built. But before he took the job, Boudreaux told officials "he would keep it in good repair but would not participate in electrocutions."[51]

Some early visitors to the new death house, who were mainly reporters, found its interior "not unpleasing."[52] As if describing a scene out of a *Good Housekeeping* testimonial, a reporter noted it was "well ventilated and light and quiet in line and color."[53] Local reporter Don Reid, who witnessed 189 Texas electrocutions, wrote in his memoir that death row was "not physically, an unpleasant place to live," describing its "airy cells, each five by ten feet, each with its own cot, toilet, water basin, and table."[54] One reporter, noting the conditions of death row, observed, "Bathing facilities have been provided and nothing left undone for the comfort of the prisoners."[55] By the time the death house was fully operational, as Reid described, it would contain "the chair, the whining generators, the condemned men, their keepers, their cells, their coffee pot, the shower stall, the barber's chair" all "enclosed in a small, one story red brick building with green doors in the courtyard of the Huntsville Unit." But the row of nine cells extending across the south end of the room to the death chamber made "the grim purpose of the place" impossible to ignore.[56]

The construction of the original electric chair did not go as smoothly as planned. It was supposed to be ready by October 10, 1923, but as that day came and went, S. J. Dean, a member of the state prison commission in Austin, was forced to concede that the chair was not yet ready, though he noted that contractors promised to have it ready by November 1.[57] The date change necessitated a week's reprieve for several men slated to be the first to be electrocuted. When asked to explain what was taking so long, Dean told reporters that the prison commission had completed the chair and death cells and done "everything it could do except installing the electric apparatus; that the contractors had made several promises but have not placed the equipment yet."[58]

Handcrafted by inmates, the oak chair dubbed "Old Sparky" and the "Thunderbolt" was affixed to the concrete floor of the death house on December 1, 1923. Texas prison historian Gary Brown called the new Texas electric chair "the most famous piece of furniture ever produced by the legions of convict craftsmen over the past century and a half ."[59] Reid later described the chair as being made of "solid oak, high backed, sturdy, held together by wooden pegs and festooned with wires and leather straps and electrodes."[60]

The adoption of the Texas electric chair met with opposition. On January 1, 1924, Captain R. F. Coleman, Huntsville prison warden and "legislatively designated executioner," turned in his letter of resignation, effective two weeks later on January 15, 1924, the day before the first scheduled execution on January 16, 1924.[61] Coleman had worked in prisons since 1888.[62] He explained his decision to reporters, lamenting, "It just couldn't be done boys. A Warden can't be a warden and a killer too. The penitentiary is a place to reform a man, not kill him."[63] Coleman was "considered one of the best criminologists in the Southwest."[64] He told one newspaper reporter that it would cause him "indescribable suffering to act as executioner and that he would lose the respect and confidence of prisoners under his care."[65] He had prepared for the next steps in his life by purchasing Huntsville's Lindley Hotel and making the transition from warden to hotelier.[66] Over the years the Lindley Hotel at 13th Street and Avenue K would host families visiting inmates on death row and became a popular stop for luminaries passing through town.[67]

Coleman's replacement, Walter Monroe Miller, on the other hand, experienced no reluctance against executing prisoners in Huntsville. A former sheriff of Johnson County south of Fort Worth, he was appointed warden February 4, 1924, and was "dismissed just eight months later."[68] Upon stepping into the warden's shoes, Miller told reporters, "It's a case of duty to me." He went on to explain his familiarity with carrying out the death penalty, commenting, "I have hanged several men while I was Sheriff and to touch the button or pull the switch on an electric chair means no more to me than pulling the levers of the gallows ... At any rate it's more humane—the chair." Just four days after taking over, he directed the execution of five Black men from rural East Texas, one after the other, in what one reporter dubbed a "harvest of death."[69]

In the month before the first electrocutions, Governor Pat Neff visited the five condemned men "who he would soon send to their deaths."[70] Neff served two terms as governor (1921–1925) and earned a reputation for opposing most executive pardons or clemency for inmates.[71] He later recounted his experience of visiting the death house in his role as governor: "A queer feeling creeps over you as you pass the death cell and pause. They knew and I realized that I held in my hand the power to save them from the electric chair."[72] Despite this epiphany, he refused to intervene.

According to Bob Storm, the master mechanic who had helped design the chair, it would take less than a minute to prepare the subject for the first dose of current, once placed in the chair.[73] It was now time for the assistant warden, N .L. Speer (1884–1937), to inaugurate the Texas electric chair. Speer had begun working at the Eastham Prison Farm in 1907 and after several years was promoted to dog sergeant, which meant he was in charge of the prison bloodhounds. By 1917, he was assistant warden at the Eastham farm and shortly after that was elevated to manager of the Ferguson farm unit. Following several other promotions, he was made assistant warden and then warden of the Huntsville Penitentiary.[74] Speer led each condemned inmate to the chair. Charles Reynolds, twenty-seven, was the first of the five men, ages twenty through thirty-nine, who were executed in quick succession on the "hot squat" between 12:09 p.m. and 2:00 a.m. on February 8.[75] According to a detailed account of the death house and the electric chair in the July 21, 1923, edition of the *Houston Chronicle*, once seated prior to the electrocution, his "head and left leg, just below the knee, have been closely shaved. His ankles, wrists, biceps of his arm, waist and chest are strapped to the chair with two and one-half inch straps."[76] An electrode is attached to his shaved left leg, and a helmet "covering the entire skull to the base" is placed over his head. The instruments "are made of heavy copper wire and lined with fine sponge which is saturated with salt water just before being used. Each has one terminal connection. A stout leather hood fastened to the back of the chair keeps the head firmly in position. The death mask is then placed over the face of the prisoner."[77] According to protocol, the executioner stood "immediately in front of two levers and at a signal from the electrician throws on the first or 'oil switch,' which runs the current up to 1600 volts. The second switch increases through rheostat to 2200 volts, sufficient to cause instant death."[78]

***

Following in the footsteps of Governor Neff, Governor Ma Ferguson visited the death chamber on April 21, 1926.[79] She wasn't shy about wanting to see the electric chair as soon as she got into the death house. To her credit, she spared the lives of six condemned men, although this did not quite balance with her letting eleven men die. She made a point of shaking the hands of all the prisoners she met and also meeting with the six men to whom she granted clemency (two of whom were white, four Black), who expressed their gratitude. Mrs. Ferguson went on to inspect the warden's quarters and visited the wagonmakers and foundrymen, as well as the mess halls and kitchens. She also took a tour through the flower gardens inside the walls, all the time passing out cigarettes and magazines to inmates. As the sun went down she became the first sitting governor to sit down and eat with the inmates. Ferguson also made sure she visited the convicts due to be executed the following month. She could see them reading bibles in their cells. Before she left, "they knelt at her feet and kissed her hand." The governor remarked that "she did not sleep the first night of an execution during her administration."[80]

***

From the moment he was sentenced to die in the electric chair, Hassell had managed to keep up the pretense of "cool indifference" to his fate. But as the day of his execution approached, "the condemned murderer [began] sending out last minute pleas for his life." Jailers couldn't help but notice him frantically writing letters to his attorney, William H. Russell, imploring him to "take immediate steps" towards requesting a new trial and a stay of execution.[81]

Upon his arrival at the Texas pen, Hassell was ushered in through the north gateway, where all condemned prisoners entered the prison, and taken across the yard to the death house. There, according to one Abilene reporter, a guard would unlock a "steel barred door and signal[ed] an inner guard" to open a second door from the inside. Prison officials considered escape impossible since one could not leave the building without guards on both sides of the doors responding to the required signals. Likewise, it was "equally impossible for a mob to gain admission by force."[82]

Once imprisoned "behind the weather beaten gray walls of the Texas state penitentiary,"[83] Hassell acquainted himself with his death row cell. The cells, according to a *Houston Chronicle* reporter, "were constructed of brick and steel bars, reinforced with copper screen wire to prevent passing any articles through the bars."[84] Each cell was eight feet by ten feet with a ten-foot-high ceiling and offered light and ventilation as well as a lavatory and a toilet.[85] The article went on to say that "on the floor is a heavy rug and other furnishings, including a bed, table and chair, and electric light with a reflector on an independent switch" in front of each cell, "affording all night light if the prisoner so desires without disturbing inmates in other cells."[86]

Hassell joined two other men on death row. Observers were struck by his demeanor, "as cool and calm as if he was sitting in his home," and how it contrasted with the other two who were "considerably more nervous."

Hassell "crouched back in a remote corner of their little eight by twelve [actually, ten] kingdom ... three souls condemned to die in the electric chair are restlessly waiting for the day they shall make the trip to 'the little room' adjoining." Guards routinely patrolled the corridor along death row at night, backlit by "three dim frosted globes." Thick rubber matting muffled their footsteps as well.[87]

It wasn't long before Hassell toned down his braggadocio and his devil-may-care attitude toward death, putting all of his efforts into converting his sentence to life in prison.[88] His jailers and others noticed that the boastful killer was beginning to come undone: "All traces of cheerfulness and indifference, which were so noticeable in the demeanor of the slayer throughout his trial have disappeared, leaving him morose and sullen. He refuses to talk and now spends his entire time constructing letters to his attorney in his last fight for life."[89] A week before his scheduled execution date, Hassell wrote to his attorney Russell, beseeching him to "do what you can, the time is growing shorter. Just think it is only February 25 when I am to die."[90]

As he sat on Huntsville's death row, Hassell penned what he thought would be a last letter to his son. Since he had no idea where James Delbert was living, he sent it care of his sister, Agnes Rister, whose husband reportedly hand-delivered it to Taylor County's *Merkel Mail* newspaper.[91] In it, Hassell said that he had been reading the Bible every day and declared that he believed "God has forgiven his sins because he has not always been a bad man." The letter was intended to offer his son "good advice," and it was published in other Texas newspapers as well:

'My Dear Beloved Son:'

Please read this letter and remember you have got a father that has loved you all these years. But by the time you get this letter, he may be in the world beyond. While you have never known me, I have shed lots of tears for you and your mother. I do hope you will stand by her, to the last, for my dear boy, you only have one mother, and she is the best friend you will ever have.

Well I felt that I must write you a few lines before I go. Listen now Delbert, remember there is only one way that will pay in this old world, and try to live a most straight and forward life and make your word your bond. The right way is the only way, and love and respect your mother and stay clear of bad company and above all leave WHISKEY alone. Be braver than your father was in that respect, always be able to say get thee behind me Satan.

Ask your mother about your dad. She will tell you he was a kindhearted husband and father; she has seen me shed tears a thousand times. I have not been bad at heart, and listen Delbert, you have one of the dearest aunts on Route 3, box 84, Aunt Dora Watson. And remember she loves you, and will always be glad to hear from you, and give you any good advice that she has.

Now Delbert, I am on my hands and knees praying that you will live what is right, and never go astray with bad company and whiskey, like your father did in his young days. Oh, if you could only see what it means! Well, Delbert, while I am sitting here in my death cell waiting for the 25th of this months to come, and then the electric chair to claim me, I am praying and I feel that I will have a chance at the morning of the resurrection, while the crime is the worst in history, I have not always been bad at heart, and I feel that God has forgiven.

But please, oh please, leave bad company and whiskey alone and love your mother and aunt till the last. Well I am glad that your grandma Hassell never lived to see this, for it would break her dear old heart. Well I have sinned, and the Bible says the wages of sin is death, so I will have to pay but for God's sake and for your dear mother's sake and your own sake and for the sake of humanity, live right and be a man.

Wherever you go, and whenever these temptations come up, remember what Christ said, 'get ye behind me Satan,' for its always Satan that brings these temptations in some way.

Well, my dear son, I will close for this time, but I want you to know, while you have not had a father's care all the time, you have had a father's love, for I have never ceased to love you and your mother.

While there has been a great wrong done you and your mother, and I have forgiven everybody, I want you and your mother to do the same. Hoping that you will read this and understand it with the same spirit that

I write it. I will close for this time, with love to you and prayer on my dying lips for you and mama.

> *Your loving father, George J. Hassell.*
> *P.S. Read St. John 3:16. I get lot of comfort from it.*

***

In the 1920s, a stay of execution during the review of capital cases in Texas was not "legally automatic" (referring to an automatic thirty-day stay of execution until the case could be reviewed), but "in practice it almost was."[92] Hassell's attorney filed an appeal of his death sentence in the Texas Court of Criminal Appeals, "the state's court of last resort for criminal cases."[93] An appeal to this court meant an automatic thirty-day stay until the high court reviewed the case.[94] In 1925, the Texas Legislature added a two-person Commission of Appeals, and both commissioners were selected by the governor. Each one was appointed for a two-year stint and was required to have at least ten years' experience as lawyers or judges.

Between 1900 and 1927, the year Hassell was tried and then appealed his sentence, there was a substantial decline in the rate of sentence reversals in Texas, which did not bode well for him. In 1900, of the non-Prohibition-related (non-liquor-related) felony cases reviewed by the Court of Criminal Appeals, 68.5 percent were reversed, one-third of them due to technical errors such as incorrect wording of indictments or jury instructions.[95] The high reversal rate undermined confidence in the criminal justice system, and by 1927 the reversal rates had noticeably diminished, down to 29.3 percent. By most accounts this was attributed to "the increased professionalism of the legal profession."[96]

Almost as soon as he was sentenced, Hassell began fighting to escape his appointment with the electric chair. He was reportedly advised that "the quickest means from dodging the chair" would be to appeal to Governor Moody to commute his sentence to life in prison.[97] Not that he knew it, but he would be bucking the odds if he received any relief from the governor. One reporter noted that "Moody has refused to save any from death in the 'smoky chair.'"[98] Indeed, during Moody's administration, "a score of persons have walked from the cell in death row through the 'little green door,' never to return."⁹⁹ The national press described the thirty-three-year-old Moody, who had beaten Ma Ferguson in the 1926 governor's race, as an "implacable foe of the Ku Klux Klan." At least one reporter suggested that he "would become the next Abraham Lincoln." But ultimately, as Texas historian Stephen Harrigan explained, Moody "turned out to be a perfectly ok governor; a little stiff, not exactly a political maestro."¹⁰⁰ Be that as it may, he held Hassell's fate in his hands.

Around 8:30 p.m. on Monday night, February 14, just eleven days away from his scheduled date with the electric chair, Hassell's appeal for a commutation of his death sentence to life in prison was formally denied. Although Moody declined to commute his sentence, the governor expressed confidence that "prison authorities or officers of the law" would make any investigations necessary "before they would execute an insane man."¹⁰¹ Moody offered a ray of hope, at least for the time being, by adding that if, between then and Hassell's execution date eleven days later, any exculpatory evidence came to light that established he did indeed suffer from a mental malady, the governor would grant him more time.

Although the plea for commutation of Hassell's sentence had already been declined by Moody on Monday, two days later, on February 16, Hassell's new attorney announced an appeal to the Criminal Court of Appeals, which when formally completed would automatically stay the execution until the high court reviewed the case.¹⁰² Also on February 16, Warden Speer received a letter from W. H. Russell, in which the Parmer County prosecutor shared his feelings about Hassell. He wrote, "This Hassell is, and has been much of a mystery to me. I am, however, not a competent judge of his mental condition. However he seems to me to be so devoid of any ordinary traits of human honor, decency, or sentiment, that his particular case should be studied by the proper alienists for the purpose of information if nothing else. I would be interested in learning what you think of him." Before he ended the letter, he added what seemed like an afterthought, telling the warden, "We understand that there is no chance of his escaping the chair, except for his mental condition."¹⁰³

Several days later, yet another effort to obtain commutation failed on Thursday, February 17, when the governor declined to accede to a personal appeal from Hassell's sister, Mrs. P. A. Watson of Crockett, Texas, on her brother's behalf. Following this turn of events, his sister left Austin for Groveton, in Trinity County, to file a petition to secure a sanity hearing for Hassell.[104] As noted previously, the governor had allowed for the possibility that he might grant a stay of execution if a sanity hearing were *arranged*, not necessarily completed, by February 25.

***

On February 19, Governor Moody received a letter from the Huntsville warden, N. L. Speer. The warden had written the governor for instructions on carrying out the execution. Enclosed in the envelope was a copy of a letter from Hassell's lawyer, W. H. Russell, and a "copy of a certificate furnished ... by the clerk of the district court of Parmer County." Moody referenced the looming execution date, which was less than a week away, as well as requests he had received from the defense for a commutation of Hassell's sentence to life in prison on the grounds that Hassell was insane. The governor explained that he would still refuse to commute the sentence based on this claim and that he had not been presented with sufficient evidence to offer any clemency.[105]

Moody was dissatisfied that the only individuals supporting an insanity plea on Hassell's behalf, referring to his attorney and sister, were heavily invested in personal relationships with Hassell and were therefore merely "interested in his welfare" rather than seeing justice served. However, the governor insisted that he did not "mean to question" the integrity of the insanity plea. He agreed that more testing should be completed before his date with the electric chair. He reminded "those who have appealed to me for a commutation of his sentence" to follow procedural dictates in the Code of Criminal Procedure "and cause the question of his sanity to be tried as the law provides."[106]

The day before he sent his letter to Warden Speer, the governor was advised by Mr. Andrew Todd "A. T." McKinney (1838–1931), a Huntsville attorney, "that Hassell's sister was going to Farwell for the purpose of beginning the proceedings."[107] McKinney asked Moody to "grant a stay of execution in this matter to the end that they might have sufficient time to try the question." Of course, the governor was well aware that between

February 21 and 25 there was insufficient time for insanity proceedings. Fortunately for the Texas Bluebeard, Hassell still had some supporters on the margins of his life, and Moody told McKinney that he "would issue a proclamation staying the execution for a sufficient length of time to allow a trial of that question."[108]

All the worrying over Hassell's insanity plea became moot when Governor Moody reiterated (in his own words) what was stated in Article 769, in the Texas Code of Criminal Procedure: "when an appeal is taken from a death penalty that the sentence shall not be pronounced but shall be suspended" until a decision is made by the Criminal Court of Appeals. Expanding upon this point, Moody argued that he did not see "how you could have a lawful warrant directing the defendant's execution, because there was no authority for the pronouncement of sentence or for the issuance of a warrant by a clerk."[109] With little more than a week until the execution date, the governor also issued a statement: "The code of criminal procedure makes provision for cases of this character. It offers orderly and safe procedure to insure society against possibility of an injustice in cases of this nature."[110]

Sometime between February 21 and 24, 1927, Huntsville warden N. L. Speer was notified by phone that Hassell had been granted a thirty-day stay of execution, pushing back his execution date to March 25. Hassell didn't make a statement when he found out, but received the news with "much apparent satisfaction."[111] It is possible Hassell was unaware of the fact that when an offender arrived on death row to await his execution date, "it was customary for the governor to grant one thirty-day reprieve to allow pardon officials to review the case. During this time many of the letters for and against additional consideration would accumulate in the inmate's file."[112] As things stood, he still faced his second date with the electric chair one month later.

On March 23, the Board of Pardon Advisors recommended that the governor give the appellant another thirty-day stay. The reasoning behind the second stay was that the Board had not received the required notice of appeal when Hassell had been sentenced to death in Farwell in January, and that this stay would rectify that miscommunication. Some of the fault for not following the usual protocol rested on the shoulders of the prisoner's attorney, W. H. Russell, who left the courtroom without returning to hear the sentencing after the jury's deliberation. Moreover, neither Russell nor the defendant filed an initial appeal, though Hassell was entitled to request one after the court adjourned. This miscommunication on the part of Hassell's court-appointed attorney and the failure to initially follow through with an appeal perhaps explains why Russell would seem to ramrod the appeals process over the following months.

Governor Moody received a telegram from Parmer County Judge Reese Tatum explaining that he had ordered Hassell to be removed from the state penitentiary pending action by a higher court: "I am this day issuing an order commanding the Sheriff of Parmer County to go to Huntsville and take George J. Hassell to some safe jail until the Court of Criminal Appeals decides his case and I am wiring the warden of the penitentiary to this effect." Huntsville warden Speer also received a telegram from the judge advising him that an officer would be there to return Hassell to Farwell pending the outcome of his current appeal.[113] No doubt, Hassell was thrilled to be leaving the death row after so many weeks in such close proximity to the electric chair.

Hassell was officially assigned a second thirty-day stay of execution from the Board of Pardons on Wednesday, March 23, just two days before his rescheduled execution would have taken place. Meanwhile, he would be returned to a North Texas jail on the grounds that the "death warrant was illegally issued, as notice to the Court of Criminal Appeals had been given after his conviction."[114] A second stay meant his scheduled execution day was pushed back once more, to April 25, 1927, unless a higher court action resulted in a reversal, which was highly unlikely at that point.[115]

If all had gone as intended after the trial, Hassell would have already been in the ground for more than a month, probably in the local state prison cemetery, which is where convicts were buried when no one claimed the body.[116] His attorneys began preparing for a sanity hearing, and he was moved again, this time to the Hale County jail in Plainview.[117]

The double mass murderer and family annihilator was now on his way back to the Texas Panhandle, for, as stated previously, it was decided to return him to a "strong jail in a North Texas city for safekeeping."[118] He was handcuffed to Deputy Marshal Sam Huffman and Parmer County Sheriff J. H. Martin on the afternoon train south to Houston. They arrived there late in the afternoon. Once they arrived in Houston, Huffman and Martin "went out to a restaurant," leaving their charge to "dine alone on sandwiches in a city jail cell."[119]

Since his appeal had not been acted on until the day before he was supposed to ride the electric chair, reporters were interested in how he had spent the hours leading up to his execution. For, after all, if things had gone as expected he would have been electrocuted twelve hours earlier. In typical Hassell fashion, he replied that he had "slept like a log." He couldn't resist adding that he had eaten a hearty breakfast once he received the stay.[120]

During his time with reporters in Houston, Hassell told them he had read the New Testament of the Bible while behind bars and "found the 15th chapter of Corinthians the greatest part of the book."[121] In the midst of the Jazz Age and the emergence of the "flapper" culture that welcomed women into more aspects of the public sphere, the child rapist and murderer felt entitled to recommend publicly that women read the eleventh chapter, "which he said dealt with bobbed hair and such things."[122]

When it came time to continue the journey after dinner on March 25, he had turned surly and declined to chat with reporters, declining to answer any questions. He told the assembled newspapermen that he was "sick of talking to reporters ... I've answered hundreds of questions, and none of em ever offered me a cigar."[123]

On June 15, Hassell's appeal for a rehearing of his case was presented to the Texas Court of Criminal Appeals.[124] The presiding judge for this appeal was Wright "W. C." Chalfant Morrow (1858–1942).[125] The appeal hinged on several issues that had also come up at his first trial. His motion for a rehearing, in the eyes of the Court, lacked persuasion. As with his failed request for a change of venue at his first trial, the appellant was unsuccessful once again.[126]

According to Hassell's motion, the denial of his request for an initial change of venue had not taken into consideration the fact that there was at least one juror who had already made up his mind by the time of his jury selection. In the appeal, Hassell's defense, W. H. Russell, argued that the juror, Dud Read, "had read in the newspapers an account of the purported confession and had heard some talk of mob violence" and "had formed an impression touching on the merits of the case." Despite Read's admission, he explained that he had actually only "formed an impression as to his guilt from what I read and heard." He pledged that if he was selected for the jury, he "could wholly disregard what [he] may have heard and read about the matter, not take that into consideration, but try the case, and decide the case solely" on its merits."[127]

The defense took issue with the juror's response as well as its acceptance by the court, commenting: "This Honorable Court knows from experience that when a juror states that he has heard all of the facts in a given case and that he has an opinion in the case, let it be as called 'fixed' opinion or merely a transient, migratory or casual opinion, and that he can 'lay its aside' or totally disregard the same in arriving at a verdict that he merely brands himself a 'superman' and into a class of evolution into which the human race has not yet reached."[128] Russell's concluding remarks on this motion to reverse the verdict for a new trial was unsurprisingly overruled on October 12, 1927.

On Thursday, June 16, 1927, almost four months after he was originally supposed to have ridden the Texas thunderbolt to oblivion, as Hassell sat brooding in the Hale County Jail in Plainview he received word that his appeal had been declined and the death sentence affirmed. One reporter claimed that when he told Hassell about the higher court's decision that morning (before Hassell was aware of it), Hassell "seemed nervous for a moment but soon regained the nonchalant attitude that he has held since his arrest" in Farwell in December the previous year.[129] Hassell was scheduled to be sent back to Farwell on July 11, where at the regular session of the district court he would be resentenced and a new date of execution determined. At this point, the convicted killer had been confined in the Plainview jail for several months.

Hassell lamented upon the reinstatement of his death sentence, "Yes, they've poured it on me again. I don't know what they will do next for me, and I don't know how long it will be before my attorneys get a hearing on the motion for a rehearing."[130] Here is another example of Hassell's psychopathic tendencies. Someone like Hassell not only lacks empathy and is probably incapable of love, but "only feels sorry" for himself while "minimizing" any suffering he causes others.[131]

At Plainview, Hassell kept himself busy making small doilies out of silk cords (see photo gallery), supposedly selling them to visitors at the jail to support his smoking habit. He shared the jail with two other convicted murderers, all "convicted of crimes that were sensations in this part of Texas." One of them, Robert Stanley Benton, a Black man from Crosbyton who killed a prominent farmer in Crosby County, would follow him onto the electric chair the following year.[132] But first, it was time to hear what the psychologists of the day had to say.

Chapter 20

Urge to Kill: Dr. Jekyll or Mr. Hyde?

"An urge to kill might have been responsible for the Farwell murders."

From the very beginning of his infamy, George J. Hassell was a subject of great fascination to students of the human mind.[1] Adding to their curiosity was his stock answer whenever he was asked why he committed his atrocities: "I wish someone would tell me why I did it."[2] Several observers in the 1920s found perhaps their best insight into his behavior in Robert Louis Stevenson's classic novel, *The Strange Case of Dr. Jekyll and Mr. Hyde*, written forty years before Hassell's Farwell massacre.[3] One reporter wrote that Stevenson's tale had found its modern-day counterpart in Hassell, the infamous "Garrotter and Slayer of 13 Persons."[4] This sensationalist reporter further wrote that Hassell was "ordinarily the smiling, jocular, and good natured farmer of the daytime, who, after taking a drink, immediately transformed into a vicious killer." Dr. Jekyll, as the story went, turned into a brutal killer after taking a simple potion, and for this reporter Stevenson's fictional story was analogous to Hassell drinking bootleg whiskey in the moments leading up to his murders, supposedly revealing his more sinister attributes.[5]

***

Research on the past, including colonial America, as well as the present has demonstrated a convincing link between violence and Hassell's potion of choice, alcohol. In 1955, the criminologist Marvin Wolfgang conducted one of the first empirical examinations linking the two. Recent research also indicates a significant connection.[6] In particular, alcohol has been strongly linked to intimate partner violence.[7] Alcohol affects people differently depending on the individual and the situation. When it comes to homicidal behavior, there is no one factor responsible for the violence. Alcohol does not *cause* violence, but it is a correlate, as in the case of Hassell. Criminologist Eric W. Hickey asserts that some violent offenders, such as serial killers, are affected by certain "predispositional factors that influence their behavior."[8] Chief among these factors is the use of alcohol, which "appears to decrease inhibitions and to inhibit moral conscience and propriety."[9] As both a stimulant and depressant, alcohol affects parts of the brain that control inhibitions and impulse control—usually reducing them.[10] It is also known to stimulate "aggressive thinking and behavior."[11] Alcohol, according to Hickey, might facilitate the actions of some serial killers, but "in all likelihood" the offenders would kill without it.[12] Hassell also was embroiled in familial conflict, another factor that can result in violence. Alcohol might have reduced his level of impulse control and judgment, if he was wired that way, but the link is not always clear.

Neighbors were almost united in their description of Hassell as "a man whose ordinary mood was that of a shrewd, pleasant man who met almost everybody with a smile and a joking mood." Still there were "those who have studied sociology, psychology, and criminology [who] marveled over the puzzling personality of the man." Moreover, some had seen Hassell's darker side and were aware that "under stress of worry with his nerves bolstered by drink, he became a heartless conscienceless creature lower than the animal of the jungle."[13] Hassell's ability to charm while hiding the monster within was part and parcel of his psychopathy. Hassell and others like him can portray ordinary folk quite convincingly, often leaving acquaintances and neighbors bewildered in the wake of their horrible crimes, making comments to reporters along the lines of "I can't believe he did that," or "that isn't the person I've known all those years."[14]

During his first trial and the initial investigation into the mass murder, Hassell was subjected to great scrutiny by several local educators, who hoped to understand what made him tick. While Hassell was waiting in Deaf Smith County's Hereford Jail, the local sheriff gave some of them permission to speak with him. It was F. W. Sawyer, superintendent of the public schools of Farwell, who came up with the idea of interviewing him first (no one else has been reported as showing interest).[15] Sawyer saw this as a case that merited further study and admitted that this was his "first time doing this." He had graduated from West Texas Teachers College and the University of Oklahoma, with bachelor's and master's degrees in sociology, and probably considered himself schooled in the burgeoning "field of criminology."

According to the trial transcript, Sawyer and another educator spent about five hours with Hassell. Parmer County Sheriff Martin introduced the men to the prisoner "in a rather informal way" and they began "swapping jokes for a while, and then sat down and told him our purpose, and he volunteered to give us any information that would be of any benefit to our study."[16] The two men listened as the killer elaborated on his version of the "history of his life."[17] The educators hoped that once they understood this, it would allow them to better understand "his heredity and environment" and "the history of his life until the commission of the crime."

The educators "found his ideas were a bit peculiar," especially when it came to his interpretation of eternity.[18] A half-century after Hassell's execution, his wife Susie's sister, Maudie Johnston, shared some information with George Turner, a reporter who was revisiting the case in a series of articles in 1978. The sister-in-law cast some light on his "peculiar" take on the hereafter, remembering, "At one time, during a family religious discussion, he became angry and began shaking with rage. 'Do you really believe that when the child dies' he indicated one of his wife's sons—'he will go straight to heaven?' Mrs. Johnston replied that she did. To wit, he replied, "Then maybe we should kill all the children and send them to heaven right now."[19]

Before Sawyer and his colleague departed, they took about twenty measurements of Hassell's head. Even as late as the 1920s the pseudoscience of craniometry was not uncommon, and there were many attempts to attribute importance to the shape and measurements of the head in the search for physical variations between criminals and noncriminals.[20] Still influenced by the work of Cesare Lombroso (1835–1909), there were many who contended that there was a "criminal type" characterized by certain physical anomalies. For example, he suggested that larger heads were usually found among murderers. In 1876, Lombroso had an epiphany while performing the postmortem of an Italian bandit. He wrote, "At the sight of the skull, I seemed to see all of a sudden ... the problem of the nature of the criminal—an atavistic [evolutionary throwback] being who reproduces in his person the ferocious instincts of primitive humanity and the inferior animal."

The educators made little headway in their investigation and ultimately, after speaking with Hassell for hours, left his cell with no better understanding of the family annihilator than when they had first met him. Just weeks away from his first scheduled execution date, Hassell was still able to smile and joke as he referred to his victims without an iota of emotion, as if they were only obstacles that had to be removed.[21]

At his 1927 trial, Hassell's attorney, W. H. Russell, asked Sawyer whether his five-hour examination of the defendant had revealed "anything about his peculiar brain formation wherein his emotional part of it may have become dormant or atrophied or diseased or anything." The best Sawyer could come up with was: "I could not tell."[22]

***

When the Amarillo newsman John L. McCarthy interviewed Hassell a year later, in the month leading up to his final date with the electric chair, he too borrowed the Jekyll and Hyde allusion to offer perhaps the best description of the duality of the Hassell persona. He wrote: "His entire life is a living lie—he is Dr. Jekyll and Mr. Hyde with a chasm deeper and wider than the Grand Canyon between his natures." Further illustrating the dimensions of the gap between Hassell's two selves, McCarthy continued: "He loves children, abhors the sight of blood, will not knowingly lie, is extremely sociable, with an infectious smile and laugh," yet murders women and children apparently without provocation." McCarthy delved as deeply as he could into the unknowable man, citing Hassell's "evil" proclivities throughout most of his past life—"he romped [with] and loved the babies he killed ... He killed and killed many times, yet he has every appearance of being a coward." Like other psychopaths and serial killers, Hassell never expressed any "remorse" or "regret" for his bloody deeds. The reporter sensed by the end of his interview that Hassell did not in fact "appear ashamed of anything he ever did" and warned that he "presents a puzzle which should be studied closely, but handled carefully."[23]

Outside of some hyperbole and a few minor factual errors, the above describes Hassell in a nutshell. From a modern perspective, we now know that serial killers and other criminals are often as adept at "presentation of self" as Hassell was.[24] However, in 1959 the sociologist Erving Goffman noted that "successful individuals in many legitimate occupations seem to have a particular knack for using self-awareness to their personal advantage."[25] So in effect, many serial killers use this skill the same way a salesman or politician might, by pretending they have the "best interests" of their targets in mind.[26] Thus, "the difference between serial killers and other successful people may not lie so much in the greater effectiveness of the former at impression management as a means to an end, but in their greater willingness to torture and kill as a result of employing the tactic."[27]

Determining mental competency before sentencing has always provided challenges to mental health experts and the judicial system, since "insanity *is a legal term*, not a psychiatric distinction."[28] Moreover, historically the common-law legal tradition has used the term "insanity" to define the state of mind of offenders at the time of their crime in order to determine whether someone is or is not guilty by reason of insanity. Established protocol requires the defense wishing to use this strategy to determine mental competency before a trial begins. This legal ploy is not used often, and when it is, it's rarely successful.

Historically, the common-law legal tradition has had to determine the offender's mind at the time the offense was committed. Criminal responsibility in American courts is based on the M'Naghten Rule of 1843. The Rule's definition of insanity has been widely accepted due to "its simplicity." What this means is that the defense must be able to convince the court that the client, at the time of the offense, was "laboring under such a defect of reason from disease of the mind as to not know the nature and quality of the act he was doing, or if he did know," was not aware that what he was doing violated the legal code.[29] This has often been described as the right-wrong rule, where all the prosecution has to prove is that the offender could distinguish right from wrong at the time of the crime. Ultimately, it is the defendant who bears the burden of proving that he was in fact insane.

The determination of sanity guidelines is not without its critics. The most common challenge to this protocol is that M'Naghten does not consider situations where offenders can distinguish between right and wrong "but are simply unable to control their behavior."[30] The closest any state has come to rectifying this conundrum has been to supplement it with what is known as the irresistible impulse test. First used in Alabama in 1887 in the case of the State of Alabama v. Parsons, it "expanded the test for an insanity plea," by recognizing that even though an offender might understand the difference between right and wrong, it is yet possible that he "succumbs to uncontrollable impulses" to kill.[31] It is then up to the defense to prove that the offender was "incapable of resisting an impulse" that led to the commission of a crime."[32]

Hassell was never able to satisfactorily explain why he killed, nor admit to how many others he might have murdered, but in the week before his execution he did confess to Huntsville assistant prison physician Dr. E. L. Angier that, as the doctor expressed it, "an urge to kill might have been responsible for the Farwell murders."[33] Hassell's use of the expression "urge to kill" has been used by other family annihilators and multiple murderers.[34] Some researchers have traced this simmering rage to intense anger bred in childhood, leading to violence later directed toward those closest to their murderers. According to psychiatrist Michael H. Stone, "the murder of an entire family is more often a crime of impulse than of long premeditation."[35]

***

Although sentenced a year earlier, an official reprieve and a legal tangle prevented Hassell's original execution date. On January 10, 1928, the Texas

Bluebeard was scheduled to return to the Parmer County court for resentencing. There were no surprises in store for him; it was merely a formality, since all his appeals had been denied. With the exception of Hassell's first trial the previous year, it was perhaps the largest crowd to ever attend a district court hearing in Farwell. In this case, they gathered to witness Hassell being resentenced to death.

Unlike the first trial, when there were rumors and undercurrents of potential mob violence, most spectators seem to have attended purely out of curiosity.[36] Nonetheless, two Texas Rangers, Privates Purvis and Moore, were sent from the violent boomtown of Borger, Texas, to observe the resentencing. Parmer County Sheriff James H. Martin was none too pleased by their arrival, confiding to one observer that "there has been no indication of any violence" and that neither he nor any other officials had requested the Rangers.[37] But Austin had ordered them to be there anyway.[38] However, there is good reason to believe that someone from Parmer County requested Ranger assistance. Indeed, Dallas Jefferson Matthews, an adjutant general of a thirty-Ranger force between 1925 and 1927 noted that "it is the policy of the Department not to send Rangers to any community without the request of the local authorities, and never without the request of the sheriff of the county."[39]

According to one chronicler of Texas sheriffs, local lawmen often "had ambivalent attitudes toward the Texas Rangers."[40] This mixed opinion was probably predicated on times when they were considered necessary for "offering valuable backup and technical assistance to county sheriffs."[41] Well aware that they had the right to intervene in community law enforcement activities, once the Rangers were on the scene it was not out of the ordinary for them to monitor the actions of city peace officers for signs of incompetence and corruption. Law enforcement agencies sometimes regarded the Texas Rangers as a mixed blessing.[42] On the one hand, since they had statewide authority, authorities could call on them when needed to cross county lines in a case. On the other hand, there were always situations where sheriffs felt the Rangers might embarrass them by intruding into county law enforcement.[43] The iconic Ranger Captain M. T. "Lone Wolf" Gonzaullas suggested that the "touchiness of citizens and local officials about the presence of Rangers in their community was largely based on a misconception" that local lawmen were often not up to the task.[44] In any case, if needed, they were on "stand-by" in Farwell, alongside Parmer County deputies equipped with sawed-off shotguns, making sure the crowds kept moving along.

At the District Court in Farwell on Tuesday, January 10, 1928, Judge Tatum resentenced Hassell for the murder of Alton, his eldest stepson and nephew. A month away from execution, the multiple murderer had lost much of his fearlessness after his spell behind bars. One reporter observed, "The gaunt rancher accepted the sentence with no outward sign of emotion. When asked if he had anything to say, he only smiled, thanked the court, and asked that his watch, ring, and clothes be returned to him."[45] Never mind that the clothes and ring were actually his victim's.

Although the term had not yet been created, "serial killers" were active in the United States in the 1920s, and they can be found throughout history.[46] Modern serial killer profilers recognize that these types of predators like to keep trophies or souvenirs that reminded them of their crimes and help them relive their murderous exploits. How much closer can a killer get to a victim than by wearing their clothes? Hassell was not queried about his predilection for wearing the clothing or other accoutrements of his victims, but it is worth speculating that this might have been the case with Hassell and his affinity for wearing the watch, ring, clothing, and shoes of at least one of his slaughtered family victims.

After being resentenced, Hassell was brought back from Farwell to the Hale County Jail in Plainview under heavy guard. Here, he would await word on when he would be returned to the Huntsville Walls for the last time. No matter the jail, be it Plainview, Hereford, or Mule Shoe, he remained a model prisoner—that is, if he was well fed and had a supply of smokes. During his time in the Plainview Jail, Sheriff Sam Faith had ample time to observe Hassell. He was proud of his new jail, which had opened earlier in 1928 and was "a freestanding jail" located on the northeast corner of the city square, featuring three floors, with the sheriff's quarters on the first.[47] Hassell had continuously hinted that he had more to confess, and he now admitted as much. Faith observed that he was "a model prisoner and seems to enjoy the environment of the jail. He has never expressed remorse or regret for his crimes and talks freely of them." Local lawmen and others were well inclined to believe "that he can throw more light on even other murders of women and children."[48] Since he had murdered two of his three wives and bragged about living with seven other women for lengths of time ranging from three months to three years, speculation was rife that he had other victims. Sheriff Faith shared with others the fact that he and his deputies were convinced Hassell had "not yet told of all of his crimes."[49] Faith commented: "That man is a puzzle. He is friendly, he is smart, a model prisoner, sociable, and apparently an all-around good fellow." Moreover, he even helped "keeping quiet and order in the jail."[50]

It was not uncommon for Hassell to get cross with reporters, especially anyone that suggested he was being untruthful. It is somewhat ironic that he became incensed so easily when branded a liar, since most of his life was based on some form of prevarication. Did he not tell his neighbors in Whittier that his family had run off to San Francisco in 1917, when in fact they were buried beneath his house? Likewise, nine years later, had he not attempted to cover up the disappearance of his nine family members in Farwell, telling neighbors they had gone off to Oklahoma, when in fact they were buried only feet away from his back door?[51]

He doubled down on his claim to truth-telling in the aforementioned interview with *Amarillo News* reporter John L. McCarthy, when he expressed apprehension about being caught in a lie: "My father who was a high up lodge member and believed to be a good man although he may have fooled the people always taught us that honesty was the best policy." Curiously, this was one of the rare times that Hassell ever brought up his father in conversation in anything resembling a laudatory manner. His excuse for clamming up on occasion and refusing to repeat his various stories to reporters was: "for fear I might not remember everything just as it was and would be called a liar." As proof, he noted that a Farwell jailer had "cussed me and called me a liar because of a statement I made in connection with the case."[52]

While the court proceedings were expected to be conducted secretly, there is no such thing as a secret in a small town like Farwell. Rumors were floated that his attorney, W. H. Russell, might ask for an immunity hearing on the strength of a recent exam by an alienist.[53] But there was nothing to it. The interview was just a required procedure before the state could take his life.[54]

He had waited almost a year to have his date of execution fixed. As usual, he presented the appearance of a "well fed, prosperous farmer," laughing and joking with fellow inmates in the Hale County lock-up and relishing his steady diet of jail cuisine (one observer commented that he "enjoys the meals"). He was fond of telling interviewers how much luckier he was than they were, because he knew his death date, while they would "never know what day you may get run over by a car or shot at or take some fatal disease."[55]

He had been in the jail for several months waiting for the regular court session. By this point, he had "abandoned his carefree attitude which he has held for more than a year and appears irritable and refuses to talk." His months behind bars in Plainview saw the confessed killer become increasingly morose and somber. As it stood, the strategy was to bring him in to court under a veil of secrecy and "rush him through the routine of sentencing and remove him immediately to the state penitentiary in Huntsville." During his last days in Plainview, Hassell gave "considerable study to the Bible. During his confinement he had been the object of many visits from curious people, who kept Sheriff Sam Faith busy as they sought to see the man who "is the author of the blackest crimes ever committed in their section of West Texas."[56]

After one of Hassell's last major interviews with journalists, Amarillo reporter John L. McCarthy made a number of interesting observations about him.[57] McCarthy found it interesting that, except for Hassell's twenty-one-year-old stepson, Alton, "all of his victims were women and children" and speculated as to how many more uncounted victims there might be. Similarly, if Hassell had killed two out of his three wives (one of whom was a common-law spouse), it raises the question, what about all the women he claimed to have lived with in twenty-seven states? Could any of these have been victims? None of his purported lovers ever came out of the woodwork to share any information about the noted killer, before or after his death. Perhaps these relationships were never more than figments of his fantasy world. But these and other claims always led authorities to speculate he had more to tell.

McCarthy suggested that with such "a twisted, perverted, repulsive career," Hassell held back much of his dark saga. The reporter was sure that "he holds the secret to other killings." Whether he tells the rest depends on his "egoistic nature. I [don't think] he cared to add more to one of the blackest pages of Texas criminology [but] it is our opinion that he can write many more cruel and gruesome details."[58]

In the days leading up to his February 10, 1928, execution, Hassell was interviewed in his death cell at the Huntsville Penitentiary by two "state-employed sanity experts." The interviewers included Dr. W. J. Johnson, the superintendent of the state mental institution in San Antonio, and Dr. C. K. Standefer, head of the one in Austin. Two days before the scheduled execution, the experts returned to Austin and assured Governor Moody that Hassell was sane, with the ability to tell right from wrong. Moreover, "he had knowledge of the nature, quality and wrongfulness of his acts and we do not believe these acts to be uncontrollable. He has very little education but is with a general intelligence commensurate with his environment. He cannot be definitely declared insane, feeble minded or epileptic."[59]

Once Hassell was apprised of their findings, he shared with a reporter his wish to "feel the searing of electric current coursing through his body without more delay." Digesting the news behind bars, he sat "slumped down on the corner of his cot" in his "little cell along a corridor which leads down to the one passage into oblivion." He picked his head up briefly, looked at his guards, and in a forlorn, tired voice told them: "I wish they would hurry up and electrocute me; a Christian man can't live on the outside these days, anyway."[60]

As noted above, these were not his first interviews with alienists. An earlier psychologist opined, "he has the brain of a man, the volatility of great historical characters and the emotions of a child. He cannot blush or cry—it is a physical impossibility." What's more, "he is exceptionally honest, refuses to tell a lie and declares he does not owe a penny." However, these conclusions do not quite jibe with Hassell's descriptions of the Whittier killings, where he went from happily frolicking in bed with his wife to suddenly being "seized with desire to kill." To another he commented that in Whittier "he suddenly had a mania to kill and couldn't resist."[61]

One reporter wrote that "alienists would tell us he is insane—that there is an abnormal side of a man who can kill ruthlessly as he did and face the consequences without emotion—criminally insane."[62] But apparently he was not clinically insane, at least according to the standards of the time: "mental tests to which he was subjected by those who studied him proved that that he arrived at conclusions as sanely as anyone. He reasoned from cause to effect as directly and soundly almost as any lawyer. Insane people lose the faculty of reasoning from cause to effect."[63]

By the late twentieth century a number of state courts abandoned the strict M'Naghten Rule in favor of the looser doctrine of diminished capacity, in which an alleged criminal may escape formal punishment if "as a result of mental disease or defect he lacks substantial capacity to appreciate the criminality of his conduct or to conform his conduct to the requirement of law."[64] But even with access to the benefits of this adaptation of the M'Naghten Rule, it is doubtful it would have made any difference in Hassell's fate.

One of the stranger aspects of Hassell's last days was his obsessive concern over what had happened to a trunk of possessions he ostensibly sent from California to Abilene years earlier. He would ask about it time and time again. One might expect that, with the electric chair pending, all of his thoughts would have gone in that direction. But his "anxiety" over the final disposition of this trunk was just one of his many quirks that left "psychologists puzzled by him." Hassell mentioned a trunk that he had sent in the care of W. J. Laughlin, the father of his first wife, Minnie, in several of his last interviews.[65] Purportedly, it contained the clothing of his first victim, Marie Vogel, his former common-law wife. Still locked inside is one of the many questions left unanswered in the life of George J. Hassell. As of 2021, it is still missing—that is, if it ever existed at all.

Chapter 21

Riding the Thunderbolt

"I'll Show Them How a Brave Man Dies."

On Saturday, January 20, 1928, Parmer County Sheriff Jim Martin and Deputy P. D. Mersfelder transported Hassell back to the state pen in Huntsville one final time. With his execution date only three weeks away, Hassell was reportedly "in high spirits." It felt like a homecoming when he got back to the old Walls Unit and its death house, as he grasped the "hands of other condemned men" and told them that "he was glad to be back with them."[1]

The death chamber was thirty-five feet long by twelve feet wide. The condemned entered through a "small heavy steel door about three feet by six feet," constructed out of "five eighths inch boiler plate and case hardened." The reporter's first impression of the room was that it "seems bare save that in the south center in sinister silence stands the electric chair," which is connected to an electric switch and panel four feet away.[2] A similar door was located in the northern portion of the room, through which passed witnesses to the execution, who were usually prison officials, physicians, spiritual advisors, friends, or relatives.

***

The Texas rules regulating the number of observers at an execution were violated just one year after the inception of the electric chair, in one of the most egregious incidents in the history of the state's death penalty. This took place on April 6, 1926, during the double execution of the brothers S. A. and Forest Robins for murder. The night of the executions, two groups of men from Houston and Dallas, mostly "special officers," were invited by the Secretary of the Texas Prison Board, Frank O'Rourke, as his special guest to witness the deaths of the brothers. By all accounts, the sixteen guests were drunk and boisterous throughout. This became public knowledge when the October 23, 1926, edition of the *El Paso Herald* featured a lead article titled, "Drunken Orgy Attends Black Terrors' Death." Described by Speer as an "all night party," it lasted well into the next day. What was probably most appalling, according to Warden N. L. Speers, was how the "drunken visitors to the death cells jeered" as the convicts made their death march to the electric chair ... Some of them feeling good: two-thirds drunk."[3]

Testifying before a committee investigating corruption in October 1926, Warden Speer was asked how this could have taken place to begin with. Speer's only answer was that "he had no authority to keep the men out." He further responded that when the prison commissioners were not there, the next highest official would have been an officer of the Texas Prison Board. In this case, Speer said, "we regard[ed] Frank O'Rourke as our next boss."[4] More disturbing information was released indicating that O'Rourke, the secretary of the Texas Board of Prisons, called Chaplain Watson "to pray" for the first to be executed, but the chaplain refused to pray for the second inmate because of the rowdy behavior of the invited witnesses. In the wake of this very public fiasco, Commissioner H. Walker Sayle, chairman of the prison commission, issued instructions that no one shall be permitted to enter the death cell during an electrocution without written permission from two commissioners, and henceforth the inebriated would be barred from witnessing an execution altogether.[5] This proclamation seemed to work, and no similar incidents were reported prior to its abolition in 1964.

***

It is doubtful that anyone has witnessed more Texas electrocutions than did Huntsville reporter Don Reid. He started out as a wire service stringer (freelance journalist) and worked his way up to become editor of the local *Huntsville Item* newspaper in 1939, which remained his role until his death in 1981.[6]

States had various rules about journalistic coverage of executions. New York, for example, initially prohibited the press from attending but relented after just a few years.[7] One journalist noted how covering executions can "spur journalists to do things they normally wouldn't dare with any story. They may dramatize, they may cry, they may write in the first person, they may opine, they become violently nauseated."[8] In 1927, the year before Hassell was executed, a young reporter named Basil Gray was selected to witness the double execution of Ruth Snyder and Judd Gray at Sing Sing Prison.[9] Warden Lewis Lawes had lined up press witnesses before the execution and asked each one to promise not to take pictures in the death chamber. Lawes was unaware that Gray had a type of small camera known as a "candid" strapped to his ankle and that by raising his trouser leg and turning his foot he could focus the camera. The shutter trigger was hidden in a pants pocket and connected with the camera by a small tube under his trouser leg.[10] What happened next set a new standard for bad taste and journalistic sensationalism, making it "the most noted camera coup with the printing of the picture taken in the death chamber just after the current was turned on." The picture was featured on the front of the New York *Daily News*, helping to sell five hundred thousand copies.[11] Gray was rewarded by his paper with a $1,000 bonus and a vacation to Bermuda, but he was barred from all the nation's major prisons from then on.[12]

When word got out there was going to be a multiple execution, interest heightened among those seeking macabre entertainment, usually resulting in an increase in requests for appointment as witnesses. One New York spectator explained the surging interest succinctly by stating, "The more there are, the better the show."[13] The number of witnesses allowed varied by state. For example, in 1940 twelve were permitted to attend an electrocution in New York and six in Pennsylvania.[14] In addition to the witnesses, there are often at least a half dozen newspaper reporters. At this time,

Massachusetts was even more exclusive, allowing only three witnesses, "always from leading wire services."[15] In many states, at least in the late 1930s, there was no limit at all in the number of witnesses.[16] One reporter observed more than seventy-five journalists and other spectators in one room during an execution.

When all Texas state executions were centralized in Huntsville in 1923, legislation established which prison system personnel and outside witnesses would be allowed to attend executions. Besides the executioner, who was usually the Huntsville warden at the time, it listed those "necessary to assist him" in the execution process, including in "the Board of Prison Commissioners, two physicians, ... the spiritual advisor of the condemned, the chaplain of the penitentiary, the county judge and the sheriff of the county in which the penitentiary was situated, and any of the relatives or friends of the condemned person that he may request, not exceeding five in number."[17]

When Huntsville reporter Don Reid witnessed his first execution in 1937, the experience was "a blur."[18] He remembered how warm the room was and how he "could smell the odor of sweat." He recalled, "I hunched my shoulders and buttoned and unbuttoned my coat ... My pulse was racing, and my blood pounded through my veins ... when the warden gave his signal to the executioner."[19] By the time Reid attended his first execution, not much had changed in the death chamber since Hassell was electrocuted in the same room nine years earlier.

Most individuals who have witnessed an electrocution, according to mental health practitioners, find that even witnessing only one "can trigger short term psychological trauma that may require professional counseling."[20] The scholar and journalist Cynthia Barnett interviewed journalists who have covered executions to get a sense of how they were affected by the experience. One Texas AP correspondent explained that when reporters called him for advice before an execution, he told them to "focus on details" in order to "get through the wrenching experience."[21] Few who cover executions come away from the experience without any visceral reaction. Another reporter, attending his first execution, told Barnett that he found himself "checking out what the other witnesses' reactions are, you're checking out the clock, the expressions on guards' faces, who's coming in the door, the color of the curtain behind the prisoner, looking at all the details ... by concentrating on those things, you subdue the emotional response." In another examination of newspaper coverage of executions, conducted by psychiatrists, it was found that "journalists who witnessed an execution experience a high prevalence of dissociative symptoms ... similar to the people who endured a natural disaster."[22] According to medical professionals at the Mayo Clinic, these symptoms are a type of "detachment," where the observer may "experience a disconnection and lack of continuity between thoughts, memories, surroundings, actions and identity."[23] It is not unreasonable to assume that those watching the Hassell execution experienced similar reactions.

Perhaps the Abilene reporter and future novelist Eddie Anderson described death in the Texas chair best. He interviewed Hassell in the Abilene jail shortly before he was to be delivered to Huntsville. It is unclear whether Anderson ever actually witnessed the chair in operation, but he heard from other prisoners that "doomed men reverently talk of the expressions dying men leave on their faces after the law has performed its ghastly ritual."[24] He went on to describe how the doomed convicts were said to be "scared into the countenance of the dead," offering "evidence of the emotion that a man feels as he totters into the great abyss. They die, these human sacrifices, in nearly every instance in the paroxysms of fear, clenching convulsively, their faces a twisted mask."

At thirty-nine years of age, George Hassell was older than the average age (thirty) of the 361 men who died in the chair between 1924 and 1964, and he was also unusual in that he was one of the 30 percent of these men who were white. However, like the majority who "rode the thunderbolt," he had a fairly episodic work history, having usually worked at some type of common labor occupation during his peregrinations through most of the United States. Most who died on Old Sparky had labored in agriculture, ranching, and related work.[25]

Between 1924 and April 5, 1926, all of the thirteen prisoners who had been executed by electrocution in Texas were people of color. On April 5, 1926, John Sidney "Pete" Welk became the first white person to die on the Texas Thunderbolt. Like Hassell, he had been a tenant farmer. The crime that put Welk on death row was much less egregious than Hassell's but was nevertheless punished as a capital crime. While Hassell was being executed for only one of his thirteen murders, Welk faced the same punishment for killing an assistant night jailer in the Dallas County jail during an escape attempt in 1923. What was most unusual in this case was Welk's final request not to shave his head until right before the execution. He was described as being "inordinately proud" of his shock of "wavy black hair."[26] On his way to the execution chamber, he asked if he could say goodbye to a friend on death row, a Black man named Lavannie Twitty. The two shook hands between the bars, and he wished Twitty "better luck than he himself had had."[27] There is, by the way, no record of Hassell having made any friends on death row.

The execution of Hassell followed an official protocol established by law in 1923. Once the death sentence had been pronounced in Farwell, a warrant was issued under the seal of the district court for the execution of the sentence of death. The warrant contained the conviction, offense, sentence of the court, and time fixed for the execution. Parmer County Sheriff Martin was handed this document in Farwell before he left the courthouse and was expected to present it to the Huntsville warden, N. L. Speer, upon arrival. Before returning to the same court that issued the warrant, it was standard procedure to bring back a receipt from prison officials.

Once ensconced on death row, Hassell would remain there until his appointed execution date. Death row inmates often wait on death row for hours, days, or even longer before their executions. But the period of the so-called death watch leading up to the execution is a block of time, usually a couple of days, during which the condemned is moved from a regular cell on death row to a cell closer to the death chamber. On death row, Hassell was prohibited from meeting with visitors outside of family members, spiritual advisors, his physician, and his lawyer. These individuals would have been on hand if the prisoner wanted to discuss his health and transact any last business that needed attending to. Family members and spiritual advisors were permitted to speak with him only at allotted times.

As his appointed time of death approached, Hassell underwent a transformation, not unlike the Jekyll and Hyde proclivities that could reportedly be unleashed after sipping his favorite whiskey. When he was moved closer to the death room, his demeanor changed dramatically from the laughing, jocular good old boy to the "sullen faced" killer of thirteen, apparently just now recognizing that he was spending his last day on earth.[28]

The criminologist L. Kay Gillespie made a study of the behavior of several condemned inmates as they came to grips with living their final hours on earth. Her data included entries from death watch logs, which offer an overview of what these last twenty-four hours typically look like. Hassell, no doubt, would have recognized many of these observations on his last day. While in isolation, the prisoner is typically under constant supervision and surveillance. He is often strip-searched, dressed in new clothes, and prevented from having physical contact with anyone.[29]

Hassell probably glimpsed the electric chair on his initial walk to his death row cell, although in some prisons there is a curtain or wall constructed to obscure the machine and avoid traumatizing the doomed inmate. Whether he saw it or not, he knew exactly where it was, just feet down the hall. Hassell probably went through the rituals typical of death row inmates during the death watch, from eating his last meal to writing some last words to a correspondent.

One can imagine that as Hassell walked into his death row cell for the last time, he gave the cell a quick look, perhaps "breath[ing] a heavy sigh."[30] Like other denizens of death row, he would notice new clothes laid out neatly on the bed. Maybe he would wash his hands in his sink and then settle on his bed to try and get some shut-eye. But he would almost certainly get up often and just pace the cell, all the time being watched by a guard. He might begin reading the Bible at some point and then try to get some sleep. However, knowing he would sleep forever soon enough, he might begin pacing again, sighing, picking up the Good Book and perhaps settling down with it again. He might think about how at that this time tomorrow he would be in the chair.

Some prisoners might be able to sleep, but only by covering their eyes from the omnipresent lights. Going over the sequence of events awaiting him, Hassell would most likely have tossed and turned, unable to find a comfortable position on his spartan bed. At 5:30 a.m. on his last day, he would take his last shower. It is not uncommon for inmates to refuse their last breakfast,[31] and Hassell might have done so as well. He might then have sought solace once more in the Bible. During the day, he would have met with a spiritual advisor and read any last correspondence that he might have received. It is doubtful, however, that a mass murderer of Hassell's ilk would have received any.

One pulp writer described Hassell as "the only man in the history of Death Row at Huntsville to gain weight."[32] It is an observation that was made by others who visited Hassell and commented on his dramatic weight gain. This was not an uncommon transformation for prisoners held in solitary confinement and with little chance for exercise. Of course, the high carbohydrate meals three times a day didn't help. One observer noted that "he ate heartily and showed no signs of remorse for the brutal killings he had committed."[33] Hassell had actually gained much of his weight during his months of confinement in the Hale County Jail in Plainview, where one visitor remarked, "Good meals and regular hours of jail life have added many pounds to his weight … From a year of carefree jail life which he has spent as a model prisoner, Hassell emerged as a changed man physically. He is as fat as a pig."[34]

Often, before a condemned prisoner notices, their last day has turned to evening. The warden will stop by and explain the protocol that awaits them and as midnight approaches, it's time for them to order the iconic last meal. In the past, some wardens have joined the condemned for their last meal. Prisoners have been known to order much more food than they can ever eat and then ask that the leftovers be distributed to other death row prisoners.[35]

Hassell's voracious appetite seems to have ended the night before his execution. When Warden N. L. Speer came by to ask him what he would like for his last meal, Hassell chuckled, telling him that he "wouldn't think of putting him to the trouble of making extra preparations for him," adding that the "regular prison meals had been fine."[36] However, the warden told his interviewer that he would have leftover chicken from lunch in any case.

On Thursday morning Hassell was taken from his old cell and measured for his burial clothes, after which he took his last bath. As he stepped out of his cell, he joked with the guards and seemed to be in "high spirits."[37] He then turned to speak to the guards outside his former cell door and found it was locked. His visage changed on a dime and did not improve when he was told that he was being moved to the adjacent cell closer to the "little green door" that housed the electric chair. He initially resisted efforts to put him in the new cell but quickly relented. He would remain in this cell until guards came for him at midnight. His former cell seemed luxurious by comparison, with his new cell furnished only with a blanket on the floor. There was no cot. This was just one of the steps that were taken to make sure he did not take his own life "and cheat the state of its legal right."

As midnight approached, Hassell's normally lighthearted attitude underwent a quick transformation. He became "sullen faced," scorning friendly conversation with his keepers. Now he seemed to have been struck "deaf and dumb," only offering "a vacant stare" that perhaps "reflected a mind in turmoil."[38] In his former cell, he had been able to see the "little green door," and usually sat facing it. Now that he was right next to it, he decided to "sit with his back toward it in his new home."[39]

The killer had "lost all of his bravado" as the minutes ticked by, no longer smiling at guards, or even communicating with them.[40] Any attempts at pacifying Hassell were met with morose mumbling to himself. He even waved off the chaplain. Around 6:30 p.m., after he had been given his last bath, the warden announced that no one else could see the doomed convict. At this time, Hassell's hair was shaved as well as his left leg. Hassell's next preparations can be assumed, since typically an inmate's newly shaven head would be doused in alcohol and in most cases he would be dressed in a "coarsely woven death suit."

According to one of his guards at Huntsville, Hassell claimed to be a Russellite, a follower of Charles T. Russell and the Jehovah's Witnesses, like his wife and victim, Susie.[41] Members claimed not to believe in the hereafter. Despite entreaties by various clergy members from other faiths "who sought to plumb the soul of the killer," he responded with only the silence of "seeming scorn." According to one reporter, after "his removal to within a few feet of the somber chamber, where grotesque shadow cast an eeried fantasy on the walls, the killer seemed to change his outlook—not, on life, but on what is after life."[42]

Just before midnight, there were twenty-five people gathered in Warden Speer's office, including state officials required to attend by law and reporters as well as "others privileged to witness the grim drama, that soon was to be enacted."[43] Demonstrating the familial enmity that characterized much of his life, according to one reporter his two sisters and cousin "expressed no desire to talk with their brother," nor did Hassell ask to meet with them.[44] For more than a week, his sister, P. A. Watson of Fort Worth, had been in the vicinity. When accosted by reporters she refused to identify her other sister nor enable them to reach her for comments. Ms. Watson secluded herself as best she could soon after arriving in the small prison town. Hassell's cousin, Sam Hassell from Crockett, Texas, had met with the throng of reporters in the warden's office shortly before the execution but "left it before [they] reached the death house."

At midnight the timeworn prison clock alerted the prison population that an execution was about to take place. When Warden Speer heard the tolling he "arose from his chair, removed his hat and led the party away [from his office] toward the execution chamber ... laughter and joking in the room ceased and the death march began." Just before the execution, music from the prison radio could be heard, "mostly stirring marches,"[45] though prisoners in the death house had been polled as to the music they favored and overwhelmingly the choice was jazz.[46] It is doubtful that any type of music would have soothed Hassell. He might have been "mentally composed," if no longer the avatar of courage, but he looked "deathly pale."[47] One reporter was struck by the "ominous quiet" following the electrocution. On the way out of the prison the witnesses were met by "hundreds of peering eyes [gazing] out of the narrow windows" in the building adjacent to the death chamber ... There was little sleep" after Hassell "walked to his doom."[48]

The death chamber is a small room lit by a "large light globe hung in the center of the room below a large white reflector, producing a harsh glare."[49] The journalist Don Reid, who remembered that on the right there was a "dark curtain hung from a runner on the ceiling, and I could see movement behind it. I surmised that it was caused by the executioner ... I noted a closed door to the left of me and wondered where it led ... the warden turned and walked several steps to the door I had noticed, tapped on it sharply with his key ring and opened it up slightly. The ear and eye of a guard appeared through the crack and the warden spoke just three words, 'we are ready.'"

The electric chair was only separated from the spectators in the room by a "large narrow rail." One reporter in the 1930s recounted entering the death chamber before midnight and standing behind the black railing "directly in front of the chair," only about four feet away: "I felt I could reach out and touch it."[50] The onlookers mostly stood. Instructions were to remain silent as soon as the condemned stepped into the room and until the prison physician pronounced him dead.[51] Thus, the only sounds made were by the nervous shuffling of their feet.

As the door to the left "swung inward and open a procession of men filed swiftly and almost soundlessly" into the room. Leading the way was a guard, who "stepped quickly to the left side of the chair." Following him were the inmate, a priest, and two other guards. The door was shut, and Reid described that the "room was full of figures and shadows and standing before me was the condemned man." One reporter described his demeanor: "Gone was his air of bravado. He looked the part of a pasty chunk of putty who stood before the veil of the unknown and hesitated to lift it."[52] His guard had to steady him when "he swayed a bit as his steps brought him closer to eternity."[53]

Hassell was dressed in a neat brown suit when he walked into the death chamber. His blue shirt was unfastened at the collar, and his broad powerful shoulders were held proudly erect. His step was firm, and he seemed to be gazing into space, away from the green door and the narrow chamber where the law would take its awful price. Instead of shoes on his feet there were the regulation gray socks meted out to prisoners in Texas.[54] If his last seconds were anything like those of past occupants of Old Sparky, he might have stared at the officials and onlookers just steps away, breaking "down the courage of spectators who bowed their heads in abasement at their own lust to witness the destruction of a fellow man."[55]

On Friday, February 10, 1928, sometime between 12:26 and 12:29 a.m.,[56] the "Texas Bluebeard" and serial mass murderer, George Jefferson Hassell, rode the thunderbolt to eternity. A minute or so before Hassell sat down for the last time, Huntsville warden N. L. Speer asked him if he had any last words. Hassell, never at a loss for words, said, "I'd like to announce to the world that I am ready to meet God. I have made my confession to God and man. Man has misunderstood some of it, but God has not. That's all." "Except for a slight tremor," his voice never wavered, and his expression never changed as he spoke his last words.[57]

As he walked to his doom, a "gray pallor overspread his features." Witnesses claimed that Hassell "walked calmly to his doom, sat down in the electric chair as if he were sitting down to a good meal." The formerly loquacious mass murderer had undergone a transformation from the smiling man to a morose version, and then, "without bowing his massive shoulders and holding his shaved head erect, sat down to face eternity."[58] As soon as he was seated, three guards fastened the confining straps across his body. They then ripped through the left leg of his trousers, baring his skin for the damp electrode that was pressed into place and fastened, followed by another electrode affixed to his head.

The warden's next duty was to draw a black curtain between the prisoner and the executioner. An attendant placed a black cap over Hassell's face and head, eclipsing the last light he would see in this world, so that "only his nose and a strip of his cheek were left bare. Hassell sat perfectly still as the death mask was adjusted. The room was so silent his labored breathing was plainly audible."[59] Once the guards had finished their work, one nodded to the warden, who then gave the executioner behind the curtain the go-ahead to start the execution. As one witness would describe an electrocution that took place about ten years later: "Then came the crunch ... The room exploded with the mounting whine of the generators ... His body slammed forward against the restraining leather straps. ... a second jolt brought an odd red glow to the skin and steam drifted from his head and chest."[60]

The spectators looked on in absolute silence, "hardly daring to move a muscle."[61] According to the reporter Ed Kilman, the lights of the prison dimmed.[62] Then, the "whine of a dynamo behind the black curtain broke the stillness." His body slumped forward as "the searing current tore through the nerves and veins of his body," and Hassell "slumped forward like a man who is immersed suddenly in cold water." One reporter noted that the "tip of his nose showed red, then white, then red as three shocks were applied."[63] His body flopped forward, "as if he were drinking in the deadly current that took the law's vengeance for his crimes ... His face was pale, and his eyes were set straight forward. No emotion could be discerned in the stolid countenance, and a firm set of the doomed giant's jaws were the only signs of the thoughts racing thru Hassell's brain in his last moments on earth."[64] The "thumb and forefingers on the hands with which he had decimated two families clenched and then fell loose. The current was turned off and his body returned to its normal position." After eight minutes and three shocks, the last current of electricity was turned off and the attendants stepped forward and unfastened the straps. In short order, "the black mask was removed, revealing the purplish countenance of the dead man." One couldn't help noticing a "scarlet burn" around the skull "where the current had crashed through to still the brain."[65]

Once the straps and electrodes had been removed, Hassell's "shaven bullet-shaped head fell down on the hairy chest, bared for the doctor's examination."[66] After checking once more, Dr. Angier nodded toward the spectators and said, "I pronounce this man dead."[67] His words were the last official entry on Hassell's record. In the prison ledger, Warden Speer wrote in red ink: "in accordance with the mandate of the law, Feb 10, 1928."[68] The body was placed on a stretcher and wheeled from the room. The spectators shifted uneasily. Newspapermen scurried to telephones. Officers turned away from the carnage. Many of the spectators were pale from the ordeal. Hassell's forehead and face were noticeably "seared by the blistering currents." Hassell became one of twentieth-century America's 4,300 criminals to die in the electric chair, more than have died by all other methods of execution combined.[69]

Hassell was only the first of two executions that February evening. It is unknown how he felt about sharing the spotlight with Black inmate Robert Lee Benton, aka "R. L. Stanley," who was slated to die the same night. Although it was the warden's decision as to who should go first, some accounts have the two men briefly discussing and deciding who would go first, with Benton showing faux respect, telling Hassell, "Mr. George, you know a white man always goes before a n****r."[70] And go first Hassell did.

Benton had been convicted of killing a white farmer near Crosbyton the previous February. As he walked into the death chamber, he was asked if he had anything to say. He smiled and said he had nothing else to say.[71]

As Benton walked to the chair, he looked at the spectators and, recognizing one of them, said, "Howdy do." He sat in the chair at 12:45 a.m., almost immediately after Hassell's demise. Three jolts of current ripped through his body and at 12:51 am he was pronounced dead. Reportedly, "he died game [bravely] without a whimper and without faltering."

In the 1930s three options were available for making burial arrangements following an execution at the Walls. Shortly before execution, the prison warden would send a form letter to the condemned man's family about picking up the body. The family could make their own arrangements, or, if they couldn't afford a burial or did not respond in time, the body would be buried in what is now Captain Joe Byrd Cemetery, known colloquially as "Peckerwood Hill." Named after a former assistant warden and executioner at the Huntsville Prison, it is the largest prison cemetery in the United States. The third option allowed the family or condemned inmate to donate his body to the State Anatomical Board for dissection and study.[72]

Once it was indicated that no one would claim Hassell's body and that the town of Farwell was uninterested in retrieving the body for burial, he was laid to rest in the prison cemetery. There is no evidence any family member attended his burial, nor in which direction his head rests.[73] Initially the family had made plans to bury the body in Palestine, Texas, but nothing came of it.[74] Shortly after the trial, the family of Hassell's murdered wife, Susan, made two requests regarding the disposition of Hassell's body. One, was that he not be buried with the rest of the family at the Olivet Cemetery in Parmer County. The other was that his head be placed pointing north, in order to mark, in Susan's father's words, "the grave of a convicted criminal." The traditional Christian method of positioning a body or coffin in a grave was to have the head pointing west and the feet to the east. According to Tom Kunesh, president of the Tennessee Ancient Sites Conservatory, the reason for this positioning is so that a deceased Christian believer in the resurrection of the dead will be allowed to see the Second Coming of Jesus face to face.[75]

According to a Hassell family manuscript, "the warden had struck up a bit of a friendship with George who had been a model prisoner, always cheerful, and a positive influence on the other inmates." On his last day,

Warden Speer visited with Hassell several times. Following the execution, Speer refused all newspaper requests for an interview "and never spoke of Hassell again."[76]

Having taken part in twenty executions, Speer had evidently tired of the smell of burning flesh and the electric whine of the electric chair, and less than two months after Hassell's execution, on April 15, 1928, N. L. Speer resigned as warden. Perhaps his last execution-related duty had been the final straw. Two days before he left office, he had to make special arrangements for the electrocution of the Bexar County killer Juan Flores a week later. According to the *Fort Worth Record-Telegram*, Speer had to have the chair adjusted because Flores' left foot, on which the electrode is fitted, had been amputated. Plans were in the works to place the electrode clamp on his remaining right leg when the time came.[77]

Speer had planned to retire several times before, but each time was convinced to stay on. During his four years as warden, he had presided over close to twenty executions and would later relate that he favored life in prison over capital punishment.[78] He was a popular figure among administrators and prisoners. However, "for some time he [had] felt under great strain because of the necessity of officiating at the execution of condemned men."[79] Speer would later trade in his warden's shield for a sheriff's badge in Walker County, Texas. Perhaps his best-known and most oft-repeated lamentation put into perspective his views on taking a life: "When I push the switch and a man's soul goes from his body, a part of me also dies."[80]

George J. Hassell paid the price demanded by the state for the murder of his stepson and nephew, Alton Hassell. There was not much more that could be done to punish him for his twelve other admitted murders. For many years, though his crimes had few equals in the criminal annals of the United States, they remained absent from the historical record. To this day, he remains the worst multiple family annihilator in US history, having taken the lives of thirteen family members in two mass killings between 1917 and 1926.

Epilogue

"The road to mass murder is long, lonely, and rocky; it takes more than an overnight journey for the killer to reach the end."

The malevolent life of the Texas Bluebeard, George J. Hassell, has few counterparts in the annals of American murder. What distinguished his crimes was the fact that he killed his two wives and eleven children over a nine-year period in three separate events. Sometime in June 1917, Hassell killed his common-law wife, Marie Vogel, and three young children in their Whittier, California, cottage. Nine years later he murdered his wife Susan and seven stepchildren, who were also his nieces and nephews, and then waited for several days to kill his remaining stepchild, his nephew, Alton—the crime that ultimately put him in the Texas death house.

Mass murder is a rare form of homicide. Conversely, "the family annihilator is the most common type of mass killer."[1] Hassell's record as America's deadliest family annihilator stood until 1987, when Ronald Gene Simmons of Russellville, Arkansas, killed fourteen family members including his wife over a period of less than two days. The timing and facts of Simmons's murders indicate that he was not a serial killer, nor multiple family annihilator, like Hassell. Several elements of both the Simmons and Hassell family mass murders, particularly the annihilation of his last family, are remarkably similar.[2]

So, not only was Hassell a mass murderer and family annihilator, but he was *also* a serial killer, according to the established rubric for these crimes. Taken together, George J. Hassell was America's worst serial *mass* murderer. There have been a few other killers that annihilated multiple families.

Several elements of both the Simmons and Hassell family mass murders mentioned above are remarkably similar.[3] Both men, for example, killed their wives first before methodically eradicating the other family members. In each instance, the father had his unsuspecting sons dig pits near their houses in the months leading up to their killing sprees.

Although both Simmons and Hassell claimed they had directed the digging of the pits for other purposes, both became abattoirs, whether planned or not.

It is probable that the Hassell and Simmons family annihilations followed allegations by family members that the father had sexually abused one of their children. Once it becomes known to family members, it often completely shatters the dynamics of the family and reveals what a monster the father in each case was.[4] Simmons impregnated his seventeen-year-old daughter, while Hassell sexually abused at least one and probably two of his nieces, who were also his stepdaughters.

Both Susan Hassell and Rebecca Simmons reportedly refused to sleep with their husbands once the sexual abuse had been revealed. Once these abuses became known, the heads of household probably lost any respect they might have had. When Ronald Gene Simmons was queried after his crime spree, he tended like other multiple murderers to deflect blame for his actions, explaining that he didn't know what came over him; like Hassell, he claimed he had an irresistible "urge to kill." It is not uncommon for serial killers and mass murderers to shift blame. According to the authors of *Extreme Killing*, Simmons attempted to distance himself from the crime, claiming, "I'm not to blame ... I couldn't help myself. I'm a victim too."[5]

Both family annihilators committed their worst murders around Christmastime and also waited for the final family victims to return home before completing their deadly slaughters. Likewise, each gave up to law enforcement without a fight, accepting their roles in the carnage, with Simmons telling officers, "I've done what I wanted to do and now it's all over ... I've gotten everybody who hurt me."[6]

***

A murderer once told Adrian Raine, a leading authority on the neurobiological factors in violence, that "it's not easy to kill a person for the first time. But once you have stepped over that threshold, the idea of killing someone else does not carry the same baggage it used to."[7] Perhaps this might explain how Hassell and other serial killers found it easier to kill once they had killed before. Hassell enjoyed tantalizing authorities till the

Epilogue

very end, telling more than one confidante that "there is more that I can tell."[8] Authorities always hoped he would "cast light on other murders of women and children that have remained mysteries." They tried to wring other confessions from the Bluebeard once he knew he had "nothing to look forward to but the fatal day."[9] But he never mentioned any others, beyond making vague insinuations. Since he never admitted to any other murders, he was probably just stringing law enforcement along.

George J. Hassell was an enigma to those who crossed paths with him. Psychologists were puzzled by his willingness to acknowledge that he did not know why he killed his victims, especially considering that he insisted he had always loved children and that he "had been a favorite with them,"[10] even though he confessed to strangling ten of his youthful victims.

In most mass murders, the killer prefers to use some type of firearm, but in family mass murders, the killers, like Hassell, usually kill the youngest children using more "personal weapons" such as stabbing and strangling, while "as age increases guns are more likely to be used."[11] This conforms to Hassell's murders of his Farwell family, in which he used a gun only on the two oldest boys and a garotte, rope, hammer, and his hands on the weaker and smaller family members.

Most evidence suggests that family mass murderers are quite deliberate in their actions. This goes against the theory by some criminologists that familicidal fathers are "always crazed and uncontrolled" at the time of the crime. There is a body of evidence that suggests that these killers are likely to be "cold, calculating, and careful in their actions."[12] Moreover, it is not uncommon for them to plan the attacks days and even months ahead of time.

The Hassell and Simmons cases illustrate that a family annihilation "is often well-planned" and "carefully considered"[13] and the perpetrator "is fully aware of his actions and their ramifications."[14] As noted previously both fathers had ready-made pits dug before they filled them with dead family members. This lends credence to the notion that they sometimes plan the attacks days and even months ahead of time. This suggests that at the time of their crimes they were capable of rational [to them] thinking and organizational planning. In Hassell's case, like other mass murderers, it is likely that he had created and followed "a mental script, one that he rehearsed [in his mind] over and over until he became comfortable with his mission" so that "when the big day arrived [he was] prepared, calm, and thrilled" to be carrying out the task he had been thinking about for some time.[15] Hassell always confessed to his killings, but never offered further insights beyond his sudden "urge to kill."

Homicide statistics reveal that being killed in one's own house by a family member is the most common type of murder. One facet of domestic homicide that is germane to gaining a better understanding of the Hassell murders in particular and domestic homicides more generally is the role played by genetic relationships between victims and perpetrators. Put another way, the vast majority of domestic homicide victims are "people who do not share the killer's genes."[16]

Raine's research suggests that one needs look no further than folklore and fairy tales featuring wicked stepmothers to get an inkling of the potential for violence between parents and stepchildren.[17] Recent research indicates that being killed by an unrelated person is eleven times more likely than by a genetic relation.[18] According to research by the Canadian evolutionary psychologists Martin Daly and Margo Wilson, "homicides perpetrated by stepfathers differ from those by biological fathers not only quantitatively, but qualitatively."[19] Biological parents who kill their "genetic offspring" are more inclined to kill their progeny with guns and asphyxiation, "methods that do not require brute force."[20] George Hassell clearly shares the attributes one would expect to find in a homicidal stepparent, since his murder methods relied on very personal acts, strangling and choking to death more than half of his victims. Put another way, one reporter observed that except for Alton, who was shot to death, "Hassell scorned lethal weapons in putting to death his victims ... either [striking] them down with a hammer, or strangling them to death."[21]

***

One glaring question needs to be addressed here. Why are legions of criminals and murderers with much less blood on their hands so well-known and Hassell all but forgotten? As mentioned earlier, he is not listed in any of the better compendiums and reference books devoted to serial and mass murderers, yet his crimes eclipsed most of those given their due.[22]

Perhaps, the popular historian Stewart H. Holbrook was onto something back in 1941, when he published *Murder Out Yonder: An Informal Study of Certain Classic Crimes in Back-Country America*. His book focused on ten old murder cases that had occurred in the rural heartland, environments not much different from Farwell, Texas. Like in the case of Farwell, these "back country crimes" were remembered because they were "settled into the tradition, the folklore, or the communities where they occurred."[23] Because Hassell committed his last mass murder in the sparsely settled Texas Panhandle, aside from several local newspapers there was little media coverage of Hassell's crimes nationwide and no chance of the saturation coverage that many other crimes invited. If he had committed these murders in Houston, Austin, or Amarillo, Texas, let alone in New York City or Chicago, instead of Whittier and Farwell, his crimes might have been chronicled in true crime books or perhaps inspired a Hollywood film or two.

Holbrook was curious about why some crimes remained part of a region's local memory. He wrote, "It is difficult to know what elements in a crime serve to preserve its memory through several generations, often for a century or more, and dignify it into minor history."[24] Perhaps because Hassell's crimes included sexual abuse and the strangling of so many young children, locals preferred to excise it from the traditional history of the region. Likewise, "if the criminal or victim becomes the subject of a singable and sufficiently maudlin ballad—preferably ungrammatical—then his name will last a long time."

George J. Hassell may never have been memorialized in song, but that doesn't mean that he has been totally forgotten. Looking back on this horrific case seventy-five years later, one Farwell area resident explained the long-lasting impact of the crime, noting, "Back then the moral fabric of our community called for everyone to think the best of your neighbors, trusting them, and always regarding them with respect. Because of this mindset it is not surprising that no one found it unusual when George Hassell had a yard sale before heading to Oklahoma. Indeed, no one wondered about the family's disappearance—as they were in fact 'literally buried within feet of the yard sale attendees, dead, sitting in hauntingly posed positions in the cellar."[25]

The murders of the nine members of the Hassell family are far from forgotten in the peaceful community of Farwell. Some might say that it is still a part of the community's "DNA." The crimes have even inspired a local theater production. For a number of years, a homeschool theater company has been performing the play *Killer Among Us* at Bovina's Fedora Theatrix. Based on the story of the Farwell serial killer George J. Hassell, the play centers around a young reporter for the local newspaper who happens to connect the dots that lead to a killer, solving a murder mystery. The theater's director and playwright, Gina Prather, explains that "some of the wonderful things of the play are its theatrical value and the connection it has to the community to this day." Prather adds, "There are still family members here in Parmer County who had grandparents, aunts and uncles who attended the Hassell family yard sale and who served on the jury during the trial."[26]

In her 2002 roman à clef about the Hassell case, novelist Rebecca Grayson tells the story of "Jefferson Bryce," a fictive version of George Hassell. She claimed to have been inspired to write the book after hearing family stories about the crime.[27] Her mother, according to Grayson, "was among the children beside the fence the day the bodies were discovered." Her brother supposedly lifted her "high enough to see in the windows" of the Hassell abattoir. She said that "a mother described the stains on the wall, this became a frightening experience for me. It was something nightmares are made of for children, and I suffered many over the years."

***

Until well into the twenty-first century, a barely legible tombstone marked the final resting place of Susan Ferguson Hassell and her eight children. The stone marker bore the engraved names of each victim, but the natural elements of the High Plains had taken their toll. As the cemetery fell into disrepair over the years, locals knew it only as the "old burying ground or potter's field."[28] By the late 1980s, it was so neglected, if not forgotten, that most residents had a hard time describing how to get there. In July

Epilogue

1988, almost exactly one century after the birth of George J. Hassell, one visitor described it as being in "shameful" condition, made even worse by the "pungent smell of a seemingly endless sea of feed lots."[29] By then, "you [could] get to it only by tromping down a lot of waist high weeds."[30]

The Farwell community had banded together in the aftermath of the awful depredations of 1926. In the twenty-first century, the community spirit rose to the challenge once more as efforts were made to support the preservation of the historic cemetery. Such a project was beyond the budget of Farwell and Parmer County, but the cemetery's historical significance was appreciated by preservation-minded locals such as Deputy Sheriff David Kube and probation officer Teresa Ancira of Texico, New Mexico.

The land was still owned by a descendent of the Hassells' landlord, J. D. Hamlin. Jane Clair Overstreet Barclay agreed to allow the Parmer County Historical Commission to clean up the cemetery, described as a "ten acre corner" of land located "behind a fence crafted of welded sucker pipe donated by a local company."[31] In 2012, the adult probation office requested and received permission from the county judge to allow the historical commission to maintain the cemetery. Out of this process emerged the Olivet Cemetery Association, which depended on local volunteers. Barclay was persuaded into deeding the cemetery to a group led by Deputy Sheriff Kube and Bonnie Warren. Over the next few years, the land was transformed, thanks to businesses and volunteers from Clovis, Texico, and Farwell donating money, time, and equipment.[32]

Preservation efforts led to the discovery of a small section where a dozen infants had been buried in the 1970s, the offspring of military families who could not afford a burial in "more expensive perpetual care cemeteries." One local farm machinery business donated the extended use of a tractor to help maintain the property, while Parmer County provided men and machinery to grade new roads.[33] Farwell chipped in by waiving any charges for dumping debris from the cleanup to the landfill.

In February 2018, Patsy Delk from the Historical Foundation of Curry County, New Mexico, led efforts to put up a new tombstone marking the final resting place of the Hassell family.[34] The headstone was donated by Steed Todd Funeral Home in Clovis, New Mexico, and

Legacy Memorial in Portales, New Mexico, did the engraving.[35] One reporter described the sight of the new stone standing next to the old one, a "formidable upright marker in grey granite."[36] One side lists the names and dates of birth of the nine victims, while the other includes a Bible verse from John 14, which starts off: "Let not your heart be troubled ..." Below is carved the simple statement "Family murdered in December 1926 by George J. Hassell."[37]

***

Several mysteries still linger. Hassell descendants, researching his life in the late 1980s, wondered whatever happened to Hassell's "assets" after he was convicted and executed. The paper trail was cold when it came to this issue. However, family members speculated on what might have happened to his car and bank accounts. One possible answer, yet unproven, is that the assets were transferred to Nora, the last living family member and the mother of his daughter. There was also some discussion of the possibility that the funeral of his slaughtered family and the original tombstone came out of his pocket. These questions remain unanswered.[38]

After the Hassell murders, the Lindops "stayed on at the murder house for about year ... until they could finish out the lease, save some money and move back to central Texas.[39] After the Lindops moved out, only one more family would live in the "murder house" for any length of time. This family, new to the area, rented it but moved out within days of hearing of its ghastly past. The house "stood empty for many years as someone worked the land" but apparently lived elsewhere. The house was moved to its final location in the 1940s and used as storage.[40]

For years after the murders, the Hassell home was regarded as the "local haunted house." High-school boys enjoyed scaring their girlfriends by driving past it "when the moon was full." The owner of the house in the 1980s, who was still using it for storage, according to Hassell family lore, did not believe in spectral goings on, but still saw "no reason to visit it at night."[41] Some locals have suggested that its reputation as a haunted house and ghostly apparition stems from a story often told by Tinnie Lindop, who testified at Hassell's trial that she had driven by the residence on December 4, which was several days after Susie and the kids were murdered, claiming that she had seen Susan waving to her while standing by the back door with her children around her.[42] The cellar pit has been plowed over for years, and the house has been torn down. In 2017, one local reporter revisited the site and found that "nothing remains but memories where murders took place."[43] However, the land there "looks flat but then in a few days a depression forms there as it has for over 60 years."[44]

Likewise, the Hassell cottage in Whittier, California, site of the 1917 murders, no longer stands. In its place on 7242 S. Whittier Avenue there is a modern four-unit apartment building. When the Whittier slayings became national news long after they took place, the house became known as the "death house" among locals but soon faded from public memory. Time tends to blur, if not evaporate, memories of events as people move on with their lives and communities change. However, in the 2000s, a woman named Sara Castro became quite "unnerved" when she was confronted with the unwelcome news "that her home for the past four years had been the site of a quadruple murder in 1917," telling a local reporter, "I was told nobody had died there."[45] Indeed, she added the caveat, "I always ask because I really don't want to live where someone has passed. It's kind of creepy." Her landlord, who had owned the building for nineteen years, had never known its infamous history either.

As for the last resting place of George J. Hassell, America's worst serial mass murderer, he will spend eternity in the very well-maintained Joe Byrd Cemetery, known colloquially as "Peckerwood Hill," in Huntsville, Texas, home to the largest prison graveyard in the country.

Appendix

List of Items for the Hassell Farm Auction Sale, Wednesday, December 22, 1926 (Plaintiff's Exhibit No. 2, Trial Transcript, 82–87)

10 Horses and Mules

1 black horse mule, 9 yrs old, 1200 lbs
1 bay horse mule, 5 yrs old, 1000 lbs
1 black mare mule, 4 yrs old, 1000 lbs
1 sorrel mare mule, 4 yrs old, 1000 lbs
2 black mare mules, 4 yrs old, 900 lbs
1 gray mare, 4 yrs old, 1400 lbs
1 bay mare, 6 yrs old, 1000 lbs
1 black saddle horse, 8 yrs old, 850 lbs
1 black Shetland pony, 8 yrs old, 650 lbs

13 Head of Cattle

2 fawn colored jerseys, 3 yrs old, giving milk
1 dark jersey, 3 yrs old, fresh soon
1 red jersey, 3 yrs old, giving milk
1 red Durham, 5 yrs old, giving milk
1 red jersey, 4 yrs old, fresh
1 jersey bull, 18 months, subject to registration
2 jersey bull calves
1 jersey heifer calf
1 jersey and Durham heifer, 1 yr old
1 red Durham heifer, 1 yr old
1 white face bull calf

FEED

13,000 bundles cane in stack
4,000 bundles hegeina in stack

IMPLEMENTS

3 three-inch farm wagons
2 hay frames
4 maize forks
2 pitch forks
2 scoop shovels
3 hoes
1 ten-inch turning plow
1 Georgia stock
1 post hole digger
Hammers, saws, brace, bits, etc.
2 28" sweeps
4 10" sweeps
1 wagon sheet and set of bows
1 good tent, 12X14

HARNESS

2 sets britching harness
2 sets chain harness
12 collars
12 bridles
5 pair lines
1 saddle
1 boy's saddle
2 riding bridles

Appendix

CHICKENS

12 pure bred Plymouth rock hens
6 pure bred Plymouth rock roosters
50 pure bred Plymouth rock fryers
3 chicken coops
6 bantams
3 guineas
6 white rabbits

HOGS

3 shoats, 4 months old

HOUSEHOLD GOODS

1 cooking stove
1 heater
1 good sewing machine
1 davenport
1 hoosier cabinet
1 safe
1 dining table
8 dining chairs
4 rockers
1 high chair
1 child's bed
1 8-day clock
1 folding bed
1 bookcase
8 window shades
1 washstand

1 chiffrobe
3 bedsteads and springs
1 2 gal. ice cream freezer
1 washing machine
1 25 gal. wash pot with furnace
1 gasoline iron
1 phonograph and records
1 dresser
1 rifle, 22 caliber
Dishes and cooking utensils
1 12 gauge shot gun, single barrel

Other things too numerous to mention.

SALE WILL BEGIN PROMPTLY AT 10 O'CLOCK A.M. TEXAS TIME

Lunch will be served at noon

Endnotes

Notes for Introduction

1. Hassell was first referred to as a "Bluebeard" in the December 31, 1926, articles "Four Bluebeard Victims Hunted" in the *San Francisco Examiner* and "Seek Other Victims of Texas Bluebeard" in the *Ardmore Daily Press*. The "Texas Bluebeard" label appeared in a number of other newspaper articles as well, including the following: "Bodies of Four Others Slain by Texas Bluebeard Found," *Arizona Republican*, February 2, 1927; "Texas Bluebeard Gets Stay of Sentence," *Arizona Republican*, February 22, 1927; "Modern Bluebeard Is Given Sanity Test by State Alienists at Government Request," *Abilene Reporter-News*, February 9, 1928; "Texas 'Bluebeard' Awaits Sentence," *Atlanta Constitution*, January 3, 1928; and "Modern Bluebeard Boasts Career with Women," *Lincoln Journal Star*, January 2, 1928.
2. Harold Schechter, *Psycho USA: Famous American Killers You Never Heard Of* (New York: Ballantine, 2012). For more on the Bluebeard legend, see Leonard Wolf, *Bluebeard: The Life and Crimes of Gilles de Rais* (New York: Clarkson N. Potter, 1980).
3. Regarding Harry Powers (1893–1932), the earliest chronicle of his crimes can be found in Evan Allen Bartlett, *Love Murders of Harry Powers: Beware Such Bluebeards* (New York, Sheftel Press, 1931). Powers was also known as the "Bluebeard of Quiet Dell," and his case was fictionalized in the roman à clef, *Quiet Dell*, by Jayne Anne Phillips (2013). By most accounts this case also inspired the classic Robert Mitchum film, *Night of the Hunter*. For more on John P. Watson (1870–1939), see Ernest Bryan Hoag and Edward Huntington Williams, "The Case of J. P. Watson, the Modern Bluebeard," *Journal of the American Institute of Criminal Law and Criminology* 12, no. 3 (November 1921): 348–59; and Katie Dowd, "'Object, Matrimony': The Forgotten Tale of the West Coast's First Serial Bride Killer," SFGate, October 4, 2019, https://www.sfgate.com/sfhistory/article/james-bluebeard-watson-serial-killer-14490554.

php. Robert S. James (1895–1942) was the last man to hang in the state of California. See Hadley Meares, "In One of L.A.'s Most Outrageous Murder Cases, A Rattlesnake was the Weapon," *Los Angeles Magazine*, December 29, 2017, https://www.lamag.com/culturefiles/rattlesnake-killer-los-angeles-robert-s-james/.
4. "Modern Bluebeard," 25.
5. The term "serial murder" dates back at least to the 1930s, when a Berlin police chief used *Serienmorder* to describe the serial killer Peter Kurten. Between the mid-1960s and the 1980s, the term became increasingly popular among homicide researchers.
6. Eric Hickey, *Serial Murderers and Their Victims*, 5th ed. (Belmont, CA: Cengage, 2010), 20.
7. According to Harold Schechter, the term serial murder can be traced back to at least 1961, when it first appeared in the *Merriam Websters Third International Dictionary*. By the middle of the decade, it had become increasingly more commonly used. However, the first-known published use of the term "serial killer" appeared in the *New York Times* magazine on May 3, 1981. See Harold Schechter, *Serial Killer Files* (New York: Ballantine, 2003).
8. Hickey, *Serial Murderers and Their Victims*, 310.
9. Ronald M. Holmes and Stephen T. Holmes, *Mass Murder in the United States* (Saddle River, NJ: Prentice Hall, 2001), 51.
10. Neil Websdale, *Familicidal Hearts: The Emotional Styles of 211 Killers* (Oxford: Oxford University Press, 2010), 19; Schechter, *Psycho USA*, 15.
11. Marieke Liem and Frans Koenraadt, *Domestic Homicide: Patterns and Dynamics* (London: Routledge, 2018), 124.
12. Schechter, *Psycho USA*, 15.
13. Randolph Roth, *American Homicide* (Cambridge: Harvard University Press, 2009), 138.
14. Websdale, *Familicidal Hearts*, 19.
15. Schechter, *Psycho USA*, 15–16.
16. Grant Duwe, "A Circle of Distortion: The Social Construction of Mass Murder in the United States," *Western Criminology Review* 6, no. 1 (2005): 59–78.

17. Jack Levin and James A. Fox, *Mass Murder: America's Growing Menace* (New York: Plenum, 1985), 204.
18. Michael H. Stone, *The Anatomy of Evil* (Amherst, NY: Prometheus, 2009), 98.
19. Adrian Raine, *The Anatomy of Violence: The Biological Roots of Crime* (New York: Pantheon, 2013), 23.
20. Before the final decision was made as to where to consign Hassell's place in the murder lexicon, I contacted the country's leading criminal profiler, John Douglas (of Mindhunter fame), to solidify my choice of "serial mass murderer." After an exchange of messages, he admitted that Hassell was "a rare one for sure" and that my choice of serial mass murderer was appropriate. John Douglas to author, text message, February 18, 2021.
21. *Shannon County Democrat*, March 8, 1928.
22. Hickey, *Serial Murderers and Their Victims*, 19.
23. Stone, *Anatomy of Evil*, 118
24. Kim Davies, *The Murder Book: Examining Homicide* (Upper Saddle River, NJ: Pearson, 2008), 77.
25. Alex Alvarez and Ronet D. Bachman, *Violence: The Enduring Problem* (Los Angeles, CA: Sage, 2021), 43; Hickey, *Serial Murderers and Their Victims*; James Alan Fox, Jack Levin, and Emma E. Fridel, *Extreme Killing: Understanding Serial and Mass Murder* (Los Angeles, CA: Sage, 2019), 45; Peter Vronsky, *Serial Killers: The Method and Madness of Monsters* (New York: Berkley Publishing, 2004), 245; American Psychological Association, *DSM-IV*.
26. Hervey Cleckley, *The Mask of Sanity: An Attempt to Clarify Some Issues about the So-called Psychopathic Personality*, 5th ed. (St. Louis, MO: C. V. Mosby, 1976). The book was revised in six editions, the last of which was published in the 1980s.
27. J. Reid Meloy, *The Psychopathic Mind: Origins, Dynamics, and Treatment* (Northvale, NJ: Aronson, 1988), 9.
28. Sarah Kramer, "Five Things Everyone Gets Wrong about Psychopaths," *Tech Insider*, August 1, 2016. https://www.businessinsider.in/5-things-everyone-gets-wrong-about-psychopaths-and-why-you-might-be-one/articleshow/53493017.cms.

29. Cleckley, *Mask of Sanity*. The psychologist and criminologist Robert D. Hare based his own Psychopathy Checklist largely on the work of Cleckley. Hare added the characteristics of grandiosity, impulsivity and juvenile delinquency, all missing from Hervey. However, his work has been challenged over its lack of empirical data. Hare, *Psychopathy Checklist*.
30. See Hassell Family, "George Hassell Murder Story."

Notes for Chapter 1

1. Most accounts of Hassell's birthplace list it as Smithville, which is located in Bastrop County. However, this is doubtful. First of all, various online ancestry sites record all of his siblings being born in Smithfield, which is in Tarrant County. George is the only one listed as being born in Smithville. It would make sense that he was probably born in the same vicinity as his siblings. Moreover, he always claimed that his "people" were in Tarrant County, not Bastrop County. The birth records for both cities in 1888 are unavailable, so the author is sticking with Smithfield, rather than the more accepted Smithville, as his place of birth. Other evidence of his birthplace is revealed in a February 3, 1927, article in the *Abilene Morning News*, "Doomed Slayer Expresses Anxiety over Trunk Sent to Abilene after Crimes." The article quotes the Huntsville warden claiming that Hassell told him "he was born in the vicinity of Fort Worth."
2. His military records indicate that he was living in Anderson County in 1909 when he first applied for his Civil War pension.
3. Ancestry.com.
4. John L. McCarthy, "Hassell Laughs and Jokes While Awaiting His Fate," *Cameron Herald*, January 5, 1928.
5. *Ibid.*
6. "Hassell Murderer of 14 Was Praying Deacon: Smiles at Death as He Goes to Electric Chair Feb 10," *Cameron Herald*, February 9, 1928.
7. McCarthy, "Hassell Laughs."

8. *Ibid.*
9. He was probably referring to Cordell, Oklahoma, in western Oklahoma, where his family relocated while he was in prison.
10. John T. Becker, Innocent Awasom, and Cynthia Henry, *Cotton on the South Plains* (Charleston, SC: Arcadia, 2012).
11. Rebecca Sharpless, "Hester Calvert: Farm Wife," in *Human Tradition in Texas*, edited by Ty Cashion and Jesus F. De La Teja (Wilmington, DE: Scholarly Press, 2001), 116.
12. "Hassell Is Ex-Convict from This County," *Abilene Daily Reporter*, December 28, 1926.
13. *Ibid.*
14. Raine, *Anatomy of Violence*, 236.
15. "Hassell Is Ex-Convict."
16. *Ibid.*
17. His convict record indicates that he began his prison sentence leased out to this company, beginning on May 12, 1907.
18. McCarthy, "Hassell Laughs."
19. Texas Convict and Conduct Registers, 1875–1945, retrieved from https://www.tsl.texas.gov/arc/convict.html.
20. McCarthy, "Hassell Laughs."
21. Walker, *Penology for Profit*.
22. *Ibid.*, 244–46.
23. According to the Texas, US Convict and Conduct Registers, 1875–1945, his leasing term began on May 12, 1907, at Burleson and Johns. https://www.tsl.texas.gov/.
24. Walker, *Penology for Profit*, 289.
25. *Ibid.*, 160–61. Burleson, originally from San Marcos, attended Texas A&M College and the University of Texas. He was admitted to the state bar in 1884 and began a state career as Austin state attorney. He would later serve as postmaster general of the United States from 1913 to 1922.
26. Steve J. Martin and Sheldon Ekland-Olson, *Texas Prisons: The Walls Came Tumbling Down* (Austin: Texas Monthly Press, 1987), 5.
27. Quoted in Crow, "Political History," 174.

28. *Ibid.*, 175.
29. Rachel Larkin, "Mewshaw State Sawmill and Maydelle CCC Camp," *East Texas History* (Sam Houston State University, 2022), https://easttexashistory.org/items/show/99.
30. Martin and Ekland-Olson, *Texas Prisons*, 8.
31. His leasing company record can be found in Texas, US Convict and Conduct Registers, 1875–1945.
32. Texas Prison Board Minutes 1907–1909, 221.
33. State Penitentiary Board Minutes, 1900–1911, Box 1998/038-1, August 1907—March 1909 file, p. 221, TSLA.
34. References to his time at farm and pen come from McCarthy, "Hassell Laughs."
35. State Penitentiary Board Minutes, 1900–1911, Box 1998/038-1, Texas Prison Board Minutes, February to June 1907 file, p. 219, TSLA.
36. Walker, *Penology for Profit*, 95n65.
37. *Ibid.*, 155. See also Rupert N. Richardson, *Colonel Edward M. House: The Texas Years, 1858–1912* (Abilene, TX: Abilene Printing and Stationary Company, 1964).
38. Robert Perkinson, *Texas Tough: The Rise of America's Prison Empire* (New York: Henry Holt, 2010), 84.
39. *Ibid.*, 98.
40. Walker, *Penology for Profit*, 99.
41. *Ibid.*, 99.
42. "Hassell's Confession," *Clovis News Journal*, January 17, 1927.
43. "Hassell Relates His Story," *Houston Post-Dispatch*, January 17, 1927.
44. "Hassell Is Ex-Convict."

Notes for Chapter 2

1. "Hassell is Ex-Convict from This County," *Abilene Daily Reporter*, December 28, 1926.
2. Sid Ross knew the family it seems and always referred to Minnie and her parents as Laughlin. Other chroniclers have suggested that her name was Lofley and that she was "the daughter of Ovalo pioneers," but they offer no substantiation.

3. Minnie Laughlin or Minnie Lofley appears on six different family trees in the leading internet ancestry sites. Although she is shown as married to George under both names, the corresponding birth dates are a year apart (1889 and 1890). The 1910 census lists her as twenty years of age.
4. Criminal Justice Historical Files (Execution Files), Box 2006/337-001, George Hassell File, Letter from James Delbert Laughlin to Richard C. Johnson [sic], Assistant Director, Texas Department of Corrections, September 8, 1964. TSLA.
5. No one by that name can be found in local records from that time period.
6. Juanita Daniel Zachry, *The Settling of a Frontier: A History of Rural Taylor County* (Burnet, TX: Nortex Press, 1980), 76–77.
7. Anderson, "Hassell, Slayer of Thirteen, 'Can't Figure It Out,'" *Fort Worth Record Telegram*, January 17, 1927, 4.
8. Raine, *Anatomy of Violence*, 17.
9. It is unclear whether she is referring to Ovalo, Winters, or Buffalo Gap, Texas.
10. In some accounts, he says he went to Oklahoma.
11. Anderson, "Hassell, Slayer of Thirteen."
12. Hassell Relates Life Story," *Houston Post-Dispatch*, January 17, 1927.
13. Riley, "Solano Chronicles."
14. Rodney K. Watterson, *Whips to Walls: Naval Discipline from Flogging to Progressive Era Reform at Portsmouth* (Annapolis, MD: Naval Institute Press, 2014), 100.
15. "Broken Romance Is Blamed by Killer," *Corsicana Daily Sun*, February 10, 1928, 10.
16. Schechter, *Psycho USA*, 15.
17. Raine, *Anatomy of Violence*, 82.
18. "Slayer of 13 Tells Life Story," *Cameron Herald*, January 20, 1927.
19. Schechter, *Psycho USA*, 15.
20. McCarthy, "Hassell Laughs."
21. Hassell Family, "Hassell Murder Story," 1. Author's collection.
22. "Hassell Is Ex-Convict."

Notes for Chapter 3

1. In another interview he claimed to have been paroled from Leavenworth prison.
2. In other accounts he says it was twenty-seven states.
3. 1910 US Federal Census for John J. Vogel.
4. "Hassell Tells Story of 13 Murders and Waits Death March," *Houston Post-Dispatch*, February 4, 1928, 1.
5. McCarthy, "Hassell Laughs."
6. "Hassell Tells Story."
7. *Ibid.*
8. According to Pittsburgh newspapers, Mrs. Sirlin visited her daughter in 1914, not 1916, and "was introduced to the ranch employees." This conflicts with the notion that George, Marie, and the kids were the only people living on the ranch at the time. Moreover, it is highly unlikely that George was in California by 1914. See for example, "Victim May Be Local Woman," *Pittsburgh Press*, December 31, 1926.
9. "Mrs. Marie Vogel," *Pittsburgh Press*, December 31, 1926, 2.
10. One story on December 31, 1926, which also included the only photo of Marie, said that she actually left in 1912 to go to California "for her health." This must be mistaken, because the 1910 population census shows her living with her husband in San Diego. *Pittsburgh Press*, "Victim May Be Local Woman," December 31, 1926.
11. "Give Clew to 4 Hassell Slew," *Fort Worth Record Telegram*, January 1, 1927.
12. "Hassell Tells Story."
13. "Skeletons of Four Victims Found," *Whittier News*, February 2, 1927.
14. "Killing Victims May Be Named," *Los Angeles Times*, January 1, 1927, 6.
15. *Ibid.*; "Skeletons of Four Victims Found."
16. "Constable Gives His History of the Case," *Whittier News*, February 4, 1927.
17. Mike Garabedian and Rebecca Ruud, *Whittier* (Charleston, SC: Arcadia, 2016), 41.

18. *Ibid.*, 58.
19. *Ibid.*, 48.
20. *Ibid.*, 50.
21. *Ibid.*, 69.
22. "Cellar Yields Victims' Bones," *Los Angeles Times*, February 2, 1927.
23. McCarthy, "Hassell Laughs."
24. "Hassell Tells Story."
25. Stone, *Anatomy of Evil*, 96.
26. Hickey, *Serial Murderers and Their Victims*, 13.
27. R. J. Vernon, "Thirteen Dead! The Startling Secret of the Unhallowed Grave," *Famous Detective Cases*, August 1935, 85.
28. *Ibid.*
29. Hassell Family, "Hassell Murder Story," 4.
30. "Hassell Admits He Murdered 13, Impulse Blamed," *Albuquerque Journal*, February 4, 1928; "Hassell Admits to Murder of 13," *El Paso Times*, February 4, 1928.
31. James Alan Fox, Jack Levin, and Kenna Quinet, *The Will to Kill: Making Sense of Senseless Murder*, 2nd ed. (Boston, MA: Pearson, 2005), 21.
32. *Ibid.*
33. *Ibid.*
34. Raine, *Anatomy of Violence*, 23.
35. "Hassell Admits He Murdered 13"; "Hassell Admits to Murder."
36. "Texas Slayer of 13 Awaits Chair Lightly," *Decatur Daily*, February 16, 1927.
37. "Cellar Yields Victims' Bones."
38. "Reveals Tomb of Four Victims," *Chattanooga Daily Times*, February 1, 1927.
39. "Officers Hope to Find Bodies of Four Victims of Texas Axe Slayer," *Modesto News Herald*, February 1, 1927.
40. "Skeletons of Four Victims Found."
41. "Confession Made by Hassell Is True," *Whittier News*, January 31, 1927.

42. "Bodies of Four Hassell Victims Are Found under House: Slayer of Nine Is Proven Murderer of Woman and Three Children," *Heraldsburg Tribune*, February 2, 1927.
43. Stone, *Anatomy of Evil*, 85.
44. *Ibid.*
45. Stone, *Anatomy of Evil*, 85–86.
46. "Hassell Tells Story."
47. "Death Cell Man."
48. *Ibid.*
49. "Constable Gives His History."
50. "Killing Victims," 6.
51. "Hassell Tells Story."

Notes for Chapter 4

1. "Hassell Tells Story of 13 Murders and Waits Death March," *Houston Post-Dispatch*, February 4, 1928.
2. "Former Valley Man Must Die," *Fresno Morning Republican*, January 14, 1927.
3. "12 Murders Admitted by Texas Killer," *Fresno Morning Republican*, December 28, 1926. The author scoured local newspapers from this period, looking for missing persons or any signs that Hassell might have committed more crimes while located there. Though it is one of the few times during which Hassell can definitely be connected to a particular area, nothing was found to suggest any criminal activities.
4. Versions given in print of the name of the tanker include *Tomaha* [perhaps *Tomahawk*], but the correct name is *Tunnehaw*.
5. Ed Kilman, "Hassell Dies at Huntsville without Break," *Houston Post*, February 10, 1928, 2.
6. Hickey, *Serial Murderers and Their Victims*, 31.
7. The State of Texas vs. George J. Hassell, District Court of Parmer County, TX, special January term, 1927. Parmer County Court Records, Farwell, TX.
8. *Hobart Democrat Chief*, December 8, 1926.

9. Nora had a second child with her first husband in 1924, before they divorced in 1925. She would spend the rest of her life in California. The following year she married Luke Breaux Guidrey (1893–1951), who was most probably the mysterious "Frenchie" alluded to in chapter six. He was from Louisiana and his surname implies some French or Acadian ancestry. They divorced in 1929. She married and divorced several more times and was buried next to her fifth husband, David Daniel Jones (1902–1967) in Riverside, California, on November 19, 1973.
10. Georgia (1922–1985) would marry Carl Pritchett Sandefur on August 28, 1952, in Santa Barbara, California. Her ancestry information lists her parents as Irby Truman McGee and Nora Lorraine Hassell Jones. Her only sibling was a sister, Betty Lorraine McGee Oddson, the second child Nora had with Irby McGee.
11. Sharpless, "Hester Calvert," 115.
12. "Mother and Eight Children, Formerly of Hobart, Slain," *Hobart Democratic Chief*, December 28, 1926.
13. "Hassell is Fifth White Person to Chair," *Fort Worth Record-Telegram*, February 10, 1928.
14. Hassell Family, "Hassell Murder Story," 2.
15. Death Certificate for Thomas V. Hassell, Oklahoma State Board of Health, available from: https://oklahoma.gov/health/services/birth-and-death-certificates/death-certificates.html. He was buried at Rose Cemetery, Hobart, Oklahoma, 73651, Lot 13, Block 35, Space 4.
16. "Inguinal Hernia," *Mayo Clinic*, https://www.mayoclinic.org/diseases-conditions/inguinal-hernia/symptoms-causes/syc-20351547.
17. "Hassell's Confession," *Clovis News Journal*, January 17, 1927.
18. "Slays Brother to Get Widow, then Kills Her and Her Eight Kids," *The Independent Record* [Helena, MT], December 26, 1926.
19. "Slayer of 13 Tells His Story," *Cameron Herald*, January 20, 1927.
20. "Farwell's Murderer to Be Given Immediate Trial," *Clovis News*, December 30, 1926.
21. Marlowe J. Churchill, "Big Smile, Good Looks—and Violent, *Eastern New Mexico News*, August 31, 2019.

22. "Hassell's Confession."
23. "Hassell Relates His Life Story."
24. Marriage Record, including Marriage License and Certificate of Marriage, State of Oklahoma, Jackson County, October 7, 1924.
25. Churchill, "Big Smile."
26. Trial Transcript, 158. Direct testimony by J.V. Ferguson.

Notes for Chapter 5

1. Stephen Harrigan, *Big Wonderful Thing: A History of Texas* (Austin, University of Texas Press, 2019), 388.
2. *Ibid.*, 536.
3. Timothy Egan, *The Worst Hard Time: The Untold Story of Those Who Survived the Great American Dust Bowl* (Boston: Houghton Mifflin, 2006), 14.
4. *Ibid*, 13.
5. Indeed, the population of their former hometown of Blair, Oklahoma, never exceeded seven hundred residents until 1950.
6. Sandra Gail Teichmann, ed., *Woman of the Plains: The Journals and Stories of Nellie M. Perry* (College Station: Texas A&M University Press, 2000), 13.
7. Zachry, *Settling of a Frontier*, vi.
8. "Murder Charge Filed against George Hassel [sic]," *Lockney Beacon*, December 30, 1926, 3.
9. *Ibid.*
10. Dan Flores, *Caprock Canyonlands: Journeys into the Heart of the Southern Plains* (Austin: University of Texas Press, 1990), 4.
11. Millie Jones Porter, *Put Up or Shut Up* (Dallas, TX: Wilkinson Publishing, 1950), 99.
12. Egan, *Worst Hard Time*, 23.
13. This semiarid region receives between seventeen and twenty inches annually.
14. Dooley-Aubry, *Why Stop? A Guide to Texas Historical Roadside Markers*. 5th ed. Providence, TX: Taylor Trade Publishing, 2005, 412.

15. J. Evetts Haley, *The XIT Ranch of Texas* (Norman: University of Oklahoma Press, 1929), 148.
16. Egan, *Worst Hard Time*, 27.
17. James D. Hamlin, *The Flamboyant Judge: James D. Hamlin*, as told to J. Evetts Haley, and William Curry Holden (Canyon, TX: Palo Duro Press, 1972), 272.
18. Teichmann, *Woman of the Plains*, 143–44.
19. Dede Weldon Casad, *Farwell's Folly: The Rise and Fall of the XIT Ranch in Texas* (CreateSpace, 2012).
20. Austin's state capitol building is the largest of its kind in the United States. Finished in 1888, it cost $3.2 million. Texas Legislative Council Research Division, *The Texas State Capitol: A History of the Lone Star Statehouse*, 7th ed. (Austin: 1998).
21. Lewis Nordyke, *Cattle Empire* (New York: William Morrow and Company, 1949).
22. Eugene V. Sofford, "History of the Farwell, Texas Community, 1905–1922," in Parmer County Historical Society, *A History of Parmer County*, 48.
23. Parmer County Historical Society, *History of Parmer County*, 35–37.
24. Haley, *XIT Ranch of Texas*.
25. Sofford, "History of the Farwell, Texas Community, 48–49.
26. June Rayfield and J. Larry Nance, *The Texas Courthouse* (Waco: Texian Press, 1971), 6.
27. Sofford, "History of the Farwell, Texas Community," 48–49.
28. *Ibid.*, 51.
29. *Ibid.*, 57.
30. George McLean, "History of Parmer County Closely Related with Early Day Merchant," in Parmer County Historical Society, *History of Parmer County*, 41.
31. Parmer County Historical Society, *History of Parmer County*, 37.
32. *Ibid.*, 35–37.
33. Sammy Tise, *Texas County Sheriffs* (Albuquerque, NM: Oakwood Publishing, 1989).
34. Sitton, *Texas Sheriff*, 57–59.

35. *Ibid.*, 61.
36. Richard Coke Hopping, *A Sheriff-Ranger in Chuckwagon Days* (New York: Pageant Press, 1952), 171–72.
37. *Ibid.*, 169–72.
38. Parmer County Historical Commission, *Prairie Progress*, 21.
39. One pioneer once said of Muleshoe, "They run out of names by the time they got to that town." In actuality there had been a ranch in the area at one time that used a mule shoe for its brand. See Porter, *Put Up or Shut Up*, 99.
40. Sofford, "History of the Farwell, Texas Community," 64.
41. *Ibid.*
42. Parmer County Historical Society, *History of Parmer County*, 64.
43. Parmer County Historical Commission, *Prairie Progress*, 17.
44. *Ibid.*
45. *Ibid.*
46. *Ibid.*
47. Fire destroyed the original two-story courthouse located where today's town water tower stands.
48. Parmer County Historical Society, *History of Parmer County*, 65.
49. *Ibid.*, 66.
50. Parmer County Historical Commission, *Prairie Progress*, 66.
51. Vernon, "Thirteen Dead!," 49.
52. Lana Payne Barnett, *Lonely Graves: A Texas Murder Trilogy* (Tulia: Texas Times Press, 2013), 70.
53. Jimmy M. Skaggs, "James Darlington Hamlin," *New Handbook of Texas*, vol. 3, 433–34. For more on Hamlin, see Hamlin, *Flamboyant Judge*. Hamlin never mentions Hassell, probably his most infamous tenant, in the book.
54. Walter Prescott Webb, *The Great Plains*, 2nd ed., (Lincoln: University of Nebraska Press, 2022).
55. Ty Cashion, *Lone Star Mind: Reimagining Texas History* (Norman: University of Oklahoma Press, 2018), 104.
56. Carl Frederic Kraenzel, *The Great Plains in Transition* (Norman: University of Oklahoma Press, 1955), 145.

57. "Slays Wife with Axe and Shoots Boys," *Santa Ana Register*, December 27, 1926.
58. Barnett, *Lonely Graves*, 69.
59. "Murder Charge Filed," 3.
60. *Ibid.*
61. State of Texas vs. George S. Hassell (Trial Transcript, 64. Richards reading confession to courtroom, prior to witnesses being called).
62. Sharpless, "Hester Calvert," 115.
63. For full list of auction items from December 22, 1926, see Appendix.
64. Trial Transcript, 75.
65. *Ibid.*
66. "Russell and Virgil Dug Graves for Victims," *Clovis Journal*, January 1927.
67. Hassell Family, "Hassell Murder Story," 5.
68. Trial Transcript, 75.
69. *Ibid.*
70. Vernon, "Thirteen Dead!," 49–50.

Notes for Chapter 6

1. Trial Transcript, 75.
2. *Ibid.*, 67.
3. *Ibid.*
4. *Ibid.*
5. *Ibid.*, 72.
6. *Ibid.*, 64.
7. Albert V. Vandenberg, "Charles Taze Russell: Pittsburgh Prophet, 1879–1909," *The Western Pennsylvania Historical Magazine* 69, no. 1 (January 1986): 3–20.
8. Trial Transcript, 66.
9. "Hassell Tells Story"; Trial Transcript, 67.
10. "Hassell Tells Story."
11. Trial Transcript, 67.
12. *Ibid.*
13. *Ibid.*

14. Hassell Family, "Hassell Murder Story," 5.
15. *Ibid.*
16. Trial Transcript, 68.
17. *Ibid.*, 69.
18. *Ibid.*, 70.
19. *Ibid.*
20. "Admits Killing Family of Nine," *Lancaster Sunday News*, December 26, 1926.
21. Hassell Family, "Hassell Murder Story," 6.
22. "George J. Hassell Petted Wives Then Slew Them, He Says," *Abilene Morning News*, February 1, 1928.
23. *Ibid.*

Notes for Chapter 7

1. Trial Transcript, 148.
2. *Ibid.*, 71.
3. *Santa Fe New Mexican*, February 10, 1928, 6.
4. Trial Transcript, 70.
5. Hassell Family, "Hassell Murder Story," 7.
6. *Ibid.*, 30.

Notes for Chapter 8

1. Vernon, "Thirteen Dead!"
2. "Feminine Curiosity Reveals Mystery," *State Line Tribune*, August 15, 1986.
3. *Ibid.*
4. Trial Transcript, 171.
5. *Ibid.*, 140.
6. *Ibid.*, 79.
7. *Ibid.*, 172.

Notes for Chapter 9

1. Trial Transcript, 99.
2. *Ibid.*

3. *Ibid.*
4. *Ibid.*, 99.
5. *Ibid.*, 101–2.
6. *Ibid.*, 101.
7. *Ibid.*, 102.
8. No other references mention him bringing food from the cellar.
9. Hassell Family, "Hassell Murder Story," 8.
10. *Ibid.*

Notes for Chapter 10

1. E. Paul Crume, "Son of Charlie Crume Grew Up in Farwell," *Dallas Morning News*, January 1, 1948.
2. *Ibid.*
3. *Ibid.*
4. *Ibid.*
5. Trial Transcript, 177. He would later receive permission from Sheriff Martin to interview Hassell for a "sociological, psychological and physiological" study.
6. Teresa Mesman, "Serial Killer Recalled," *State Line Tribune*, April 12, 2001, 9.
7. *Ibid.*
8. *Ibid.*
9. "Feminine Curiosity Reveals a Mystery," *State Line Tribune*, August 15, 1986, reprint from December 23, 1926.
10. Morley, "Mantrap Woman!," 23.
11. *Ibid.*, 24.
12. *Ibid.*
13. Trial Transcript, 82–87. Auction Sale, Plaintiff's Exhibit II.
14. Morley, "Mantrap Woman!," 24.
15. Vernon, "Thirteen Dead!," 50.
16. *Ibid.*
17. Trial Transcript, 102.
18. "Feminine Curiosity."
19. Trial Transcript, 87.

20. Hassell Family, "Hassell Murder Story," 9.
21. *Ibid.*
22. Trial Transcript, 152.
23. *Ibid.*, 96.
24. *Ibid.*, 170.
25. "Slays Wife with Axe."
26. Vernon, "Thirteen Dead!"

Notes for Chapter 11

1. Selective Service Registration Card, in which he claimed an exemption from the draft in 1917–1918. Accessed through Ancestry.com: US World War I Draft Registration Cards, 1917-1918 for James H. Martin.
2. Vernon, "Thirteen Dead!," 50.
3. Hassell Family, "Hassell Murder Story," 10.
4. Trial Transcript, 115.
5. Hassell Family, "Hassell Murder Story," 10.
6. Trial Transcript, 116.
7. *Ibid.*
8. *Ibid.*
9. Vernon, "Thirteen Dead!," 50.
10. *Ibid.*
11. Trial Transcript, 116.
12. *Ibid.*, 117.
13. Morley, "Mantrap Woman!," 25.
14. *Ibid.*
15. Vernon, "Thirteen Dead!," 51.
16. *Ibid.*
17. *Ibid.*
18. Hassell Family, "Hassell Murder Story," 9.
19. Morley, "Mantrap Woman!," 25.
20. Vernon, "Thirteen Dead!," 49.
21. Trial Transcript, 102.
22. *Ibid.*

23. Hassell Family, "Hassell Murder Story," 10.
24. *Ibid.*

Notes for Chapter 12

1. Trial Transcript, 102.
2. *Ibid.*
3. *Ibid.*, 103.
4. *Ibid.*
5. *Ibid.*
6. Vernon, "Thirteen Dead!," 49.
7. *Ibid.*, 48.
8. *Ibid.*
9. *Ibid.*, 51.
10. *Ibid.*
11. *Ibid.*
12. *Ibid.*
13. The Clovis sanitarium still stands and has been converted into an antique store, its operating room still intact.
14. Trial Transcript, 160.
15. *Ibid.*, 161.
16. *Ibid.*, 165.
17. "George J. Hassell, Doomed to Die in Electric Chair for Confessed Slaying Leaves for Penitentiary," *Abilene Reporter-News*, January 17, 1927.
18. "Hassell Tells Story."
19. Raine, *Anatomy of Violence*, 236.

Notes for Chapter 13

1. Morley, "Mantrap Woman!," 24.
2. Trial Transcript, 92.
3. Vernon, "Thirteen Dead!" His presence is noted nowhere else. I suspect he misremembered this and that he confused him with Dr. Clark, who is mentioned in other places.

4. "Feminine Curiosity."
5. Trial Transcript, 92.
6. However, another witness remembered otherwise, claiming that it was the newspaper reporter Graham's spade that "uncovered a quilt." Vernon, "Thirteen Dead!," 52.
7. Mesman, "Serial Killer Recalled," *State Line Tribune*, April 12, 2001, 4.
8. Hassell Family, "Hassell Murder Story," 11.
9. Trial Transcript, 92.
10. Vernon, "Thirteen Dead!," 52.
11. Trial Transcript, 130.
12. *Ibid.*
13. *Ibid.*
14. "'13' Killer Heartless; Calmly Awaits Chair," *Pomona Progress Bulletin*, February 3, 1927.
15. "George J. Hassell Petted Wives Then Slew Them, He Says," *Abilene Morning News*, February 1, 1928, 4.
16. Trial Transcript, 138.
17. *Ibid.*, 130.
18. *Ibid.*
19. *Ibid.*, 121.
20. *Ibid.*, 138.
21. Hassell Family, "Hassell Murder Story," 10.
22. Trial Transcript, 121.
23. Hassell Family, "Hassell Murder Story," 10.
24. Trial Transcript, 131.
25. *Clovis Journal*, December 30, 1926, 2.
26. Hassell Family, "Hassell Murder Story," 10.
27. *Clovis Journal*, December 30, 1926, 2.

Notes for Chapter 14

1. Vernon, "Thirteen Dead!," 52.
2. *Ibid.*
3. *Ibid.*, 52–53.
4. Vernon, "Thirteen Dead!," 53.

5. "Think Accused Hassell to Live," *Dallas Morning News*, December 26, 1926, 1.
6. "A Look Back at Most Infamous Moments in Parmer County History," *State Line Tribune*, December 20, 2001.
7. "Spirited from Farwell," *Dallas Morning News*, December 30, 1926; "Increase Guard on Man," *Waco News Tribune*, December 28, 1926.
8. "A Thrust at Governor," *Sweetwater Daily Reporter*, December 29, 1926.
9. Vernon, "Thirteen Dead!," 53.
10. *Ibid.*, p. 85
11. Trial Transcript, 35–36.
12. It has never been determined who the name "Maggie" referred to.
13. "Murder Charge for Ranchman Whose Family Is Found Dead," *Albuquerque Journal*, December 25, 1926, 1.
14. "Hassell's Former Wife at Jarrell," *Abilene Daily Reporter*, December 29, 1926.
15. While researching this story in Farwell, Texas, I was able to get copies of the trial transcripts and miscellaneous items held in the County Clerk's office. I had failed to discover what happened to Minnie and James Delbert, despite an exhaustive search on ancestry sites and elsewhere. I had almost given up, when serendipity struck. Among materials I had collected was a 1964 letter to the Criminal Court Records in Farwell asking for materials on the Hassell trial. It was signed by John Laughlin, from Lampasas, Texas. His signature was a perfect match with the signatures on both his World War Two draft card, serial number 3355, Order number 3791, and his Ohio marriage record, No. 1097. John Benjamin Hodge died in 1981, so it seems more than plausible to conclude that this was George's son trying to learn more about his family background.
16. "Hassell in New Statement Admits Killing 13 Persons," *Los Angeles Times*, December 28, 1926.
17. "Is Placed in the Hale County Jail Wed," *Abilene Daily Reporter*, December 29, 1926.
18. *Ibid.*

19. "Hassell Relates Life Story," January 17, 1927.
20. "Murderer of 13 Wants to Be in Condition for Electric Chair," *El Paso Herald*, January 1, 1927, 1.
21. "Hassell to Remain in Jail at Plainview," *Dallas Morning News*, January 4, 1927.
22. Amarillo Public Library, https://hrlc.ent.sirsi.net/en_US/search/asset/1331/0.

Notes for Chapter 15

1. State of Texas vs. George J. Hassell, Murder Indictments, January 4, 1927, Nos. 187, 189–195. Parmer County Court Records, Farwell, Texas. Each case has a separate indictment number and describes the specifics of the death of each family. Susie Hassell (187), David (189), Samuel (190), Nannie (191), Russell (192), Virgil (193), Maudie (194), and Johnnie (195). Alton's indictment is missing from this file but is included in the murder indictment files of the case (188). Hence the missing number between Susie and David above. Alton's indictment is listed as no. 4 on the Index page. Since Alton's murder was the only one of the nine indictments that the state decided to go forward, it was moved from the rest of the indictments into the body of the Trial Transcript and Index. Alton's case No. 188 is located on pages one to five of The State of Texas vs George J. Hassell, In the District of Parmer County Texas, Special Term, January, 1927. The indictments were all originally dated January 4, 1927. All of the indictments can be found in the George J. Hassell file at the Parmer County Courthouse, Farwell, Texas.
2. State of Texas vs. George J. Hassell, No. 188, January 4, 1927. This typed document can be found with the indictments.
3. Sitton, *Texas Sheriff*, 61.
4. Bessie Patterson, *A History of Deaf Smith County from 1890–1964* (Hereford, TX: Pioneer Publishers, 1964), 113. Russell continued his practice until dying of heart failure on May 17, 1950.
5. Trial Transcript, Index, 7.
6. The State of Texas vs. George J. Hassell, No. 188, January 7, 1927.

7. *Ibid.*, 66.
8. James Somerville McEachin, *McEachin's Annotated Civil Statutes of the State of Texas*, Vol. 2, Section 62.007 (Chicago: The Flood & Company, 1913).
9. Parmer County Historical Commission, *Prairie Progress*, 449–50.
10. *Ibid.*, 237.
11. Parmer County Historical Society, *History of Parmer County*, 253.
12. "Selecting Grand Jurors," Trial Transcript, 3.
13. Neal, *From Guns to Gavels*, 231.
14. Bill Neal, *Sex, Murder and the Unwritten Law: Courting Judicial Mayhem, Texas Style* (Lubbock: Texas Tech University Press, 2009), 117.
15. George J. Hassell (appellant) v. The State of Texas (appellee), Brief for State, No. 10908, p. 3, Parmer County Courthouse, Farwell, Texas.
16. Neal, *From Guns to Gavels*, 231. For more on Texas trials in the nineteenth and twentieth centuries, see also Neal, *Getting Away with Murder*, and Neal, *Sex, Murder and the Unwritten Law*.
17. Neal, *From Guns to Gavels*, 231.
18. "Hassell Now Facing Trial at Farwell," *Dallas Morning News*, January 7, 1927.
19. Order Summoning Petit Jurors, The State of Texas vs George J. Hassell, No. 188, January 7, 1927, 7–8.
20. In the trial transcript he is listed as Reeves on 43–47, and in Parmer County Historical Society, *History of Parmer County*, 332–337, as "Floyd W. Reeve." Further research found that the name was Reeve and that Reeves in the trial transcript is in error.
21. "Marvin Whaley," Parmer County Historical Society, *History of Parmer County*, 359. See also Connie Slagle, "Marvin and Beulah Whaley," in Parmer County Historical Commission, *Prairie Progress*, Parmer County Historical Commission, *XIT Ranch to XXI Century*, 299–300.
22. Trial Transcript, 48–53.
23. *Ibid.*, 3, 56.

24. Trial Transcript, G.W. Atchley, 20.
25. Trial Transcript, 23–24; See "About the J. L. Landrums," in Parmer County Historical Commission, *Prairie Progress*, 296; "JL Landrum Family, Some Olden Day Happenings," in Parmer County Historical Society, *History of Parmer County*, 295–98.
26. Trial Transcript, 29–31.
27. *Ibid.*, 32–34.
28. *Ibid.*, 35–37; Prairie Progress, "Crawford Family," 204-205.
29. He was interviewed for Hassell Family, "Hassell Murder Story."
30. "History of Goodwine Family," Parmer County Historical Society, *History of Parmer County*, 255–62.
31. Bill Ellis, "Goodwine Recalls Details of Trial," *Friona Star*, October 8, 1978, 1.
32. Ellis, "Goodwine," 6.
33. Ellis, "Goodwine," 1, 6.

Notes for Chapter 16

1. "Sentiment Hot on Eve of First Hassell Trial," *Houston Post-Dispatch*, January 7, 1927.
2. "Hassell's Plea of Not Guilty Not Accepted," *Marshall Messenger*, January 7, 1927.
3. "They Sent Him Farther East," *State Line Tribune*, May 6, 1988.
4. Neal, *Sex, Murder and the Unwritten Law*, 34.
5. Trial Transcript, 63.
6. *Ibid.*
7. *Ibid.*, 66.
8. *Ibid.*, 67–72.
9. *Ibid.*, 72–73.
10. "Hassell Hears His Statement Read to Jury," *Houston Post-Dispatch*, January 11, 1927.
11. Trial Transcript, 58.
12. *Ibid.*, 57.
13. As mentioned previously, also present were Sheriff Martin and Sheriff Kennedy of Clovis, Mr. W. W. Holmes (court reporter), and possibly Jake McLain.

14. "Death Chair for Hassell," *Clovis Journal*, January 12, 1927.
15. *Ibid.*
16. Trial Transcript, 60.
17. *Ibid.*, 61.
18. Judge James Darlington Hamlin married Miss Kate Nichols in 1906. Their marriage lasted thirty years, until they parted ways in 1936. They remained on good terms until her death in 1940. In Hamlin, *Flamboyant Judge*, he only mentions Kate two times, despite a marriage of thirty years. Hence, what little is known about her comes mostly from her trial testimony and the role she played in helping uncover Hassell's crimes.
19. Trial Transcript, 74.
20. *Ibid.*, 75.
21. "Russell and Virgil Dug Graves."
22. Trial Transcript, 75.
23. State Exhibit Number 2.
24. Trial Transcript, 93.
25. *Ibid.*, 94.
26. *Ibid.*, 94.
27. *Ibid.*, 95.
28. *Ibid.*, 91.
29. *Ibid.*, 100–1.
30. *Ibid.*, 109.
31. *Ibid.*, 104.
32. *Ibid.*, 106.
33. *Ibid.*, 110.
34. *Ibid.*, 111.
35. *Ibid.*, 112.
36. *Ibid.*, 118.
37. *Ibid.*, 117.
38. *Ibid.*, 121.
39. *Ibid.*, 133-34.
40. *Ibid.*, 136.
41. *Ibid.*, 139; "Closing Hours of the Hassell Trial," *Clovis Journal*, January 13, 1927.

42. Trial Transcript, 139.
43. *Ibid.*
44. *Ibid.*, 141.
45. *Ibid.*, 143.
46. *Ibid.*, 143.
47. *Ibid.*, 143.
48. The trial transcript has her listed incorrectly as Nora Gigler.
49. "Closing Hours of the Hassell Trial."
50. *Ibid.*
51. Trial Transcript, 155.
52. *Ibid.*
53. *Ibid.*, 156.
54. *Ibid.*
55. *Ibid.*
56. *Ibid.*, 158.
57. *Ibid.*, 161.
58. *Ibid.*, 161–62.
59. *Ibid.*, 163.
60. *Ibid.*, 162.
61. *Ibid.*, 164.
62. *Ibid.*, 164.
63. *Ibid.*, 165.
64. *Ibid.*, 165.
65. *Ibid.*, 168.
66. *Ibid.*, 169.
67. *Ibid.*
68. *Ibid.*, 170.
69. *Ibid.* Parentheses in original.
70. *Ibid.*
71. *Ibid.*, 171.
72. "Insanity Defense in Hassell Trial," *Houston Post-Dispatch*, January 12, 1927.
73. Trial Transcript, 177.
74. *Ibid.*, 176.
75. *Ibid.*, 178.

76. *Ibid.*, 179.
77. *Ibid.*, 180.
78. "Insanity Defense."
79. Trial Transcript, 189–90.
80. *Ibid.*, 191.
81. *Ibid.*
82. *Ibid.*, 194.
83. *Ibid.*, 195.
84. "Closing Hours of the Hassell Trial," *Clovis Journal*, January 13, 1927.
85. "Death Chair for Hassell."

Notes for Chapter 17

1. Hassell Family, "Hassell Murder Story," 12.
2. "Hassell Execution," 1.
3. Hassell Family, "Hassell Murder Story," 12.
4. "Death Chair for Hassell," 1.
5. Trial Transcript, Index, 9. Hyperbolic newspaper accounts quote the judge as ending his judgment with "dead, dead, dead." Examples include the *Clovis Journal* article taunting the murderer about being electrocuted "till you are dead, dead, dead" ("Hassell Execution Feb 25," January 13, 1927).
6. "Hassell Execution Feb 25," *Clovis Journal*, January 13, 1927.
7. *Ibid.*
8. Ellis, "Goodwine."
9. Trial Transcript, Index, 9.
10. McCarthy, "Hassell Laughs."
11. "Death Chair for Hassell."
12. "Confessor Upon Killing Thirteen Found Guilty," *Sedalia Democrat*, January 14, 1927, 18.
13. "Jury Returns Verdict after Deliberating Less Than Two Hours; Defendant Unmoved," *Vernon* [TX] *Weekly Record*, January 13, 1927, 1.
14. James W. Marquart, Sheldon Ekland-Olson, and Jonathan R. Sorensen, *The Rope, the Chair, and the Needle: Capital Punishment in Texas, 1923–1990* (Austin: University of Texas Press, 1998), 69.
15. Marquart, Ekland-Olson, and Sorenson, *Rope*, 71.

16. *Ibid.*
17. *Ibid.*
18. *Ibid.*, 79.
19. *Ibid.*
20. *Ibid.*
21. Ed Blackburn Jr., *Wanted: Historic County Jails of Texas* (College Station: Texas A&M University Press, 2006), 316. Built by the Pauly Jail Building and Manufacturing Company, it would be replaced in 1931 by a modern Art Deco structure five stories tall.
22. "George J. Hassell Doomed to Die in Electric Chair for Confessed Slaying Leave for Penitentiary," *Abilene Reporter-News*, January 17, 1927.
23. Anderson, "Hassell, Slayer of Thirteen."
24. Edward E. Anderson, "Slayer of Thirteen, on Way to Death Cell, Dwells Upon his Happiness and Sorrows," *Abilene Morning News*, January 15, 1927, 1.
25. *Ibid.*
26. Anderson, "Hassell, Slayer of Thirteen, on Way to Death Cell."
27. Patrick Bennett, *Rough and Rowdy Ways: The Life and Hard Times of Edward Anderson* (College Station: Texas A&M University Press, 1988), xiv. As this is Anderson's only biography thus far, it is unfortunate that it includes no mention of his reportage during the Hassell era.
28. Anderson, "Hassell, Slayer of Thirteen, on Way to Death Cell."
29. *Ibid.*
30. *Ibid.*
31. *Ibid.*
32. *Ibid.*
33. McCarthy, "Hassell Laughs."
34. Anderson, "Hassell, Slayer of Thirteen, on Way to Death Cell."
35. *Ibid.*
36. *Ibid.*
37. *Ibid.*
38. *Ibid.*

39. *Ibid.*
40. *Ibid.*
41. *Ibid.*
42. "George J. Hassell Doomed to Die."
43. J. B. White, "I Will Tell Everything before I Die," *Cameron Herald*, January 20, 1927. It should be mentioned that this was about the only newspaper coverage that got Hassell's place of birth right: Smithfield, instead of Smithville.
44. *Ibid.*
45. *Ibid.*
46. *Ibid.*
47. *Ibid.*
48. *Ibid.*
49. *Ibid.*
50. *Ibid.*
51. "George J. Hassell Doomed to Die."

Notes for Chapter 18

1. See for example "Slayer of Nine," (Roseburg, Oregon) *News Review*, February 18, 1927.
2. Several newspaper accounts mention these letters. See, for example, "Traces Found in excavation," *Los Angeles Times*, February 1, 1927, 20.
3. She told police she only had one copy and requested its return when finished using it. By most accounts they did send it back. "Execution Taken as a Matter of Course," *Pittsburgh Press*, February 2, 1927.
4. "Slayer Keeps Quiet about Those Killed," *Houston Post-Dispatch*, January 1, 1927.
5. "Killer Admits He Took Lives of 13 Persons," *Miami News Herald*, December 28, 1927.
6. "Is Awaiting Execution," *El Paso Herald*, February 1, 1927.
7. "Cellar Yields Victims' Bones."
8. *Ibid.*
9. "Says Santa Ana Is Town to Find Hassell's Slain," *Billings Gazette*, January 3, 1927.

10. *Ibid.*
11. Vernon, "Thirteen Dead!," 85.
12. *Ibid.*
13. *Ibid.*
14. "Cellar Yields Victims' Bones."
15. *Ibid.*
16. *Ibid.*
17. "Search Is Continued Here for Death House," *Whittier News*, February 1, 1927.
18. "Murderer is 'Glad' as Four Bodies Found," *Los Angeles Evening Post-Record*, February 2, 1927.
19. *Ibid.*
20. "Skeletons of Four Victims Found."
21. "Officers Hope to Find Bodies."
22. "Cellar Yields Victims' Bones."
23. "Diggers Expect to Find Bones of Murdered Woman," *Los Angeles Times*, February 1, 1927.
24. "Police Digging under House to Find Bodies," *Great Falls Tribune*, February 1, 1927.
25. "Bones of Hassell's California Victims Found Beneath House," *Clovis Journal*, February 3, 1927.
26. "Police Digging."
27. *Ibid.*
28. "Diggers."
29. "Cellar Yields Victims' Bones."
30. *Ibid.*
31. "Diggers.'
32. "Skeletons of Four Victims Found."
33. "Texas Murderer Says He Wiped Out Two Families Killing 12 Persons," *Evening News Harrisburg*, February 2, 1927.
34. "Four More Hassell Victims are Found in California," *Clovis Journal*, February 3, 1927; "Grave Gives Up Victims of Hassell," *Arizona Republic*, February 2, 1927.
35. "Skeletons of Four Victims Found"; "Death Cell Man Leads Officers to Ghastly Find," *Lubbock Morning Avalanche*, February 2, 1927.

36. "Texas Murderer."
37. "Four More Hassell Victims Are Found in California," *Clovis Journal*, February 3, 1927; "Grave Gives Up Victims of Hassell," *Arizona Republic*, February 2, 1927.
38. "Texas Murderer Says He Wiped Out Two Families Killing 12 Persons," *Evening News Harrisburg*, February 2, 1927.
39. "Murderer is 'Glad' as Four Bodies Found."
40. Of all the lawmen who were involved in investigating the murders of George J. Hassell, none was more versed in murder investigations than William James Bright (1884–1943). He was a peace officer and county jailer for thirty-five years and was well known in the Los Angeles area for his detective work on famous cases, including the Clara Phillips axe murder case (1922), the Gordon Northcott "murder farm" case (1926–1928), the William Hickman kidnapping and rape case (1927), the Los Angeles River "torso slaying" case (1929), the disappearance of the evangelist Aimee Semple McPherson (1931), and many others. In 1921, he organized the Sheriff's homicide squad, which he commanded, and from 1935 to 1940 he was chief of the Sheriff's Criminal Division.
41. "Slain Family's Burial Delayed," *Los Angeles Times*, February 3, 1927.
42. "Texas Killer Tells of Murdering Thirteen," *Oakland Tribune*, February 4, 1927.
43. *Ibid.*
44. "'13' Killer Heartless."
45. *Ibid.*
46. "Hassell's Victims"
47. "'13' Killer Heartless."
48. *Ibid.*
49. "Slain Family's Burial"; "Texas Slayer of 13."
50. "Slain Family's Burial."
51. *Ibid.*
52. "Slain Family's Burial Delayed"; "Four Victims of Murder Disinterred," *McKinney Weekly Democrat-Gazette*, February 10, 1927.
53. "Four Human Skeletons Hide Secret," *Pasadena Evening Post*, February 2, 1927.

Notes for Chapter 19

1. John D. Bessler, *Death in the Dark: Midnight Executions in America* (Boston, MA: Northeastern University Press, 1997), 23.
2. *Ibid.*
3. Austin Sarat, *Gruesome Spectacles: Botched Executions and America's Death Penalty* (Stanford, CA: Stanford University Press, 2014), 201.
4. *Ibid.*, 63.
5. *Ibid.*
6. *Ibid.*, 181.
7. *Ibid.*
8. For a list of botched American executions from 1890 to 2010, see Sarat, *Gruesome Spectacles*, 179–210.
9. David M. Horton and Ryan Kellus Turner, *Lone Star Justice: A Comprehensive Overview of the Texas Criminal Justice System* (Austin, TX: Eakin Press, 1999), 266.
10. *Ibid.*
11. *Ibid.*
12. *Ibid.*, 266–67.
13. *Ibid., Lone Star Justice*, 267.
14. Sandra E. Rogers, *Electrocutions in Texas:1924–1964* (Huntsville: Texas Prison Museum, 2018), 5.
15. *Ibid.*
16. Gilbreath, *Death on the Gallows*, ii.
17. Once the transition was mandated by law in Texas, it was time to remove the gallows that remained in various counties.
18. "Prisoners Sleep around Trap Door of Jail Gallows," *Houston Post*, October 26, 1923.
19. "Prisoners Sleep."
20. According to the Lynching in Texas Project, "In December 1940, officials from the National Association for the Advancement of Colored People (NAACP) and the Association of Southern Women for the Prevention of Lynching (ASWPL) met at Tuskegee Institute to

discuss lynching. Together, they established the following definition of the crime:
1. There must be legal evidence that a person was killed.
2. That person must have met death illegally.
3. A group of 3 or more persons must have participated in the killing.
4. The group must have acted under the pretext of service to justice, race, or tradition" (www.lynchingintexas.org).

21. Jeffrey L. Littlejohn, "One Family's Photo Album Includes Images of a Vacation, a Wedding Anniversary, and the Lynching of a Black Man," *The Conversation*, May 30, 2022, https://theconversation.com/one-familys-photo-album-includes-images-of-a-vacation-a-wedding-anniversary-and-the-lynching-of-a-black-man-in-texas-183704.
22. Marquart, Ekland-Olson, and Sorenson, *Rope*.
23. Perkinson, *Texas Tough*, 185–86.
24. Marquart, Ekland-Olson, and Sorenson, *Rope*.
25. Just five months later, Kentucky executed seven men in its electric chair on the evening of July 13, 1928. The electrocutions took place between midnight and 1:30 a.m., See "Four White Men and Three Negroes Pay Death Penalty," *Corsicana Daily Sun*, July 13, 1928, 1.
26. Frederick Drimmer, *Until You Are Dead: The Book of Executions in America* (New York: Citadel Press, 1990), 10. For more detail on the electric chair, see Richard Moran, *Executioner's Current: Thomas Edison, George Westinghouse, and the Invention of the Electric Chair* (New York: Knopf, 2002); Mark Essig, *Edison and the Electric Chair* (New York: Walker, 2003); and Thom Metzger, *Blood and Volts: Edison, Tesla, and the Electric Chair* (New York: Autonomedia, 1996).
27. Drimmer, *Until You Are Dead*, 10.
28. *Ibid*.
29. Metzger, *Blood and Volts*.
30. Essig, *Edison and the Electric Chair*, 160.
31. *Ibid*.
32. Bryan Vila and Cynthia Morris, *Capital Punishment in America* (Westport: Greenwood, 1997).
33. Quoted in Vila and Morris, *Capital Punishment in America*, 68.

34. Essig, *Edison and the Electric Chair*, 252.
35. *Ibid.*, 253.
36. *Ibid.*, 252–53.
37. Drimmer, *Until You Are Dead*, 15.
38. *Ibid.*, 16.
39. Essig, *Edison and the Electric Chair*, 161.
40. *Ibid.*, 157.
41. "Far Worse Than Hanging," *New York Times*, August 7, 1890.
42. Essig, *Edison and the Electric Chair*, 259.
43. Scott Christianson, *The Last Gasp: The Rise and Fall of the American Gas Chamber* (Berkeley: University of California Press, 2010).
44. State of Texas, Senate, *Journal*, 38th Legislature, 2nd Called Session, 1923, 221–23.
45. Minutes of Board of Prison Commissioners, January 7, 1924, TSLA. There are 23 files in each box in chronological order, this one can be found in file labeled Minutes, October 1923–March 1924.
46. Quoted in Rogers, *Electrocutions in Texas*, 6.
47. *Ibid.*, 5.
48. *Ibid.*, 213.
49. "Walton Puts Ban on Electric Chair while Governor," *Houston Post*, April 2, 1923, 1.
50. "Texas Death Chair Ready on August 14," *Houston Chronicle*, July 22, 1923, quoted in Rogers, *Electrocutions in Texas*, 5.
51. Rogers, *Electrocutions in Texas*, 214.
52. Don Reid, *Eyewitness: I Saw 189 Men Die in the Electric Chair* (Houston, TX: Cordovan, 1973), 10.
53. "Texas Death Chair Ready on August 14," *Houston Chronicle*, July 21, 1923.
54. Reid, *Eyewitness*, 10–11.
55. "Texas Death Chair Ready."
56. Reid, *Eyewitness*, 11.
57. "Electric Chair To be Ready for Huntsville Executions November 9," *Houston Post*, October 10, 1923.
58. *Ibid.*

59. Gary Brown, *Singin' a Lonesome Road: Texas Prison Tales* (Plano: Republic of Texas Press, 2001), 16.
60. Reid, *Eyewitness*, 10.
61. Rogers, *Electrocutions in Texas*, 35.
62. *Ibid.*
63. "Ex-Warden Sleeps as Five Negroes Die," *Dallas Morning News*, February 8, 1924.
64. Rogers, *Electrocutions in Texas*, 35.
65. *Ibid.*, 214
66. "Captain Coleman Resigns as Head of State Prison," *Houston Post*, January 5, 1924, 1–2.
67. Rogers, *Electrocutions in Texas*, 214.
68. "Midnight Appeal Causes a Pause in Harvest of Death," *Austin American*, February 7, 1924. See also Marquart, Ekland-Olson, and Sorenson, *Rope*, 15.
69. *Ibid.*
70. Pat M. Neff, *The Battles of Peace* (Fort Worth, TX: Pioneer, 1925), 176.
71. Perkinson, *Texas Tough*, 186.
72. *Ibid.*
73. Rogers, *Electrocutions in Texas*, 215.
74. "Warden Speer, Who Started Prison School and Baseball Team, Is Mourned by Many," July 18, 1937, newspaper clipping, N. L. Speer file, Texas Prison Museum. Speer resigned in 1928 and successfully ran for Walker County Sheriff. He claimed he had become "averse to throwing the switch" by then.
75. Marquart, Ekland-Olson, and Sorenson, *Rope*, 15.
76. "Texas Death Chair Ready."
77. "Texas Death Chair Ready."
78. *Ibid.*
79. "Mrs. Ferguson Visits Prison," April 21, 1926, newspaper clipping, Execution file, Texas Prison Museum.
80. "Mrs. Ferguson."
81. "Slayer Dodges Chair."

82. "Hopes of Escaping Death Chair Dimmed for Hassell with Supreme Court Denial," *Abilene Morning News*, October 13, 1927.
83. "Three Men Await Death in Prison," *Houston Post*, February 12, 1927.
84. "Texas Death Chair Ready."
85. *Ibid.*
86. *Ibid.*
87. "Three Men."
88. "Three Men"; "Slayer Dodges Chair Feb. 2," *Clovis Journal*, February 17, 1927.
89. "Slayer Dodges Chair."
90. *Ibid.*
91. "Hassell Approaching Electric Chair, Writes His Son ... To Read Bible," *Cameron Herald*, March 17, 1927.
92. Paul M. Lucko, "Texas Court of Criminal Appeals," *New Handbook of Texas*, vol. 6 (Austin: Texas State Historical Association, 1996), 312n48.
93. Lucko, "Texas Court of Criminal Appeals," 312–13; "Attorney for Hassell Files Notice of Appeal," *Abilene Reporter News*, February 16, 1927.
94. "Hassell Starts Fight to Escape the Chair," *Dallas Morning News*, February 15, 1927.
95. Keith Carter, "The Texas Court of Criminal Appeals," *Texas Law Review* 11 (December 1932, February, April, June 1933): 196.
96. Neal, *Getting Away with Murder*, 18–20. By the year 2000, the reversal rate in Texas was less than 10 percent.
97. "Hopes of Escaping Death Chair."
98. "Hassell Again Dodges Death Chair," *Clovis Journal*, March 24, 1927.
99. "Hopes of Escaping Death Chair."
100. Harrigan, *Big Wonderful Thing*, 537.
101. "Slayer Dodges Chair."
102. Proclamations for Various Convicts, 2007/170-81, January 18, 1927—February 23, 1930, Governor Dan Moody Papers, TSLA.
103. *Ibid.*
104. "No Clemency for Hassell" *Dallas Morning News*, February 18, 1927; "Court without Authority to Execute Hassell: Appeal Was Made

before Writ Issued," *Cameron Herald*, March 3, 1927. This comes from a February 21, 1927, letter from Watson that was published in Farwell's *State Line Tribune*; "Hassell Lunacy Plea Is Planned by Sister," February 18, 1927.

105. "Court without Authority." This article contained a letter from the governor, originally printed in Farwell's *State Line Tribune*, addressed to Mr. N. L Speer.
106. *Ibid.*
107. Andrew Todd McKinney (1838–1931) graduated from Princeton University (1858) before studying law in Knoxville, Tennessee. He served in the Confederate Army and was disabled in the field in 1863. He served the State of Texas in the Texas Legislature (1883–1911) as well as in a variety of other capacities during his law career in Walker, County. See Sam McKinney, "McKinney, Col. Andrew Todd," in *Walker County History* (Dallas: Curtis Media Company, 1986), 553.
108. *Ibid.*
109. *Ibid.*
110. "Hassell Is Denied Plea for Mercy," *Houston Post*, February 15, 1927, 1.
111. "Hassell Granted 30 Days Respite," *Houston Post*, February 22, 1927; "Moody Delays Hassell Death," *Fort Worth Record-Telegram*, February 22, 1927.
112. Marquart, Ekland-Olson, and Sorenson, *Rope*, 28.
113. "Hassell Now Is to Leave Death Cell," *Dallas Morning News*, March 23, 1927.
114. "Stay of 30 Days Is Granted Hassell," *Dallas Morning News*, March 24, 1927.
115. "Moody Gives Hassell 30 Days of Grace," *Houston Post-Dispatch*, March 24, 1927.
116. "Hassell's Body to be Buried at Prison," *Fort Worth Star-Telegram*, February 10, 1928. See also Marquart et al, *The Rope, the Chair, and the Needle*, 29, for Texas state burial options over the years.
117. "Shadow of Chair Fades for Hassell," *Houston Post-Dispatch*, March 23, 1927.
118. "Hassell, Leaving Death Cell, Advises Women to Read Writings of Paul," *Cameron Herald*, April 7, 1927.

119. "Hassell Silent while in Houston," *Houston Post-Dispatch*, March 26, 1927.
120. "Hassell Leaving Death Cell."
121. *Ibid.*
122. *Ibid.*
123. "Hassell Silent."
124. Court of Criminal Appeals of Texas Trial Transcript and Narrative, #10908 *Hassell v. State*, Vol 298 SW Reports, October 12, 1927. PCCR.
125. Morrow was the presiding judge at the Texas Court of Criminal Appeals from 1921 to 1939.
126. Court of Criminal Appeals of Texas Trial Transcript and Narrative, #10908 *Hassell v. State*, Vol 298 SW Reports, October 12, 1927. PCCR.
127. "Opinion on Motion for Rehearing," Bill number 2, Appeal from Parmer County, George Hassell, Appellant, No. 10,908, The State of Texas, Appellee, Texas State Archives Copy. PCCR. See also Court of Criminal Appeals of Texas Trial Transcript and Narrative, #10908 Hassell v. State, Vol 298 SW Reports, October 12, 1927, 293–95. PCCR.
128. No. 10908, George J. Hassell Appeal from Parmer County to Texas Court of Criminal Appeals by W.H. Russell, document is not paginated but it is page 3, June 15, 1927, Parmer County Courthouse Records.
129. "Hassell Must Die in Electric Chair," *Clovis Journal*, June 16, 1927.
130. "Hassell, Slayer of 13, Nonchalant When He Learns Appeal Lost," *Fort Worth Star-Telegram*, June 17, 1927.
131. Davies, *Murder Book*, 77-78.
132. "Hassell, Slayer of 13"; "Hassell Calm as Plea Lost," *Fort Worth Record-Telegram*, June 1, 1927.

Notes for Chapter 20

1. Too little is known about Hassell's early life, making it all but impossible to determine what environmental elements or biological conditions might have contributed to his penchant for violence.

Recent research in genetics and other areas biological science suggests that impairments to the parts of the brain responsible for controlling a person's ability "to experience fear, make good decisions, and feel guilt predispose us to violence." Raine, *Anatomy of Violence*, 269.
2. "Hassell Tells Story of 13 Murders and Waist Death March," *Houston Post-Dispatch*, February 4, 1928.
3. "Was Hassell a Dr. Jekyll and Mr. Hyde," *Clovis Journal*, January 20, 1927; McCarthy, "Hassell Laughs."
4. "Was Hassell a Dr. Jekyll."
5. "Was Hassell a Dr. Jekyll."
6. Marvin Wolfgang, *Patterns of Criminal Homicide* (Philadelphia: University of Pennsylvania Press, 1958). See also Kai Pernanen, *Alcohol in Human Violence* (New York: Guilford Press, 1991).
7. Pernanen, *Alcohol in Human Violence*.
8. Hickey, *Serial Murderers and Their Victims*, 106.
9. *Ibid.*, 111.
10. Alvarez and Bachman, *Violence*, 83.
11. Hickey, *Serial Murderers and Their Victims*, 112.
12. *Ibid.*, 114.
13. "Was Hassell a Dr. Jekyll."
14. Stone, *Anatomy of Evil*, 86.
15. Trial Transcript, 178.
16. *Ibid.*, 177–79.
17. *Ibid.*, 179.
18. *Ibid.*, 178.
19. Turner, "It All Seems Like a Dream."
20. For more on craniometry, see Nicole Rafter, *The Criminal Brain: Understanding Biological Theories of Crime* (New York: New York University Press, 2010); and Stephen Jay Gould, *The Mismeasure of Man* (New York: W. W. Norton, 1996).
21. Trial Transcript, 180.
22. *Ibid.*
23. McCarthy, "Hassell Laughs."

24. Fox, Levin, and Fridel, *Extreme Killing*, 75.
25. Ibid., 76.
26. Ibid., 76.
27. Ibid., 76.
28. Hickey, *Serial Murderers and Their Victims*, 58. Emphasis in original.
29. Ibid., 58–60.
30. Ibid., 60.
31. Vronsky, *Serial Killers*, 242.
32. Neal, *Getting Away with Murder*, 273–74 n37.
33. "Hassell Does Not Wish Last Special Meal," *Marshall News Messenger*, February 10, 1928.
34. When thinking about book titles, *Urge to Kill* was one of my possibilities. However, a cursory search of titles on Amazon showed at least seven books with this title or subtitle published since 1974.
35. Stone, *Anatomy of Evil*, 90.
36. "Hassell May Be Sentenced This Evening," *Amarillo-Globe Times*, January 10, 1928.
37. Ibid.
38. "Crowds Wait in Vain for Sight of Hassell at Farewell Courtroom," *Amarillo-Globe Times*, January 8, 1928; "Hassell May Be Sentenced."
39. Charles H. Harris III and Louis R. Sadler, *The Texas Rangers in Transition: From Gunfighters to Criminal Investigators, 1921–1935*. Norman: University of Oklahoma Press, 2019), 223.
40. Sitton, *Texas Sheriff*, 56.
41. Ibid.
42. Sitton, *Texas Sheriff*, 57.
43. Sitton, *Texas Sheriff*, 56–57.
44. Malsch, *Captain M. T. Gonzaullas*, 83.
45. "Man Who Slew Dozens Smiles Hearing Doom," *Shreveport Times*, January 11, 1928.
46. Peter Vronsky, *Sons of Cain: A History of Serial Killers from the Stone Age to the Present* (New York: Berkley, 2018).
47. Blackburn, *Wanted*, 146.

48. McCarthy, "Hassell Laughs."
49. *Ibid.*
50. *Ibid.*
51. *Ibid.*
52. *Ibid.*
53. As mentioned previously, when the term "alienist" was coined in the nineteenth century, it was understood to refer to the study of people whose minds had become alienated from society.
54. "Rangers Sent to Protect Killer of 13," *El Paso Herald*, January 10, 1928; "Rangers to Farwell to Keep All Quiet," *Austin Statesman*, January 11, 1928.
55. "Hassell Now at Plainview Awaits Fate," *Abilene Reporter-News*, January 1, 1928.
56. "Smiles and Thanks Court; Asks Return of Clothes, Watch," *State Line Tribune*, January 10, 1928.
57. McCarthy, "Hassell Laughs."
58. *Ibid.*
59. "Hassell Given Insanity Test," *Fort Worth Record Telegram*, February 8, 1928. This article listed Mr. and Mrs. V. F. Kripperfdorf of San Antonio instead of Dr. Standefer from Austin, but the claim, which may by a typesetting error, is not substantiated anywhere else. See also "Hassell Sane and Must Pay Penalty Rules Governor Moody," *Austin American*, February 9, 1928.
60. "Hassell Denied Clemency Hope," *Houston Post*, February 8, 1928.
61. "Hassell, Murderer of 13, was Praying Deacon: Smiles as He Goes to Electric Chair Feb 10," *Cameron Herald*, February 9, 1928.
62. "Was Hassell a Dr. Jekyll and Mr. Hyde," *Clovis Journal*, January 20, 1927.
63. *Ibid.*
64. Roger Lane, *Murder in America: A History* (Columbus: State Ohio University Press, 1997), 334.
65. "Doomed Slayer Expresses Anxiety over Trunk He Sent to Abilene Wife after Crimes," *Abilene Daily Reporter*, January 21, 1927.

Notes for Chapter 21

1. "Place George Hassell in Huntsville Prison," *Dallas Morning News*, January 24, 1928, 9.
2. "Texas Death Chair Ready."
3. "Drunken Orgy Attends Black Terrors' Death," *El Paso Herald*, October 23, 1926, 1.
4. "Officials Tell of Alleged Wild Party in State Prison," *Austin American*, October 23, 1926, 1; "Drunken Orgy."
5. "Drunken Orgy"; "Officials Tell of Alleged Wild Party"; "Told in Quiz; Chief Describes Carousal at Pen," *McKinney Weekly Democrat-Gazette*, October 28, 1926, 3.
6. Reid (1906–1981) was first tasked with watching executions in 1937, almost a decade after Hassell was executed.
7. Leo W. Sheridan, *I Killed for the Law: The Career of Robert Elliott and Other Executioners*. New York: Stackpole Sons, 1938), 55.
8. Cynthia Barnett, "Covering Executions," *American Journalism Review* 17, no. 4 (May 1995): 27–31.
9. Sheridan, *I Killed for the Law*, 55.
10. *Ibid.*
11. Bessie, *Jazz Journalism*, 117.
12. Sheridan, *I Killed for the Law*, 55.
13. Elliott, *Agent of Death*, 230.
14. *Ibid.*, 55.
15. *Ibid.*
16. Elliott, *Agent of Death*, 231.
17. Texas Senate Bill 63 Chapter 51, Thirty-Eighth Legislature, Section 7, June 4, 1923.
18. Reid, *Eyewitness*, 38.
19. *Ibid.*
20. Robert Johnson, *Death Work: A Study of the Modern Execution Process* (Belmont, CA: Wadsworth, 1998), 58n79.
21. Barnett, "Covering Executions."
22. Johnson, *Death Work*, 8n79.

23. "Dissociative Disorders," Mayo Clinic, https://www.mayoclinic. org/diseases-conditions/dissociative-disorders/symptoms-causes/ syc-20355215.
24. Eddie Anderson, "George Hassell's Burning Ambition to Go to Death for Many Murders with a Smile of Contempt on Lips," *Abilene Reporter-News*, January 22, 1928, 1.
25. Marquart, Ekland-Olson, and Sorenson, *Rope*, 23.
26. Alice Adams, "From Unsuccessful Moonshiner to a Texas First," *Dripping Springs Century News*, January 21, 2020, 5.
27. See also Rogers, *Electrocutions in Texas*, 17–18. https://www. drippingspringsnews.com/features/unsuccessful-moonshiner-texas-first.
28. "Texas Butcher of Two Families Goes to Chair at State Prison," *Houston Post*, February 10, 1928, 44.
29. Gillespie, *Inside the Death Chamber*, 44.
30. *Ibid.*, 45.
31. *Ibid.*, 46.
32. Morley, "Mantrap Woman!," 59.
33. Parmer County Historical Society, *History of Parmer County* (Quanah, TX: Nortex Press, 1974), 69.
34. "Prisoners Sleep around Trap Door of Jail Gallows," *Houston Post*, October 26, 1923.
35. Gillespie, *Inside the Death Chamber*, 47. Today, last meals are limited to food on hand or just regular prison fare. At some point, bacon was prohibited because it was too expensive.
36. "Slayer of 13 Is Executed," *Blackwell [OK] Morning Tribune*, February 10, 1928, 1.
37. "Texas Butcher."
38. *Ibid.*
39. *Ibid.*
40. "Millikin Death Hour," *Austin American*, November 5, 1927.
41. "Texas Butcher."
42. "Texas Butcher."
43. Kilman, "Hassell Dies at Huntsville," 2.

44. "Hassell Goes to Chair for Murder of Young Stepson," *Austin American*, February 10, 1928.
45. "Confessed Murderer of 13 Executed in Texas Prison," *San Bernardino County Sun*, February 10, 1928.
46. "Jazz Is Popular in Death House at Huntsville," *El Paso Evening Post*, December 3, 1928.
47. "Hassell Goes to Death in Chair without Remorse for Murder of Two Women, 11 Children," *Albuquerque Journal*, February 10, 1928.
48. "Hassell Dies at Huntsville without Break," *Houston Post*, February 10, 1928.
49. Reid, *Eyewitness*, 36.
50. Ibid., 37.
51. *Ibid.*, 36–37.
52. *Ibid.*, 38.
53. "Hassell Like 'a Pasty Chunk of Putty,' as He Goes to His Death," *Amarillo Globe-Times*, February 10, 1928.
54. According to Hassell Family, "Hassell Murder Story," 14, Hassell family members claimed that George had gained seventy pounds on death row, which is doubtful since he was only on death row for a month. Likewise, the family account claims that because Hassell "could not fit into standard prison clothes," an official supposedly went into Huntsville and purchased him a "pair of bib overalls and two white shirts to wear toward the end of his stay." This too is highly unlikely. At 5'8" and less than two hundred pounds, there were surely many much bigger convicts behind bars and there would have been prison clothes on hand and no need for a trip into town to dress him.
55. "Thirty Men Have Met Death behind the Walls of Texas Penitentiary," *Bryan Weekly Eagle*, September 2, 1926.
56. Accounts differ as to the exact time. According to the *Dallas Morning News*, for example, it was 12:29 a.m., while according to the *Houston Post*, it was 12:26 a.m.
57. "Goes to Chair at 12:29 for 1 of 13 Killings," *Amarillo Daily News*, February 10, 1928; "Hassell Like 'a Pasty Chunk of Putty.'"
58. Kilman, "Hassell Dies at Huntsville," 2.

59. *Ibid.*, 37.
60. Reid, *Eyewitness*, 38.
61. Kilman, "Hassell Dies at Huntsville."
62. The flickering of lights outside the prison during an electrocution is mostly myth, since the prison has its own generator.
63. "Hassell Like 'a Pasty Chunk of Putty.'"
64. Kilman, "Hassell Dies at Huntsville."
65. "Slayer Fills Appointment with Death," *Waxahachie Daily Light*, February 10, 1928; "Confessed Murderer of 13 Executed in Texas Prison," *San Bernardino Sun*, February 10, 1928; "Hassell Like 'a Pasty Chunk of Putty.'"
66. "Hassell Like 'a Pasty Chunk of Putty.'"
67. Hassell Goes to Chair for Murder of Young Stepson," *Austin American*, February 10, 1928.
68. "Hassell and Negro Electrocuted," *Corsicana Daily Sun*, February 10, 1928.
69. Moran, *Executioner's Current*, 228.
70. "Hassell Like 'a Pasty Chunk of Putty.'" Original without asterisks.
71. "Negro Dies Game," *Houston Post*, February 10, 1928, 2.
72. Marquart, Ekland-Olson, and Sorenson, *Rope*, 29. Only eighteen electrocuted inmates were turned over to the Anatomical Board of Texas, and these took place between 1950 and 1962. Rogers, *Electrocutions in Texas*, 238.
73. Hassell Family, "Hassell Murder Story," 13.
74. "Hassell's Body to Be Buried at Prison," *Fort Worth Star-Telegram*, February 10, 1928, 14.
75. www.tngenweb.org/darkside/facing-east.
76. Hassell Family, "Hassell Murder Story," 23.
77. "Change Required for 'Death Chair,'" *Fort Worth Record-Telegram*, April 13, 1928, 1. It appears that Flores might have had his sentence changed, or at least was not electrocuted. His name is missing from Rogers, *Electrocutions in Texas*. Rogers's book is considered the most complete record of Texas electrocutions.
78. "Speer Believes in More Life Terms," *Austin American*, April 5, 1928.

79. "Executions Irk Speer, Resigns," *Galveston Daily News*, April 5, 1928; "Speer Believes."
80. "Told in Quiz." When Speer originally tendered his resignation on April 15, 1928, he had already told a prison administrator that he had bought a chicken ranch near Huntsville and intended to go there immediately to work his stock of chickens for the season. According to a letter from W. W. Mead to the Board of Pardons, "He has a negro here named Jack Preson working for him as a house man and desires to have this man paroled out to him to use on the chicken ranch ... It would be very pleasing personally if this could be done for Mr. Speer ... I think this request should be granted." Letter, W. W. Mead to Board of Pardons, April 10, 1928, Governor Dan Moody Papers, TSLA. It is unknown whether this came to pass, nor can it be determined how well he did in the chicken business. However, he did become county sheriff and remained in that role until 1932 when he was forced to resign, after which time he was sentenced to a short stint in prison for embezzlement. His wife was appointed to fill her husband's unexpired term as sheriff in February 1932, becoming the first female Walker County sheriff. It must have been a poignant moment for him as he "unpinned his star from his vest and handed it to his wife, who stood beside him in the courtroom, and thrust into her hand the pistol he had worn." "Name Wife of Speer as Walker County Sheriff," *Dallas Morning News*, February 14, 1932.

Notes for Epilogue
1. Holmes and Holmes, *Mass Murder*, 60.
2. Moore, *Rampage*.
3. See Moore, *Rampage*.
4. Kelleher, *Flash Point*, 49.
5. Fox, Levin, and Fridel, *Extreme Killing*, 123.
6. Charles Patrick Ewing, *Fatal Families: The Dynamics of Intrafamilial Homicide* (Thousand Oaks, CA: Sage, 1997), 134. Besides his fourteen family members, he also killed two other people at businesses he

formerly worked at. For the best account of the Simmons family killings, see Moore, *Rampage*.
7. Raine, *Anatomy of Violence*, 129.
8. "Hassell Now at Plainview Awaits Fate," *Abilene Reporter-News*, January 1, 1928.
9. "Hassell Now at Plainview," *Abilene Reporter-News*, January 1, 1928.
10. "Doomed Slayer Expresses Anxiety over Trunk He Sent to Abilene Wife after Crimes," *Abilene Daily Reporter*, January 2, 1927.
11. Davies, *Murder Book*, 180.
12. Alvarez and Bachman, *Violence*, 102.
13. Kelleher, *Flash Point*, 154.
14. Kelleher, *Flash Point*, 41.
15. Fox, Levin, and Fridel, *Extreme Killing*, 170.
16. Raine, *Anatomy of Violence*, 23.
17. *Ibid.*
18. *Ibid.*
19. Fox, Levin, and Quinet, *Will to Kill*, 21.
20. Quoted in Fox, Levin, and Quinet, *Will to Kill*, 21.
21. "Hassell's Body to Be Buried at Prison," *Fort Worth Star-Telegram*, February 10, 1928.
22. For example, nary a mention in Michael Newton, *Hunting Humans: An Encyclopedia of Modern Serial Killers* (Port Townsend: WA: Loompanics Unlimited, 1990); nor in the more recently published books by Harold Schechter, *Psycho USA: Famous American Killers You Never Heard Of* (New York: Ballantine, 2012); and *Serial Killer Files: The Who, What, Where, How, and Why of the World's Most Terrifying Murderers* (New York: Ballantine, 2003).
23. Stewart H. Holbrook, *Murder Out Yonder: An Informal Study of Certain Classic Crimes in Back-Country America* (New York: Macmillan, 1941), 220.
24. *Ibid.*, 219.
25. Mesman, "Serial Killer Recalled," *State Line Tribune*, April 12, 2001.
26. "Hassell Family Murder Play to Be Presented in Bovina," *Friona Star*, October 20, 2017.

27. "New Novel Is Based on Parmer County's Most Infamous Crime," *State Line Tribune*, January 11, 2011.
28. David Grieder, "New Headstone Marks Family Grave," *Eastern New Mexico News*, February 18, 2018.
29. "Volunteers Reviving History at Farwell Cemetery," *Clovis News Journal*, September 6, 2014.
30. Hassell Family, "Hassell Murder Story," 22.
31. Robin Fornoff, "Volunteers Reviving History at Farwell Cemetery," *Clovis News Journal*, September 6, 2014.
32. *Ibid.*
33. *Ibid.*
34. Teresa Ancira, interview with the author, Farwell, TX, March 15, 2021.
35. Teresa Ancira, telephone interview with the author, March 30, 2021.
36. Grieder, "New Headstone Marks Family Grave."
37. *Ibid.*
38. Hassell Family, "Hassell Murder Story," 12.
39. *Ibid.*, 11.
40. *Ibid.*
41. *Ibid.*
42. *Ibid.*
43. David Stevens, "Man Does Not Understand It at All," *Clovis News Journal*, April 23, 2017.
44. Hassell Family, "Hassell Murder Story," 11.
45. "Death House Slayings Gain Attention," *Whittier Daily News*, February 24, 2007, updated August 30, 2017.

Bibliography

Primary

Amarillo Public Library
George J. Hassell photo file.

Criminal Justice Department Historical Files [Execution Files], George Hassell File, Box 2006/337-001.
Convict's Biography.
Final Disposition, Condemned Men, No. 37, February 10, 1928.
The State of Texas vs. Geo. Hassell, no. 27527, Taylor County District Court, File No. 3206, March 13, 1907, embezzlement case.
Texas State Penitentiaries, Description of Convict When Received, January 23, 1928.
Texas Department of Health, George J. Hassell Death Certificate.

Oklahoma
Marriage Record, George J. Hassell and Susan Hassell, State of Oklahoma, Comanche County, October 7, 1924.
Thomas V. Hassell, Medical Certificate of Death, Oklahoma State Board of Health, July 3, 1924.

Parmer County Court Records, Farwell, Texas
(All of the following documents may be found under No. 188, State of Texas vs. George J. Hassell in the District Court of Parmer County, Texas, Special January Term AD 1927, Parmer County Court Records, Farwell, Texas.)
Court of Criminal Appeals of Texas Trial Transcript and Narrative, #10908
Hassell v. State, Vol 298 SW Reports, October 12, 1927.
State of Texas vs. George J. Hassell, Murder Indictment [Susan], No. 187, January 4, 1927.

State of Texas vs. George J. Hassell, Murder Indictment, [Alton], No. 188, January 4, 1927.
State of Texas vs. George J. Hassell, Murder Indictment, [David], No. 189, January 4, 1927.
State of Texas vs. George J. Hassell, Murder Indictment, [Samuel], No. 190, January 4, 1927.
State of Texas vs. George J. Hassell, Murder Indictment, [Nannie], No. 191, January 4, 1927.
State of Texas vs. George J. Hassell, Murder Indictment, [Russell], No. 192, January 4, 1927.
State of Texas vs. George J. Hassell, Murder Indictment, [Virgil], No. 193, January 4, 1927.
State of Texas vs. George J. Hassell, Murder Indictment, [Maudie], No. 194, January 4, 1927.
State of Texas vs. George J. Hassell, Murder Indictment [Johnnie], No. 195, January 4, 1927.
District Court Minutes, Vol. II, 373–74, January 4, 1927.
Commissioners Court Minutes, Vol. 2, 333, November 9, 1927.
Letter, John Laughlin to Criminal Court Records, Parmer County [Court] House, September 15, 1964.

Texas Prison Museum
Execution file.
N. L. Speer file.

Texas State Library and Archives, Austin
Criminal Court of Criminal Appeals (CCA #10908).
　1993/088–782.
Governor Dan Moody Papers.
　Proclamations for Various Convicts, 2007/170–81, January 18, 1927—February 6, 1930.
Minutes of Texas Board of Criminal Justice, 1900–1919.
　File, Minutes, February–June 1907.
　File, Minutes, August 1907—March 1909.
State Penitentiary Board Minutes, 1900–1911.

Box 1998/038-1, Files: February 1906—Feb 1907; February–June 1907; August 1907—March 1909; May 1909—January 11.

Texas Department of Criminal Justice Death Row Files (execution files).

Box 2006/337-001, File Execution #37, letters from 1927, 1928, 1955, 1964. Hassell Bertillon card.

Texas Department of Criminal Justice (Texas, Convict and Conduct Registers, 1875–1945 database).

Convict Record Ledgers and Conduct Registers.

Texas First Court of Appeals Records: An Inventory of First Court of Appeals Records Case Files, 1891–1975.

Boxes 2004/228-1 and 2004/228-2.

Texas Senate Bill 63 Chapter 51, Thirty-Eighth Legislature, June 4, 1923.

US Federal Census Reports, 1880–1920.

Secondary

American Psychological Association. *DSM-IV and DSM-5 Criteria for the Personality Disorders*. American Psychological Association: 2012. https://www.psi.uba.ar/academica/carrerasdegrado/psicologia/sitios_catedras/practicas_profesionales/820_clinica_tr_personalidad_psicosis/material/dsm.pdf.

Barnett, Cynthia. "Covering Executions." *American Journalism Review* 17, no. 4 (May 1995): 27–31.

Barnett, Lana Payne. *Lonely Graves: A Texas Murder Trilogy*. Tulia: Texas Times Press, 2013.

Becker, John T., Innocent Awasom, and Cynthia Henry. *Cotton on the South Plains*. Charleston, SC: Arcadia, 2012.

Bessie, Simon Michael. *Jazz Journalism: The Story of the Tabloid Newspaper*. New York: E. P. Dutton, 1938.

Bessler, John D. *Death in the Dark: Midnight Executions in America*. Boston, MA: Northeastern University Press, 1997.

Blackburn, Ed, Jr. *Wanted: Historic County Jails of Texas*. College Station: Texas A&M Press, 2006.

Brown, Gary. *Singin' a Lonesome Road: Texas Prison Tales*. Plano: Republic of Texas Press, 2001.

Carter, Keith. "The Texas Court of Criminal Appeals." *Texas Law Review* 11 (December 1932, February, April, June 1933).

Casad, Dede Weldon. *Farwell's Folly: The Rise and Fall of the XIT Ranch in Texas*. CreateSpace, 2012.

Churchill, Marlowe J. "Big Smile, Good Looks—and Violent." *Eastern New Mexico News*, August 31, 2019.

Cleckley, Hervey. *The Mask of Sanity: An Attempt to Clarify Some Issues about the So-called Psychopathic Personality*. 5th ed. St. Louis, MO: C. V. Mosby, 1976.

Crow, Herman Lee. "A Political History of the Texas Penal System, 1829–1951." PhD diss., University of Texas, Austin, May 1964.

Daly, Martin, and Margo Wilson. *Homicide*. Hawthorne, NY: Aldine, 1988.

Davies, Kim. *The Murder Book: Examining Homicide*. Pearson, 2007.

Dooley-Aubry, Betty, and Claude Dooley. *Why Stop? A Guide to Texas Historical Roadside Markers*. 5th ed. Providence, TX: Taylor Trade Publishing, 2005.

Egan, Timothy. *The Worst Hard Time: The Untold Story of Those Who Survived the Great American Dust Bowl*. Boston: Houghton Mifflin, 2006.

Elliott, Robert G. *Agent of Death: The Memoirs of an Executioner*. New York: E. P. Dutton, 1940.

Essig, Mark. *Edison and the Electric Chair*. New York: Walker, 2003.

Ewing, Charles Patrick. *Fatal Families: The Dynamics of Intrafamilial Homicide*. Thousand Oaks, CA: Sage, 1997.

Fox, James Alan, Jack Levin, and Kenna Quinet. *The Will to Kill: Making Sense of Senseless Murder*, 2nd ed. Boston, MA: Pearson, 2005.

Fox, James Alan, Jack Levin, and Emma E. Fridel. *Extreme Killing: Understanding Serial and Mass Murder*. Los Angeles, CA: Sage, 2019.

Freinkel, Andrew, Cheryl Koopman, and David Spiegel. "Dissociative Symptoms in Media Eyewitnesses to Execution." *American Journal of Psychiatry* 151, no. 9 (1994): 1335–39.

Garabedian, Mike, and Rebecca Ruud. *Whittier*. Charleston, SC: Arcadia, 2016.

Gilbreath, West. *Death on the Gallows: The Encyclopedia of Legal Hangings in Texas*. Fort Worth, TX: Wild Horse Press, 2017.

Gillespie, L. Kay. *Inside the Death Chamber: Exploring Executions.* Boston, MA: Pearson, 2003.

Hamlin, James D. *The Flamboyant Judge: James D. Hamlin.* As told to J. Evetts Haley, and William Curry Holden. Canyon, TX: Palo Duro Press, 1972.

Hare, R. D. *The Hare Psychopathy Checklist—Revised (PCL-R).* 2nd ed. Toronto: Multi-Health Systems, 2003.

Harrigan, Stephen. *Big Wonderful Thing: A History of Texas.* Austin, University of Texas Press, 2019.

Harris III, Charles H., and Louis R. Sadler. *The Texas Rangers in Transition: From Gunfighters to Criminal Investigators, 1921–1935.* Norman: University of Oklahoma Press, 2019.

Hassell Family. "George Hassell Murder Story." Unpublished manuscript, c. 1988. Photocopy belonging to author.

Hickey, Eric. *Serial Murderers and Their Victims.* 5th ed. Belmont, CA: Cengage, 2010.

Holbrook, Stewart H. *Murder Out Yonder: An Informal Study of Certain Classic Crimes in Back-Country America.* New York: Macmillan, 1941.

Holmes, Ronald M., and Stephen T. Holmes. *Mass Murder in the United States.* Saddle River, NJ: Prentice Hall, 2001.

Hopping, Richard Coke. *A Sheriff-Ranger in Chuckwagon Days.* New York: Pageant Press, 1952.

Horton, David M. and Ryan Kellus Turner, *Lone Star Justice: A Comprehensive Overview of the Texas Criminal Justice System*, Austin, TX: Eakin Press, 1999.

James, Bill, and Rachel McCarthy James. *The Man from the Train: The Solving of a Century-Old Serial Killer Mystery.* New York: Scribner, 2017.

Johnson, Robert. *Death Work: A Study of the Modern Execution Process.* Belmont, CA: Wadsworth, 1998.

Kelleher, Michael D. *Flash Point: The American Mass Murderer.* Westport, CT: Praeger, 1997.

Kraenzel, Carl Frederic. *The Great Plains in Transition.* Norman: University of Oklahoma Press, 1955.

Liem, Marieke, and Frans Koenraadt. *Domestic Homicide: Patterns and Dynamics*. London: Routledge, 2018.

Lucko, Paul M. "Texas Court of Criminal Appeals." *New Handbook of Texas*, vol. 6. Austin: Texas State Historical Association, 1996, 312–13.

Malsch, Brownson. *Captain M. T. Gonzaullas, Lone Wolf: The Only Texas Ranger Captain of Spanish Descent*. Austin, TX: Shoal Creek, 1980.

Marquart, James W., Sheldon Ekland-Olson, and Jonathan R. Sorenson. *The Rope, the Chair, and the Needle: Capital Punishment in Texas, 1923–1990*, first paperback edition. Austin: University of Texas Press, 1998.

Martin, Steve J., and Sheldon Ekland-Olson. *Texas Prisons: The Walls Came Tumbling Down*. Austin: Texas Monthly Press, 1987.

McKinney, Sam. "McKinney, Col. Andrew Todd," in *Walker County History*. Dallas: Curtis Media Company, 1986, 553.

Meloy, J. Reid. *The Psychopathic Mind: Origins, Dynamics, and Treatment*. Northvale, NJ: Aronson, 1988.

Metzger, Thom. *Blood and Volts: Edison, Tesla, and the Electric Chair*. New York: Autonomedia, 1996.

Moore, Jim. *Rampage: America's Largest Family Mass Murder*. Fort Worth, TX: Summit Group, 1992.

Moran, Richard. *Executioner's Current: Thomas Edison, George Westinghouse, and the Invention of the Electric Chair*. New York: Knopf, 2002.

Morley, Clyde. "Mantrap Woman!" *Line-Up Detective*, October–November 1951, 22–25, 59.

Neal, Bill. *From Guns to Gavels: How Justice Grew Up in the Outlaw West*. Lubbock: Texas Tech University Press, 2008.

———. *Getting Away with Murder on the Texas Frontier*. Lubbock: Texas Tech University Press, 2006.

Neff, Pat M. *The Battles of Peace*. Fort Worth, TX: Pioneer, 1925.

Parmer County Historical Commission. *Prairie Progress*. Dallas, TX: Taylor, 1981.

———. *XIT Ranch to XXI Century*. Amarillo, TX: Whitney Russell, 2010.

Parmer County Historical Society. *A History of Parmer County Texas*. Vol. 1. Quanah, TX: Nortex Press, 1974.

Perkinson, Robert. *Texas Tough: The Rise of America's Prison Empire.* New York: Henry Holt, 2010.

Porter, Millie Jones. *Put Up or Shut Up.* Dallas, TX: Wilkinson Publishing, 1950.

Raine, Adrian. *The Anatomy of Violence: The Biological Roots of Crime.* New York: Pantheon, 2013.

Reid, Don. *Eyewitness: I Saw 189 Men Die in the Electric Chair.* Houston, TX: Cordovan, 1973.

Richardson, Rupert N. *Colonel Edward M. House: The Texas Years, 1858–1912.* Abilene, TX: Abilene Printing and Stationary Company, 1964.

Riley, Brendan. "Solano Chronicles: 'Old 84' on Mare Island was Navy's First Prison." *Vallejo Times-Herald*, January 6, 2019. https://www.timesheraldonline.com/2019/01/06/brendan-rileys-solano-chronicles-old-84-on-mare-island-was-navys-first-prison/. Retrieved September 1, 2020.

Rogers, Sandra E. *Electrocutions in Texas:1924–1964.* Huntsville: Texas Prison Museum, 2018.

Sarat, Austin. *Gruesome Spectacles: Botched Executions and America's Death Penalty.* Stanford, CA: Stanford University Press, 2014.

Schechter, Harold. *Psycho USA: Famous American Killers You Never Heard Of.* New York: Ballantine, 2012.

———. *Serial Killer Files: The Who, What, Where, How, and Why of the World's Most Terrifying Murderers.* New York: Ballantine, 2003.

Sharpless, Rebecca. "Hester Calvert: Farm Wife." In *Human Tradition in Texas*, edited by Ty Cashion and Jesus F. De La Teja, 115–28. Wilmington, DE: Scholarly Press, 2001.

Sheridan, Leo W. *I Killed for the Law: The Career of Robert Elliott and Other Executioners.* New York: Stackpole Sons, 1938.

Sitton, Thad. *The Texas Sheriff: Lord of the County Line.* Norman: University of Oklahoma Press, 2000.

Sofford, Eugene V. "History of Farwell, Texas Community, 1905–1952." Master's thesis, Eastern New Mexico University, 1955. [In Parmer County Historical Society, *A History of Parmer County, Texas.* Quanah, TX: Nortex, 1974, 46–78.]

Spikes, Nellie Witt. *As a Farm Woman Thinks: Life and Land on the Texas High Plains, 1890–1960*. Edited by Geoff Cunfer. Lubbock: Texas Tech Press, 2010.

Stone, Michael H. *The Anatomy of Evil*. Amherst, NY: Prometheus, 2009.

Teichmann, Sandra Gail, ed. *Woman of the Plains: The Journals and Stories of Nellie M. Perry*. College Station: Texas A&M University Press, 2000.

Tise, Sammy. *Texas County Sheriffs*. Albuquerque, NM: Oakwood Publishing, 1989.

Turner, George. "It All Seems Like a Dream to Me—Hassell." *Amarillo Globe News*, October 1978.

Vernon, R. J. "Thirteen Dead! A Texas Horror." *Famous Detective Cases*, August 1935, 48–53, 85.

Vila, Bryan and Cynthia Morris, *Capital Punishment in America*. Westport: Greenwood, 1997.

Vronsky, Peter. *American Serial Killers: The Epidemic Years, 1950–2000*. New York: Berkley, 2020.

———. *Sons of Cain: A History of Serial Killers from the Stone Age to the Present*. New York: Berkley, 2018.

Walker, Donald R. *Penology for Profit: A History of the Texas Prison System, 1867–1912*. College Station: Texas A&M University, 1988.

Watterson, Rodney K. *Whips to Walls: Naval Discipline from Flogging to Progressive Era Reform at Portsmouth*. Annapolis, MD: Naval Institute Press, 2014.

Websdale, Neil. *Familicidal Hearts: The Emotional Styles of 211 Killers*. Oxford: Oxford University Press, 2010.

Zachry, Juanita Daniel. *The Settling of a Frontier: A History of Rural Taylor County*. Burnet, TX: Nortex Press, 1980.

Index

A

Abilene jail, Taylor County, 166–69
Alcohol, connection to violence, 210
Alienists, 220
Ancira, Teresa, 243
Anderson, Edward E., 167–69, 225
Angier, Dr. E. L., 35, 214
Atchley, G. W., 140

B

Baptist Sanitarium, 127
Badger game, 37, 38
"Baker, George G.," alias, 39, 175, 179–80, 182, 184
Barnett, Cynthia, 224–25
Benton, Claude (Deaf Smith County sheriff), 160
Benton, Robert Lee, executed after Hassell, 233
Blair, Oklahoma, 111
Bluebeards, 1–2
Bluebeard, Texas, 1–2, 237, 251 n. 1
Bovina, Texas, 140
Burleson, Albert Sidney, 19
Burleson and Johns Share Farm, 18

C

Cameron, Texas, 170
Campbell, Thomas M. (governor), 19–20
Capital punishment. See Executions.
Capitol Freehold and Investment Company of Chicago. See Capitol Syndicate.
Capitol Syndicate, 64
Capitol Syndicate Hotel, 68
Cleckley, Hervey, 7, 16, 28, 31

Cotton farming and gins, 15–16
Crume, E. Paul, 101–102

D

"Death house," Whittier, 44, 245
Death Penalty, Texas, 188–89
Delk, Patsy, 243
"Delocalization" of executions, 189
Domestic homicides, 240
Douglas, John, 253 n. 20

E

Electric chair, 193
    adopted in U.S., 189
    behavior condemned inmates last night, 227–28
    naming the device, 191
Electric chair, New York, 190–91
    and first use, 191
    Gerry Commission, 190
    and Southwick, Dr. Alfred, 190
Electric chair, Texas, 193, 221
    and Coleman, R. F., warden, 193, 195–96
    first used, 196–97
    and Miller, William Walter, warden, 196
    and Neff, Governor Pat proposes, 189
    "Old Sparky," 195
    opposition to, 195
    and Sayle, Walker, 193
    and Storm, Robert T., 193–94, 196
    "Thunderbolt," 195, 225
Electric power, 189–92
    and battle of the currents, 189
    and Edison, Thomas A., 189–91
    and Westinghouse, Sr., George, 189–90, 192

Electrocutions. See Electric chair.
Executions, America, 187
    and bungled hangings, 188
    and deterrence value, 187
    and electric chair, 193
    and hangings, 187–88

F

Faith, Sam (Plainview sheriff), 133, 216–18
Familicide, 3–4, 184, 240
Family annihilation, 3–4, 235, 237–39
Farwell, Texas, 59
    and impact of Hassell murders, 241–43
    and cemetery and funeral, 125–27
    and exhumation of bodies, 121–27
    incorporation, 64–65
    and jail, 66, 69
    and mass murder there, 1, 5, 77, 81–84, 99
    Prohibition in, 62–63
Farwell brothers, 63–64
Ferguson, J. V., 57
Ferguson, Miriam "Ma" (governor), 59, 197, 202
Ford, J. O., 70, 92–93, 106, 109, 122–23
Ford, Mrs. J. O., 105
Fowler, Carl, 140
Fort Leavenworth Penitentiary, 30

G

Gas chamber, 193
"George Hassell Murder Story," 9
Gillespie, L. Kay, 227
Goodwine, Clyde, 141–43, 161, 163
Great American Desert, 62
Guidry, Nora. See Hassell, Nora

H

Hamlin, James Darlington, 61, 71–72
Hamlin, Mrs. Kate, 75–76, 92, 94, 98, 103, 111, 158
    and suspicions, 105–106, 108
    watches pit being dug, 75
Hanging executions, 187–88
Hassell, Alton, 123–24, 155, 164
    murder of, 87–90
Hassell, George Jefferson, 1, 4–6, 8–24, 109–113, 127, 129
    at Abilene, Texas, 28
    appeals for commutation, 202
    argues with Susan, 74
    and background, 12, 13, 254 n. 1
    "Baker, George G," alias, 39
    buries first family, 49
    California employment, 49–50
    chewing tobacco, 13
    and confession, 130–31
    convicted of fraud and desertion, 30
    in courtroom, 163–64
    and death row, first trip, 170
    and death row, last time, 221, 226
    death sentence, 164
    depersonalizes victims, 7
    deserts first family, 27
    and embezzlement arrest (1907), 17
    and execution of, 232–33
    as family annihilator, 235
    and farm auction, 101–106
    and farming methods, 70
    and Farwell marriage deteriorating, 79
    and Farwell mass murder, 81–84, 99
    and father, relationship with, 15
    and first stay of execution, 204

height, 18
and insanity plea, 204
and last meal, 228
and last words, 231
and Laughlin, James Delbert, son, 26, 31–32, 35, 199–201
and Laughlin, Minnie, first wife, 25–26, 29, 32
and local impressions of, 73
makes doilies at Plainview, 208
and Merchant Marine corps chef, 50, 54
and military desertion, 24, 29
and military enlistment, 23–24, 29
as model prisoner, 216
moved off death row, 205
and move to Farwell, 61
and prison farms, 18–20
and prison records, 18
psychopathic tendencies, 207, 210, 213, 239
released from prison, 23
and reconciliation with first wife, 31, 35
resentenced to death, 216
and scratches on face, 94
sells out to Lindops, 97–100
and sexual abuse of Maudie, 77–79, 81
and sexual abuse of Nora, 77–78
and sister, P. A. Watson, 203, 230
"Stovall, George" alias, 23
and suicide attempt, 115–19
suspected of killing brother, 55
and suspicions of Farwell neighbors about, 91–95
and trial for Farwell murders, 135–143
and victim selection, 218
visits brother Thomas in Oklahoma, 52–53
and Vogel, Marie, 36–41
and weight gain, 228

and Whittier mass murder, 40–46, 129–30, 177–78, 180–81
and whiskey, 15, 80–81, 88
and women, 14
as worker, 70
and writing letter to son, 199–201
Hassell "Farwell murder house," 73, 244
Hassell murder trial, 145–161
    change of venue argument, 136–37
    confession read by prosecution, 146–48
    grand jury, 137–38
    incest with nieces, 146
    indictments, 135
    and Martin, Sheriff J. H., 148, 154
    petit jury selection, 138
    picking jury, 135–143
    Russell, W. H., defense, 146, 148
    J. D. Thomas, 147–48, 152–53
    verdict, 163–73
Hassell, Maudie, 120, 149–50, 164
Hassell, Nora, 52, 147–48, 155
Hassell, Sammie, 122
Hassell, Susan, 229
    argues with George, 74
    as farm wife, 53, 55, 74
    marries George, 55–56
    as Russellite, 229
    and sister, Maudie Johnston, 211
    and work routine, 74
Hassell, Thomas V., brother, 51
    death investigation reopened, 165
    dies mysteriously, 51, 53–54
    George visits in Blair, Oklahoma, 51, 55–57
    marries Susan Ferguson, 51
    and work history, 52

Hawkins, R. V., 110, 116–17, 122, 154–55
Hickey, Eric, 2, 6, 41, 210
Hoffman, Gertrude, 46, 175–76, 180, 185
    identifies Hassell as "Baker," 175, 179–80, 182, 184
    investigates Vogel disappearance, 175–76, 180, 185
Holbrook, Stewart H., 241
Hopping, Richard Coke (Parmer County sheriff), 67
House, Edward M., 22
Hurston, Zora Neale, 22

I

Imperial sugar company, 19
Insanity defense, 213–14
Insanity experts, 213–14, 219

J

Jekyll and Hyde, 6, 134, 209–210, 212

K

Kube, David (deputy sheriff), 243

L

Landrum, J. L., 141
Lark, Myrtle (neighbor), 40, 179–80
Laughlin, James Delbert, 26, 31–32, 35, 131–32
    and Hassell tries to kill him, 27, 29
Laughlin, Minnie (first wife), 25–26, 29, 32, 131–32, 220
    and Hassell tries to kill her, 27, 29
    at Ovalo, Texas, 25, 28
Leaward, L. L. (Walker County sheriff), 176, 181
Lindop, Nicholas Albert "N. A.," 97–100, 122
Lindop, Mrs. N. A. "Tinnie," 73, 106, 113, 244
Lombroso, Cesare, 212
Lynchings, Texas, 189

M

Mare Island Naval Prison, 30–31
Martin, Sheriff James H., 107, 109–110, 112, 116, 118, 121, 130, 206, 215, 221, 226
Mass Murder, 3, 5, 81–84
McCarthy, John L. (reporter), 18, 168, 212–13, 217–19
McKinney, Andrew Todd "A. T.," 203
Mersfelder, Bill, 65–66
Mersfelder, P. D., 221
Milam County Jail, Cameron, 170–72
M'Naghten Rule, 213–14, 220
Moody, Dan (Texas governor), 201–203, 219
Muleshoe Jail, 119, 264 n. 39

N

Neff, Pat (governor), 196
Norfolk Marine Disciplinary Barracks, 30, 35

O

Oil fields in Whittier, California, 40
Olivet Cemetery Association, 243
O'Rourke, Frank (prison board member), 222
Overstreet, Hamlin, 109–110

P

Parmer County, 69–70
Parmer County District Court, 133–34, 215
Parmer County Historical Commission, 243
Plainview jail (Hale County), 131, 133, 138, 165, 205, 207–208, 216, 218
    and Hassell as model prisoner, 216
    and Hassell has wounds dressed, 133
    and Hassell makes doilies, 208
Psychopaths, 6–8, 31, 41, 119, 153, 207–208, 210, 213
Psychopathy checklist, 7, 17

R

Railroad lines, 71–73
Raine, Adrian, 7, 35, 42
Read, Dud, 140, 207
Reeve, F. W., 140, 164
Reid, Don (reporter), 194–95, 223–24, 230
Ross, Sidney Petters "Sid," 16–18, 27, 33
Ross and Malone, 24–25
Russell, William H. (defense attorney), 93, 136, 142, 198, 202–203, 205–206, 212, 217
Russellites, 80, 110, 229

S

Sawyer, F. W., and psychological study of Hassell, 159–60, 211–12
Schechter, Harold, 251
Serial killers, 2–3, 5, 216, 238
Serial mass murderers, 237
Shanker, Clara (neighbor), 43, 45–46
Sheriffs, Texas, 66
Smith, Albert "Blackie," 122–23
Smith, Dr. E. L., 118, 156–57
Sneed, C. V. (undertaker), 122, 125
Sociopaths, 7
Speer, N. L. (Huntsville warden), 183, 222, 226, 228, 231, 233
State Line Tribune, 103
Stepparents and homicide, 4, 42
Stone, Michael H., 4, 6, 41, 45, 214
Storm, Bob, 196
"Stovall, George," alias, 23, 29, 35

T

Tatum, Judge Reese, 133, 136, 139, 164, 205, 216
Taylor County jail, Abilene, 166–68
Texas Board of Pardon Advisors, 204–205

Texas Court of Criminal Appeals, 201–206
Texas death penalty, 165–66
    and profile of death sentenced inmates, 225–26
    and Texas Electrocution Bill, 193
Texas execution protocol, 228–34
Texas Penitentiary Investigating Committee, 23
Texas prison leasing and farms, 18–20
    Brazoria prison farm, 23
    Camp Wright, 20–21
    contract lease system abolished, 23
    Texas Turpentine Company, 21
    Trinity and Brazos Railroad, 20–21
Texas Rangers, 215–16
Texas statehouse construction, 63–64
Texas State Penitentiary and death house, Huntsville, 188, 194, 227–28
Texas State Prison System, 18
    and Rusk Prison iron foundry, 20
Thomas, J. D., 41, 71, 109–110, 116–18, 121, 123–25
Thomas, Sr., John William "J. W.," 188
Travis County Jail gallows, 188
Turner, George (reporter), 211
Tuscola, Texas, 16–17

V

Vogel, Marie, 36–39, 41, 175, 220
    and badger game, 37–38
    and children, 36–37, 41–42, 175
    and disappearance of family, 176
    and Hoffman, Gertrude, sister investigates, 175–76, 180, 185

W

Walton, J. C. (Oklahoma governor), 194
Way, Bob (constable), 46, 176–77, 179–80, 182–83
Whaley, Martin, 140

White, J. B., 171–72
Whittier, California, 35–47
Whittier mass murder, 41–46, 175–82, 184–85
Witnesses to executions, 230–31, 233, 235
    Massachusetts, 224
    New York, 223
    Snyder, Ruth, execution, 223
    and trauma from watching, 224
Wolfgang, Marvin, 210

X

XIT Ranch, 63, 68